THE HISTORY
OF THE
SUPPLY SHIP

by Victor Gibson

La Madrila Press

La Madrila Press

A Division of:

Ships and Oil Ltd,
Bon Accord House,
Greyhope Rd,
Aberdeen AB11 9RD

www.shipsandoil.com

ABERDEEN and MADRID

Published in 2007.

© VICTOR GIBSON

This volume is dedicated to my wife, Maria de la Natividad Santana Zapatero, who tolerates my enthusiasm for all things relating to supply vessels with patience and good humour.

All rights reserved. No part of this publication may be reproduced in any material form (including photocopying or storing in any medium by electronic means and whether or not transiently or incidentally to some other use of this publication) without the written permission of the copyright holder except in accordance with the provisions of the Copyright Designs and Patents Act 1988 or under the terms of a licence issued by the Copyright Licencing Agency Ltd, 90 Tottenham Court Rd, London, England W1P 9HE.

ISBN NO 978-0-9557002-0-0

Design, Layout and Production by:
Big Sky, Findhorn

www.bigskyprint.com

Acknowlegements

Back in 1998 I set up a website which was intended to provide information about supply vessels, for my own interest, and for the interest of professionals in the business and enthusiasts outside it.

I ran a number of photographic competitions and then less onerously, just published the photographs people had sent in on the website. As a result I collected a library of offshore photographs of considerable size, and many of these photographs have been used in the book, with what I believe is good effect. I was also helped by Peter Barker and David Dodds who were good enough to put me in touch with Paul Gowen and Ken Turrell who held libraries of photographs from the past.

Major contributors of photographs to the website, and hence to the book were Derek Mackay, David Styles, Tony Poll, Oddgeir Refvik, Ron Jansen and Wullie Bremner. Other contributors were Roy Krakevik, Win Kosten, Kenny Polson, Bob Beegle, Peter Barker, David Bland, Daren Green, Keith Ricketts, Geir Jarnes, Tim Roberts, Charles Baker, Fergus Mack, Graham Medhurst, Neil Holland, Andrew Woodrow, Sandy Stewart, Jaques Carney, Hayden Brown, SC Brand, Mark Warren, Bjart Tronsden, Christian Borges, Paul Slingsby, Robert Nilsen, Robert Smith, Stephen Green and Jan Plug.

Deserving of a special mention are James Mclellan who contributed two outstanding photographs from the antipodes and George Craigen who as well giving me the use of some pictures of Star Offshore vessels in action, was good enough to read through the manuscript to ensure that it contained no glaring errors or omissions. My thanks are also due to those who gave up some of their time to talk to me about their experiences and as a result have made what could be a pretty dry subject, a little more interesting. These included Captains Dave Bland and Cliff Roberts.

I also used information from the internet, and since I uploaded the first picture of an offshore vessel in 1998, there have been many other sites developed dedicated to the industry, as well as those operated by the major ship-builders and ship-owners. I visited many of them over the last couple of years. My special thanks are due to Tim Colton of the Colton Company who has gone to the trouble of cataloguing the construction of every ship built at every American shipyard since the second world war. He provided me with a wonderful source if information on the Gulf of Mexico activities.

I also received a little help, albeit reluctantly, from one or two ship-owners and ship builders, some-what in contrast to the assistance I received when I visited the Tidewater offices in Canal Street, New Orleans in 1982, when the idea of writing this book was nothing more than that. They went to considerable trouble to provide me with information and invited me to visit their base in Morgan City. What they gave me twenty-five years ago, has been invaluable today.

And finally my thanks go to my designer in Posthouse Printing, Karin Thain who has tolerated my changes of mind, layout and text with considerable stoicism.

Victor Gibson
Madrid. October 2007.

Introduction

This book attempts to chronicle the development of the supply ship since it first appeared in the 1950s. This is not a life's work, so sometimes there are gaps in the narrative and the information, but it is to be hoped that there is a tenuous thread from the beginning to the present day, that offers a taste of the environment. Unfortunately, even after a mere fifty years, the records are sometimes sparse, and sometimes people are just not interested in telling us what happened or even what is happening now. The American supply ship owners remain particularly reluctant to share information about their current fleets, and in some cases about their past.

It is difficult to avoid Tidewater in America, and Maersk in Europe, since both companies have had a considerable influence on the development of ship types, and both own large numbers of ships. Tidewater in particular has seen its fortunes wax and wane, but has gradually increased in size by taking over other companies. A British engineer who contributed his recollections to this book went to work originally for International Offshore Services (IOS) and thereafter worked for two other companies, all of which were taken over by Tidewater. So in his career he was taken over three times by the same company.

If there are omissions of important developments then apologies are due, but like virtually all other historical narratives the writer must concentrate on what he has discovered and what he already knows, and must hope that the glimpses into the activities and events of the times will be enough to give the reader a flavour of what was happening.

During the development of the book a number of structures were considered, but in the end it was decided that a division of chapters by approach would be the best. Hence each chapter can be read individually and is complete in its own right. But the information in each one contributes to the whole.

Every effort has been made to include ships and events from all over the world, although being resident in Europe, it has been easier to find things out here, but it is hoped that the words which follow will give the reader some idea of the more or less headlong progress that has been made in the development of offshore vessels.

I use the term "supply vessels" to describe the typical vessels. They are the small ships which support oil rigs and platforms with all the services that they need, and it is probably only in the last years of the period that anchor-handlers have really become a different type of ship. And of course by the year 2000 they were ceasing to be so small.

The increase in size of the ships has been prompted not only by the tasks required (and here it is difficult to tell whether the rigs and platforms are venturing out into deeper water because of the availability of larger ships, or whether the ships are being developed to follow the rigs) but also by the increasing power offered by an engine of given dimensions and by the increase in sophistication of all the equipment carried on the vessels.

I started writing this book in 2005, hoping that its publication would coincide with the fiftieth anniversary of the appearance of the Ebb Tide, but it was not to be. The increase in the oil price which prompted the ordering of many new supply vessels, also necessitated my involvement in aspects of the operation of mobile drilling units at previously unexpected levels. So time has elapsed, but all being well it should be published in 2007.

Writing this book in the 21st Century has offered me a number of advantages, particularly the internet as a research tool. However I have not shirked from using the information which has been published by others. Many of the sources have been acknowledged at the back of this volume, and some have been acknowledged in the text. But in most cases it has been a labour of love to actually extract the required information. For instance, a visit to Great Yarmouth library produced a fund of information and identified a number of specialist books. It was easy to use the books on the Norfolk fishing boat and standby boat owners by Malcolm White; more difficult were the books of individual pictures from Great Yarmouth's past which included a single shot of two US Gulf supply ships and the vague title "Two survey ships visit Great Yarmouth in 1962". I read the names off the sterns and included them in the narrative.

Indeed the task of research became almost a reward in itself, and I began to understand what motivates researchers into genealogy. A tiny discovery can take one down a whole new avenue, littered with all sorts of nuggets of information, but in the end one has to be disciplined. This is one book, and it must be small enough to fit on the coffee table, and of sufficient interest for the reader to want to carry on reading.

My own involvement in the business started in the 1970s when I was working as a cargo superintendent for a small shipping line operating out of the port of Barry in South Wales. It was hard going and as time passed I began to realise that although I had a shore job, something a bit like gold dust in those days, I was still seeing nothing of my family. On the other hand I was seeing much of the quayside of Barry docks and was becoming used to breakfasting in the docker's canteen, having made a start at six am, and stumbling off to the pub at some time after six in the evening to talk over the day's disasters with similarly oppressed managers.

I was usually in the office before anyone else, which gave me the opportunity of reading Lloyds List, which often had the latest in supply vessels on its front page. Although not much was being said about what these craft actually did, it seemed that it might be exciting and require a high level of seamanship, and so when being a cargo superintendent got to be too much, and the ships in the North Sea started offering equal time off for time worked, I decided to make a change. I wrote to a number of ship-owners. OIL were the first to reply and pretty soon I found myself on an anchor-handler making up the team which moved the Victory class semi-submersible Ocean Kokuei.

A little over a year later I was in command of an anchor-handler, often being scared out of my wits, but enjoying the challenge of handling a ship which was constantly at odds with the environment and being asked to undertake tasks which were frankly beyond it, or any other ship which was around at the time.

My last ship in the North Sea was the wonderful UT734, the Star Sirius, which I brought out of the shipyard in Kristiansund in 1985 and put to work for Amoco out of Aberdeen. I learnt of the rather charming Norwegian custom of offering congratulations to the Captain of a new ship, and enjoyed the pleasure of commanding a well-designed and powerful vessel, and gaining the gratitude and sometimes the admiration of our charterers. I left in December 1986, but the Star Sirius and its sister ship, the Star Spica, spent more than a decade as the Shell term anchor-handlers in the North Sea.

The ten years I spent supplying rigs and towing them around the North Sea were followed by twenty years as a marine consultant, during which time I retained an interest in offshore vessels, their development and capabilities. From being a professional I became an enthusiast, and I hope both are obvious in the pages of this book.

Contents

Chapter 1	THE OFFSHORE OIL INDUSTRY	9
Chapter 2	IN THE BEGINNING	27
Chapter 3	SUPPLY WORK	39
Chapter 4	THE SEMI-SUBMERSIBLE	49
Chapter 5	THE NORTH SEA	65
Chapter 6	RIG SHIFTING	87
Chapter 7	DEEP WATER	103
Chapter 8	THE AMERICAN REVIVAL	121
Chapter 9	THE NEW MILLENIUM	137
Chapter 10	DEEP WATER MOORING	153
Chapter 11	TO BOLDLY GO	167
	AFTERWORD	180
	TIMELINES	182
	REFERENCES	185
	GLOSSARY OF TERMS	186
	INDEX	195

The Far Grimshader at a platform in the North Sea. The culmination of a number of years of exploration and development. Picture: Derek Mackay.

Chapter 1

THE OFFSHORE OIL INDUSTRY

This book is the history of the supply ship, in its broadest sense. It will be its job to chart the development of this particularly specialised marine activity associated with the offshore oil industry, and so those already familiar with the business should be patient while the uninitiated are given the opportunity of catching up.

Before 1955, a significant year as we will discover, ships carried out certain defined activities. The majority carried cargo and passengers from one place to another, whether they were ferries, liners, tramps, puffers or tankers. Some of their voyages were a few minutes long, others several weeks, but the tasks were essentially the same. These ships made up the merchant services of the world. Operated in parallel by most countries, even some without sea coasts, were the navies, which in the case of the larger nations were composed of fighting and support ships as well as numbers of auxiliary services. At their most fundamental level, the navies existed to protect the merchant fleets.

In addition to these basic tasks, large numbers of small craft towed, pushed and pulled larger vessels and barges, and in some cases rescued them when they broke down. These tugs were small ships and due to their size could be relied on to be able to manoeuvre close to larger vessels without crashing into them, and it was from this basic principle that the supply vessel was developed.

Seismic Ships

The offshore exploration process starts with the acquisition of seismic data. Seismic ships are used to collect the information and like the other types of marine craft involved, they have developed over the years. Early seismic ships were ex-trawlers towing a single short cable behind them, with one seismic receiver, or geophone, on it which received signals from the explosive charges lobbed over the stern by an intrepid seismic company employee. Today's vessels are large, purpose built and sophisticated, towing eight or ten streamers behind them, up to eight kilometres long, and receive information in what is known as 4D seismic, where the fourth dimension is time.

Watch-keepers on other ships find it difficult to comprehend the sheer scale of a seismic operation, and have a tendency to run over the cables, so these ships are usually provided with chase vessels whose job it is to warn off approaching craft. In addition, the deployment and recovery of the seismic streamers is a lengthy and complicated marine operation, and this has resulted in seismic ships being supported by small ships which store and refuel them, thereby removing the need for port visits. Like many of the larger marine craft engaged in oil exploration and development, most seismic ships are today provided with helidecks so that they can crew change on the move.

The Western Regent a modern seismic vessel. They deploy multiple streamers and need to be extremely powerful to haul the whole set-up through the water. Picture: Derek Mackay

Once the seismic information is collected, the geologists employed by the oil companies can determine the likely areas where it may be worthwhile drilling for oil. Most of the world's oceans have now been mapped by the seismic fleet, but the data keeps getting better, so it may be necessary to do the job again, and possibly again.

It is common for seismic companies to run long widely-spaced lines over likely areas which are due to be auctioned, and to sell the data to any oil company who may have an interest. This allows the company to make a more positive analysis of the value of the block on offer. These lines can be thirty kilometres long and several kilometres apart, and their function is to confirm the geologist's general ideas of the formation of the sub-strata.

In the simplest terms they are searching for a dome shaped substructure holding beneath it the oil-bearing rock, and in the event of preliminary surveys giving this impression, more detailed seismic work is carried out using shorter lines, closer together. These may be 10 kilometres long and 1 kilometre apart, and may be run in several directions.

This data is then analysed by the oil company's geological team and, assuming that they still consider the area productive, they will identify a spot where an initial hole is to be drilled. This will usually be where they consider the centre of the field to be.

Positioning an Exploration Rig

An exploration rig will then be hired, or taken from another area on completion of its work, and towed into the precise position defined by the geologists. It will then be sunk to the sea-bed, jacked up on its legs, or anchored, depending on what type of rig it is and the depth of water. Alternatively it may maintain station by dynamic positioning, a technique which has found great favour since the development of GPS – the global positioning system.

Apart from the DP drill ships, other types of rig will have been towed to the location by one or more anchor-handlers or tugs, and in the case of moored semi-submersibles the anchors will have been run using anchor-handlers. In very deep water the anchor-handler may have been used to locate suction piles or other specialist anchor points to which the rig's moorings will be connected, sometimes using ropes of various sorts.

The DP drill ships remain the most independent of the group. They can move from one place to another under their own steam, and when they arrive at the selected location they just stop moving forward, lock themselves into the GPS and stay exactly where they are for as long as it takes to drill the hole.

Assuming that the first hole is productive, the rig may then be moved to other spots in the field to determine the overall structure; the more complex the structure the more holes have to be drilled. In the event of a particularly worthwhile field more than one rig may be used, and drilling will continue until the company is satisfied that they know exactly what lies beneath the earth's crust.

Spudding In

Once on the location the rig will "spud in" – the very first stage in the drilling programme. Reservoirs may be found at any depth up to 30,000 feet and the speed with which drilling takes place depends on the hardness of the strata being penetrated, complete holes taking anything from six weeks to six months, so that the exploration of a field may be measured in years in some cases.

The initial phase of the drilling operation requires the rig to extend a 36" drill bit on the end of the drill string to the seabed. The depth of the hole drilled depends on the part of the world where the operation is being carried out. In some places, including the Gulf of Mexico, the hole is effectively jetted out with high pressure water to a depth of several hundred metres, but at the very least a hole is drilled deep enough to receive about 100 metres of 30" casing. The carriage of this casing is the first supply task to be carried out by one of the operator's chartered vessels; the casing may be lifted aboard the rig while the initial hole is being drilled.

The top of the 30" casing is fitted with the wellhead connector, and the whole length is cemented into place, the cement being injected through the drill string with a suitable connection. The rig then goes through one of its more onerous processes, the installation of the blow-out preventer (BOP) and the riser. The BOP and its associated subsystems can weight at much as 160 tonnes, and by one means or another this large lump of metal is suspended or supported under the drill floor, while the first joint of the riser is manoeuvred from the riser storage area into the derrick.

Deploying the Riser

On a drilling rig, as the name suggests, everything happens in the derrick, which up until recently was a lattice, with the blocks suspended under the centre. Every piece of tubular of any sort must therefore be heaved up off the deck through what is known as the V door and then the end attached to the hook on the travelling block. The driller then heaves away on drawworks and the tubular is lifted up until it is vertical.

At this point in the operation the end is lowered through a hole in the centre of the drill floor until it can be connected to the top of the BOP. Alarmingly, at least for the uninitiated, making this connection involves people hanging from wires under the drill floor wielding large spanners. If the rig is moving at all, they will be swung about, as will the BOP unless it is supported from beneath. While this is going on there may be a standby vessel close by, ready to rescue anyone who falls into the water; this is true of the North Sea and a few other places, where the provision of standby vessels has become a specialised activity.

Once the BOP is connected to the first joint of riser the whole lot is lowered away until the top of the joint can be held in place while the second joint is heaved into the derrick and connected to the top of the first joint. This is then lowered away, and so on. Finally the BOP will be positioned above the wellhead connector and can be lowered into place. Once in position the hydraulic connectors are activated and the rig is connected to the seabed.

The Stena Don, a fifth generation dynamically positioned semi-submersible mobile drilling unit, on location in the Norwegian sector of the North Sea. Picture: Roy Krakevik

Of course, on a semi-submersible, or a drill ship, some movement must be allowed for, and this is achieved by means of a slip joint - which is just what it sounds like, moving in and out like the slide on a trombone. Once the drill string has been extended down the riser this is kept on the bottom despite the movement of the rig by means of a compensating system consisting of hydraulic rams at the top of the derrick moving the whole of the block and tackle system up and down.

When the riser is in place the drilling cycle proper commences. The technique varies in different parts of the world. In the North Sea a 26" drill bit is used to drill a thousand feet into the sub strata, then the drill string is pulled out of the hole and the casing run. The casing lines the hole and once in position cement is pumped from the bottom up so that it is firmly held in position. Then a 17 1/2" bit is used and drilling starts in earnest.

Drilling Fluid - Mud

As the drill bit rotates, oil-based mud is pumped down the centre of the drill string and allowed to flow back up the outside, carrying with it the debris and providing a hydrostatic head. Drilling fluid requirements vary depending on water depth but at least 2000 barrels is normally required; hence nearly all supply vessels are designed to carry at least this amount, and some can carry much greater volumes in order to support deep water drilling.

The make-up and provision of drilling fluid is a science all of its own. The fluid needs to be heavy and should be able to lubricate the drill bit and coat the hole to prevent it from collapsing. Drilling fluid, or mud, is the first barrier to a blow-out, the second of course being the blow-out preventer. Up until the 1970s the mud was water-based, the liquid being mixed on board the rig and then pumped down the hole. On the rig it is held in what are known as "mud pits", essentially open topped tanks containing the mixing devices, like very large liquidisers.

Like many other items of rig equipment, the name "mud pit", originates on the plains of Texas, where the oilmen would dig holes in the ground, line them with tarpaulins and then fill them with mud. During the 1970s the industry began to experiment with diesel as the medium in which the baryte was suspended. The fluid proved to be better at doing everything in the well than water-based mud had been, but it was much more difficult to carry, and the development of transportation for mud from the shore to the rig and back again is a saga in itself.

By the year 2000 pseudo oil-based mud was being used, with chemicals added to water to raise the viscosity, so that it could hold in suspension the quantity of barytes required to provide the weight. As well as providing good lubrication this new compound has other essential qualities, the primary one being that it does not react with any of the substrata, as water-based mud sometimes does.

As well as supplying the rigs with "mud" and its constituents, base oil, baryte and bentonite the ships also carry cement in bulk – several hundred tons of it, and the pumping of cement out of the ship's tanks up into the silos on board the rigs has been one of the many areas of technical development in the industry, requiring as it does large volumes of compressed air at high pressure.

Once drilling has reached a depth of about 4000 feet, the drillers will call for 9 5/8" casing. The amount and variety of casing used to be the cause of considerable distress aboard the supply vessels, for two reasons. Firstly it was usually called for far in advance of the time when it would be required, necessitating the ship remaining at the location for long periods while space was made on the rig, and secondly all casing must be measured individually, so that the exact length will be known to the drillers when it is connected together and lowered into the hole.

Because of the limited deck space available on the rig it was customary for each length to be measured during unloading from the supply vessel, making the discharge time extremely lengthy, between twelve and twenty-four hours. In certain parts of the world there would not be much of a problem. The ships could, and still can, tie up, and if the weather is calm, switch off the engines and relax until the discharge is complete. In less benign conditions, even if tying up is possible, the master has to remain at the controls, alert for any changes in wind direction, swell or current.

Riser being discharged from the Sun Wrestler to the Ben Reoch at a deep water location in the Mediterranean. The riser connects the rig to the seabed and allows the return of drilling fluid. Picture: Victor Gibson.

Additionally, as we will see, the technique of snatching, or remaining positioned under the crane without actually being attached to anything, has become more and more necessary with the passing of time, not least because modern platform ships must align themselves sideways with offshore installations so that the cranes can reach everywhere on the deck.

Drilling continues and once a depth of about ten thousand feet has been reached the 9 5/8" casing is run. After this drilling resumes with an 8 1/2" drill bit to a depth of up to seventeen thousand feet, when the same procedure continues with 7" casing.

General Supply

During the drilling phase the rig must be supplied with the commodities needed for the job, which include casing, mud, chemicals, cement, fuel, drill water, potable water and food for the crew. In times past the operation was made more complex by the fact that the semi-submersibles had difficulty moving from operating to transit draft and back again without discharging most of the top weight, so the assigned vessels would load up with the rig's riser and drill pipe and transport it all to the shore, then dash back again to carry out the move. Once the rig had arrived

The drill floor of a drilling rig. This is an iron roughneck which is used to connect and disconnect drill pipe instead of the chains and spanners used in years gone by. Picture: Victor Gibson

at its new location and had been anchored up safely, the ships would then bring all the stuff out again. By the mid 1990s virtually all semi-submersibles had been upgraded so as to be able to carry a greater load on deck – 'variable deck load' as it is known, and so this particular phase of the operation became unnecessary; now anchor-handlers are often only hired for the move, and platform ships (normally part of a larger operation) carry out the supply duties. Most importantly, the marine riser, the length of tube connecting the wellhead to the rig, could remain on board the rig.

Well Testing

If oil has been discovered, a supply vessel will be required to transport quantities of equipment to allow for the rate of flow of oil to be tested. The equipment includes portable pipework, separators for separating gas and water from the oil, and storage tanks, all of which must be pressure rated for the expected pressures of the well. While the oil is flowing, it is burnt off using flare booms deployed by the rig. Once this is done the well can be capped and the rig is ready to move on. If the hole turns out to be dry it is plugged with cement, and the top section of casing blown off with explosives and retrieved, leaving the seabed level.

Well testing can also be carried out via a support vessel, with the well fluids being conducted by a long hose onto the ship, although at the time of writing only a few such vessels exist, and two built specifically for the task have never operated commercially in a way which returned the money invested in them. It is however possible to see some trends in this direction, and the key would appear to be that a complete set of test gear can fit onto the deck of a large platform ship, and many platform ships are now fitted with DP equipment.

Once the well testing has been done, or not, anchor-handlers are recalled and the anchors recovered, and the rig towed away to another location. This then is the basic task carried out by mobile units and the tasks described for the support vessels are the basic tasks which they can carry out.

Drill ships

Drill ships, which are ship-shaped monohulls with a derrick and a moonpool in the middle, are sometimes used in climatically benign areas of the world, and in very deep water. Drill ships have the disadvantage of being more vulnerable to adverse weather (because they are ship-shaped) but in any water depths they have the advantage of being able to carry a much greater load of drilling equipment and chemicals than other mobile units. Hence in past years moored drill ships were commonly used, particularly in South East Asia, but as the carrying capacity of semi-submersibles increased, so they became less popular.

The move into deeper water has increased the enthusiasm of the oil companies for DP vessels, including drill ships, which under the best circumstances do not need to be supported by any other marine vessels. In addition, the development of satellite navigation systems, especially GPS (the Global Positioning System) has made their operation as DP vessels much more viable. They can move from place to place under their own power, leaving a location and positioning themselves at a new one using GPS, and so require the minimum of outside intervention.

To service this market, a number of very large drill ships have been constructed, and some of them can test the results of their work and store the produced oil in tanks on the ship, then return to port to discharge.

These vessels and other DP units are able to carry the vast quantities of equipment required to carry out the drilling operation. They can drill holes 30,000 feet under the sea and in water depths of 10,000 feet. To do this they will have to carry the 10,000 feet of riser (the tube connecting the vessel to the seabed) as well as the drill pipe and other chemicals and equipment.

Deep Water Semi-submersibles

In addition to the operation of DP vessels in deep water, the industry has developed means of mooring semi-submersibles in depths of up to 10,000 feet. This system uses suction anchors and fibre ropes connecting the ends of the ropes to the mooring systems of the rigs. The particular advantage of using a mooring system is that it ceases to be totally dependent on the rig, and the actual operation of mooring the rig takes no more than 24 hours.

The technique used is to lay a set of moorings, using either a patent form of drag embedment anchor or else suction anchors, and then disconnect the rig from its current set of moorings and move it to the new position and connect it up to the new set of moorings. The ships will then be sent back to the previous set of moorings, now buoyed off, and move them to a new location to await the arrival of the rig. This technique is being used both in the Gulf of Mexico and off the coast of Brazil and is being contemplated in the deep waters off the coast of the UK.

In addition to the use of fibre moorings, there are semi-submersibles being moored using their own mooring systems in water depths of up to 7,000 feet.

Casing being discharged at a jack-up. Over the duration of a drilling programme thousands of feet of tubulars will be discharged to the rig. Picture: David Styles.

A well test. Flaring off indicates that the drilling programme has been successful and that the next stage will be production. Picture: Tony Poll.

Dynamic Positioning

We have now mentioned dynamic positioning a number of times without providing a suitable explanation. Curiously, while the marine industry knows much about the technicalities of DP vessels, they are less aware of the capabilities of these craft, and indeed why there are now so many of them about. DP systems allow some platform ships to remain in a precise position on the earth's surface, with the assistance of an electronic referencing system, some interfacing by computer and the provision of engines, rudders and thrusters; the last probably at both ends of the craft.

DP, as a concept, was originally developed by Shell in the Gulf of Mexico. The first DP vessel was the Eureka built by Sedco. It was an extremely small vessel, and somewhat optimistically named, but it did the job for the developers and paved the way for the Sedco 445, which was the first genuinely operational DP drill ship, in 1971. It soon became apparent that the system could be used for diving ships, which usually maintained position by means of clump weights on the seabed connected to a taut wire. The referencing system in this case was the sensor, which detected changes in the angle of the wire from the vertical and restored the angle to what it was before by moving the ship.

In addition, when these vessels were operating within an oilfield, it was normal for one or more of the platforms in the field to have some form of positioning system installed. Some systems transmitted signals from three platforms, giving the computer on the ship a triangular fix, the most prominent of these being "Syledis". This was a long-range system capable of being used at ranges of up to 80 kilometres. For shorter range work "Artemis" systems were often installed. Artemis consisted of two motor-driven dish aerials, one on the ship and one on the platform. When locked in, they would track each other, providing direction and distance.

Global positioning systems have done much to reduce the requirement for these aerial systems, and the Artemis principal has been more or less subverted by the "Fanbeam", where the motor-driven aerial is only fitted to the ship, and this locks onto an inactive aerial on the rig.

Today DP systems at various levels of complexity are becoming common on all types of support vessel.

Diver Intervention

In the sixties and seventies virtually every semi-submersible was fitted with a diving habitat, a diving bell and all the accoutrements. The divers were required to make connections between the blow-out preventer and the wellhead, and the blow-out preventer and the marine riser. Divers were also used extensively as the concept of the 'satellite well' developed, and platforms became collecting points for wells drilled at a distance. Such wells had their own termination on the seabed (known as a 'manifold'), and their own small pipe known as a flow-line. The divers would connect up all the hardware, which resulted in a technically advanced vessel with a crew of up to fifty people, costing many thousands of dollars a day, being used to put a single man with a spanner on the seabed.

But as the offshore industry moves into deeper and deeper water the possibility of diver intervention is reduced, and the likelihood of the fields being operated through platforms with their feet on the seabed decreases. There was some development in the mid-seventies of dry habitats, which it was felt would solve some of the problems relating to work with divers. Such habitats would allow workers to descend to the seabed at surface pressure, enter the habitat, also at surface pressure, carry out the work which was required and then return to the ship. No endless days in a decompression chamber would be required.

Today there is talk of drilling wells from the seabed, and as the systems on board drilling rigs become more automated, such ideas get closer to reality. Such a drilling system would be carried, launched from and operated by a surface ship on DP. This is not a million miles away from film "The Abyss", where the main characters are housed in an underwater drilling unit supported by surface craft.

Developing Offshore Oilfields

Having gone through the process of exploration, once the company has decided that the field will be productive they will apply to the government under whose jurisdiction the area of the seabed lies, for permission to develop it. They will then decide what sort of means are to be used to extract the oil, process it, and transport it.

The next step depends on water depth and location, and in shallow waters such as the edge of the Gulf of Mexico and in the Arabian Gulf, further wells might be drilled and capped and small diameter pipes led over the seabed to central collecting platforms. Elsewhere, until the end of the 1970s, once it had been established that there was a reservoir sufficiently large to be worthy of exploitation, construction of a platform would take place.

Diving ships are often used to complete wells by installing items of subsea equipment, which when connected up will flow the well to an adjacent platform.
Picture: Victor Gibson

When the jacket in put in place in the traditional way a heavy lift vessel is called in to install the topsides. This is the Balder on its way to another job with Njord following. Picture: Wim Kosten.

The base unit, known as the jacket, would be towed out to the location either relying on its own buoyancy or else on a barge, and once there, in one way or another, it would be set upright and pinned to the seabed. Thereafter the modules would be shipped out on barges and lifted into place with a heavy lift crane. Next a large number of wells would be drilled from the platform, all of them directed to different places in the reservoir.

This basic process continues, although the technology is changing. Operators everywhere but in the Gulf of Mexico are tending to avoid large and tall platforms, and in many cases the jacket can be placed in position by the same jack-up which drilled the holes, or at least by one of the modern heavy lift barges which are capable of picking up and positioning lifts of 10,000 tonnes.

The heavy lift barge has itself made a difference to the speed of construction of offshore installations, and one can see what has motivated developments in the area of platform construction. From the moment when it has been decided that a field will be developed, a race against time begins. It becomes essential that the field be brought on stream soon as possible, presumably because once a great deal of money has been invested in the platform structure, immediate payback is required.

The ability to drill the wells before the platform arrives, and for the crane barges to lift a complete topside in one lift, have made a massive difference to the speed at which fields are brought on stream, although of course the level of marine support has consequently been reduced.

In some cases the platforms arrive on location complete, with their topsides already in position. This has always been so in the case of concrete platforms and also uniquely in the case of the Maureen platform, which is a steel jacket, but which was towed to location vertically with the topsides in position, buoyancy being achieved by flotation units. Concrete platforms have been constructed in Norway and in locations on the West coast of Scotland, both areas having the necessary ingredient of deep water. Concrete platforms are constructed vertically, being ballasted down to keep the work area close to the sea surface, and during the construction of the North Sea platforms in Loch Kishorn back in the 1970s, numbers of supply vessel acted as utility craft, some of them even being given the role of mobile canteen – this a tent on the afterdeck. Curiously this very basic task seems now to be echoed in the use of large, sophisticated, dynamically positioned platform ships to provide construction worker's accommodation at offshore locations in West African waters.

Tension leg platforms have been developed to enable the structure to be completed close to the shore and then towed out into position. So far the only one in the North Sea - the Hutton TLP - has proved successful, but there are now a number of different tension leg designs being used in the deeper waters of the Gulf of Mexico.

This is an accommodation module for the Scott platform on its way out of Invergordon on a Heerema barge in 1994. Picture: Victor Gibson

Traditionally once the platforms are in position they will be connected by pipeline to the shore. This is Ninian Central with the Viking Piper pipelaying barge in the 1970s. Picture: Victor Gibson

FPSOs and Subsea Completions

In addition to drilling wells to be positioned beneath the platforms, latterly even in deep water, wells have been drilled at a distance from the central platform and the product directed to it by means of flow-lines. The process is not simple. The wells have safety valves installed beneath the surface which can be operated at any time by those who are receiving the flow of hydrocarbons, and the flow-lines must be protected from dropped objects, which are an ongoing problem for those installing these systems. The protection sometimes takes the form of a solidly built steel structure over the wellhead, and the pipelines are either buried beneath the surface of the seabed, or else covered with linked concrete slabs, known as mats. Occasionally a rock dumping vessel is called in to lay a pile of rubble over the pipe.

The rock dumpers usually extend a fall pipe towards the seabed,. On the end of it is the fall pipe ROV, which provides the means for the operator to locate the end of the pipe precisely over the flow-line. Once in position the rock is discharged over the pipe to be protected.

Many of the systems consist of a number of wellheads connected to the final collection point (which may be a platform or a floating unit) and in one or two cases may actually be on shore. The valves can be operated from a remote position, allowing some or all of the wells to be flowed at one time. Some of the fields are also provided with water injection wells, also operated remotely as part of the same system.

Sometimes the collection points for subsea systems are FPSOs. Floating production and tanker off-take systems have been used for many years. Such systems are used in the North Sea, on the Atlantic margin and in the deep waters off the coast of Brazil and West Africa. In the US Gulf of Mexico, a variety of floating objects and very tall platforms are in use, with pipeline connections to the shore, principally because the distances are short. All of these systems have one objective, which is to get the oil or gas from its source under the earth's crust to a point on the land where it can be refined into the many products for which hydrocarbons are used.

There are two means of transporting the hydrocarbons from the field to the shore, the first by pipeline and the second by tanker. Early fields in the Gulf of Mexico and the Arabian Gulf relied on pipelines to get the liquid ashore, while the first fields in the North Sea relied on tankers which swung round offshore loading buoys for weeks at a time. Today the FPSOs have resulted in a much faster turn-round time for tankers, which can arrive, load and depart in less than 48 hours.

Once platforms are operating they have a constant need for intervention from Remote Operating Vehicles (ROVs) which are deployed from DP vessels. Picture: Derek Mackay.

Pipe-laying

Of course to lay the pipe, pipe-layers are required, this task traditionally being carried out by large barges which are moved slowly forward on multiple anchors. The pipe is welded together on the deck and when a weld is complete the vessel will move forward laying the welded pipe over the stern. Meanwhile small vessels will be engaged in moving the anchors forward as if manipulating the limbs of a giant insect, and pipe carriers will be providing a constant supply of lengths of pipe.

Over the passing of time this operation has become more sophisticated and complex. Sometimes the pipe has to be buried under the seabed and so a trench has to be dug, and sometimes the water is so deep that the angle at which the pipe leaves the vessel is close to the vertical.

Like many other activities, trenching is a task which has developed over time. During the 1970s and '80s trenching machines were like very large bulldozers which were lowered over the stern of a support vessel and which then trundled along on the seabed making the hole, powered by hydraulics on the surface, but by the millennium the task was being carried out by very large high-power anchor-handlers which towed a plough behind them. The pipe would then be laid in the trench and buried and where necessary construction vessels might be used to lay concrete mats over vulnerable points.

There has also been an increase in the number of vessels laying pipe from reels. Initially ships were used to lay flexible flow-lines over short distances, but the increased size of supply ships, and the availability of GPS and DP systems, has made it viable to lay flexibles and solid steel pipe from reels over long distances. The first of these reel ships was the Apache, built in 1979, and the latest is the Skandi Navica. The great attraction of the Apache and other ship-shaped vessels is the speed of mobilisation, although this attraction is, in a way, reduced, because special loading points are required. Hence there is probably an optimum pipe size for this type of ship. One can for instance see the attraction in having 30 miles of 6" pipe reeled into the ship, all of which can be laid in one shot in 200 ft of water.

Once constructed and connected the platforms may operate for many years. This is the Brent Field, established in the 1970s and still producing in 2007. Picture: Victor Gibson.

Brownfield Activities

With the maturity of the industry, the incidence of brownfield activities, the rejuvenation of old fields, has become the order of the day, and old wells are routinely cleaned up and made to operate better. Of course, if the original field has used the technique of drilling a number of wells through a subsea manifold, then when these wells need cleaning up a mobile unit must be towed into position over the manifold and anchored. The well must then be re-entered and the necessary work done.

In shallow waters all over the world jack-ups are eased into position very close to the small platforms which host a single well. There are places where it is necessary to constantly test the flow rate from individual wells, and since each well surfaces under a small platform fitted with its own helidecks, a ship fitted with a full set of well-test kit is required to tie up to the platform and flow the well for a couple of hours though the equipment; thereafter either burning off the results or storing it in tanks.

When the clean-up is being carried out it is not uncommon for the job to be done by a 'Frac' vessel which of course does a "fracturing" job. These ships carry large quantities of sometimes noxious substances which are pumped down the well at high pressure, and their use makes the whole job easier. The alternative is to transport pumps and tanks of the fluids out by supply vessel and lift the lot up to the drilling unit deck and then do the job. There are of course risks involved in both processes and the personnel involved in the operation will weigh one set of risks against the other.

Inspection and Maintenance

We have already mentioned diving and DP ships, but it is in the inspection and maintenance of fields that supply ships come into their own. Back in the early days divers were used for most stages of the operations. Many aspects of field developments required diver intervention and some fields still do. However, the ROV has more or less taken over from the diver as the means of carrying out work under water.

Initially ROVs were used for pipeline inspections and the like but as the technology has improved so the work carried out by ROVs has increased, and now most mobile units will be provided with an ROV by the clients. ROV ships are sent out to do all sorts of maintenance and inspection work and some vessels, including the anchor-handlers, which lay the suctions anchors and attach the fibre moorings, carry an ROV of their own which attaches and detaches the rope.

In some locations the oil is collected at a floating production, storage and offtake vessel (FPSO). It is moored using the largest anchor-handlers available, in this case Maersk Assister. Picture: Wullie Bemner.

Supplying Platforms

In addition to all these exciting and innovative activities, a field with manned platforms operating needs to be supplied. This basic task now inevitably involves a few large platform ships and some sort of specialised logistics supply company, and is a long way from how it once used to be. Back in the early days oil companies would have their own fleets of vessels, which would probably be a mixture of platform ships and anchor-handlers.

In the Gulf of Mexico and the Arabian Gulf, and almost anywhere where the distances from the base port to the field are limited, the vessels used have remained small, but in places where the fields are more distant they tend to be larger. In the Arabian Gulf for instance, the distance of the farthest field from the main base port is not much more than 6 hours and the closest fields are not more than 2 hours away. Contrast this with the North Sea, where some of the fields are 24 hours away from the base port.

At some times during the last fifty years the ability of ships to operate with minimal fuel consumption has been a major factor, something which one might be forgiven for thinking would be of no interest to the oil companies. At times this resulted in the Chief Engineers keeping hidden stores of fuel, which was not too difficult to do and depended on how rigorous the surveys were at the end of charters. If necessary some fuel from this hidden store could be used to apparently minimise fuel consumption. Today there is considerable interest in environmentally effective platform ships, which genuinely use less fuel in their day-to-day operations.

De-commissioning

The phases of the operation so far covered are data acquisition, exploration, appraisal, construction and production, and these will shortly be followed by destruction, for which as yet no well-defined marine procedures have been established, although some platforms had been removed by the year 2005.

Notable amongst these are the Maureen platform in the North Sea and the Hutton TLP. The former is still to be found tied up to a pier in Norway and the latter was towed off to Northern Russia where parts of it are once more to be used for oil production. Some small platforms have also been removed by the simple expedient of lifting them up with a very large crane. At oil shows round the world people with ideas, backers and money propose exciting marine craft which they hope will be used to remove the topside of large platforms in one hit and then transport them to the shore. There they can be refurbished. Whether this, or in fact any other technique will work for the platforms which were constructed in the early seventies, like vast Lego edifices, remains to be seen.

Emergency Response and Rescue Vessels

So far only the briefest mention has been made of the standby vessel, or as they are known in the UK sector of the North Sea ERRVs (Emergency Response and Rescue Vessels). In a number of areas of the world these craft are required by law to save the chaps on the rigs if they fall over the side, to rescue numbers of them if their helicopter fall into the sea and to rescue large numbers of them if their offshore structure or vessel should sink. They are used in many offshore areas under the jurisdiction of a number of governments. In Europe these include the UK, Norway, Holland and Denmark and elsewhere some are used in the Gulf of Mexico, and their presence is mandatory off the coast of Newfoundland.

The first ships to be employed as Standby Vessels were in almost all cases redundant fishing vessels, partly because they became available due to the reduction in deep-sea fishing, and partly because of their sea-keeping qualities. However most legislations have developed rules for standby vessels which have necessitated an improvement in their capabilities. In addition there have been developments as operators have attempted to optimise the use of resources, one vessel often covering a large area containing several structures. Both in the UK and Norway there are now large vessels in service which do many things, although the basic task has not changed.

How then do the guys out there carry out the basic task? If a helicopter falls into the sea within their area of jurisdiction, they will launch one of their FRCs (Fast Rescue Craft) and make way as fast as possible to the vicinity of the crash, where they will try to pull the survivors out of the water.

As these ships became employed to look after more than one structure, but it was evident that the ships could not be in more than one place at a time, the concept of the "daughter craft" was developed. Daughter craft are large FRCs with cabins in which the crew are able to remain for a number of hours, and are hence, to a degree, autonomous. Of course the larger the craft is, the more difficult it becomes to launch and recover, and where it is too difficult to launch an FRC it is often impossible to fly helicopters, so most standby vessels are fitted with a glorified shrimp net called a 'Dacon Scoop' . The Dacon Scoop in theory allows the vessel to pick survivors out of the sea without the necessity of launching an FRC but it has yet to be tested in anger, apart from the tests carried out by its inventor who apparently routinely threw himself into the sea and had himself scooped out of the water by an intrepid standby vessel master.

Sophisticated Operating Systems

It should be clear to the reader by now that operating ships in support of the oil industry is an expensive business. All the craft require a degree of sophistication unheard of previously and even currently in much of the marine world. Most merchant ships are still built with a single propeller and a single engine, the objective being to get their cargo from A to B at the cheapest possible price. Complex systems, as well as requiring extra money, also require a greater degree of skill in operation.

The largest tanker in the world under construction in 2004 had one engine and one propeller, which seems less than adequate in reality. Contrast this with a modern anchor-handler, which will be provided with four engines and two main propellers and a number of thrusters.

These ships will also have two rudders which can be operated independently, and while it is pretty obvious what the tanker master does with his one engine and one rudder it may not be evident to all what an anchor-handler master does with the multiple systems at his disposal.

Of course, these multiple systems are provided to allow the ships to manoeuvre extremely close to offshore installations, other ships and platforms and of course in port without needing to use tugs. Almost all offshore supply and other support vessel are provided with two conning positions, one facing forwards and one facing aft and overlooking the after deck.

When the ships are engaged in point-to-point voyages the watch-keepers look out of the forward windows, and manoeuvre the ship as necessary from the forward conning station, which is usually provided with a seat and more than one radar. If the ship is provided with multiple engine the voyage will often take place using only two of four or possibly one of two if the correct subsystems are available.

On arrival at the offshore location the ship will be stopped and manoeuvred using the aft controls, a wholly different and possibly unique skill, and rather surprisingly becoming more rare as the technical development of control systems continues apace.

Sophisticated Control Techniques

The traditional technique of tying up the ship to an offshore installation is now used only in shallow and benign conditions and elsewhere ships do what used to be called 'snatching', but which now is considered to be the normal mode of operation in the North Sea and the deeper waters of the Gulf of Mexico. Of course, even if the water is too deep for the use of the anchor, it may still be possible to lie alongside an offshore installation, as many photographs from the Gulf of Mexico show.

It is said that the technique of keeping a ship on station in a wind or current is not far away from the process of keeping a helicopter hovering over a fixed object. It is done most easily if the stern of the ship is facing the wind because, without wanting to go too deeply into the mystique of ship handling, if the ship is being propelled astern it will naturally back into the wind. Therefore to maintain station it would appear to be sufficient only to go very slowly astern. Beam to wind things are a little different. The accommodation has more windage than the low stern but fortunately there are usually more thrusters at the bow, so really all that is necessary to maintain station beam to wind is to ensure that there is enough thrust being used both forward and aft to maintain the position. Of course if there are no thrusters aft then the propellers and rudders have to be used to create a side thrust without the ship moving forward or aft.

If there is a current from a different direction then a more complex level of control is required, in some cases turning the rudders inwards so that they act against each other, and in order to make these more complex controls easier a computer will often be used to interface with the engines and rudders, allowing them all to be operated by a single collective control known as a joystick. Many technically advanced vessels are fitted with joysticks.

Basic supply vessel and anchor-handling operations are carried out with the ship driver, and the task is known as 'driving', facing the stern. This is difficult to get used to, considering the fact that all the controls appear to be acting in exactly the opposite way to the manner in which they are operated when the driver is facing forward.

The History of the Supply Vessel

This then is the environment in which the supply vessel operates. And the term "supply vessel" includes its derivatives, which are anchor-handlers of all sorts, including the small vessels used for moving pipe-barges, and some of the larger craft which might be described by some as field maintenance vessels. The narrative which follows can only be a strand of loosely connected events wending its way through the decades to the present day. To do anything other would create a very large volume which would be boring in the extreme.

The history of this curious ship type is unusual in that the industry which it supports is also very new, so the normal marine traditions have hardly been applied to it. And if they had it would be difficult to imagine that the job could have been done at all. Today it has become a day-to-day event for a ship to pull a subsea plough along the seabed using over 20,000 bhp or for a platform supply vessel to use between six and ten thousand horsepower to maintain station a few metres from a vast offshore structure in a near gale.

We have reached this point from the beginning, when an ex WWII landing ship (tank) struggled to get alongside a wooden platform in the shallow waters off the Mississippi delta. It is a story of technical innovation, and bravery, both on the part of those who invested in the new ship designs and those who sailed on them.

The Ebb Tide set the style for all the supply vessels which were to follow – this photograph seems to have been taken before the vessel departed for Lake Maracaibo. Picture: Tidewater Archives.

Mr Charlie, not the first but possible the most famous submersible designed by Doc Laborde and built for Odeco in 1954. Picture: Kenny Polson

CHAPTER 2

IN THE BEGINNING

Paddling in the Shallows

At the end of the 19th century the oil industry, already mature onshore in America, put its toe into the shallows at the sea edge of the coast of Summerland, California; and drilled holes (from a variety of odd structures) on Lake Eirie. Neither development was sustained and they contributed little to the collective knowledge of the offshore industry. However, drilling at a third location, on the border between Louisiana and Texas was a different proposition.

Gas had been bubbling to the surface of Lake Caddo for as long as any of the locals could remember. When it finally seemed possible to search for oil over water in 1904, the first well was drilled into the lake bed. It was a duster, but during the drilling of the second well in 1905 the gas caught fire. This was the first ignited blow-out. In the following years, the gas ignited on a number of occasions, causing the intrepid oil men to abandon the wells, still burning, and to move on to another spot. Some wells continued to burn for years, and although exploration continued there was never any productive use made of the gas. It was looked upon as an unwelcome impediment to the pursuit of oil.

In 1910, during the process of increasing regulation of oil exploration activities, Gulf Oil obtained the exploration rights to the whole of Lake Caddo and their drilling superintendent devised a formal plan for drilling over water. Drilling equipment was transported by barge up the Red River from Baton Rouge and platforms were built using trees from the lake shore for piles. By the end of 1911, Gulf had eight wells in production on the lake.

The book "50 Years Offshore" mentions the fact that Gulf operated a special fleet on the lake, but gives no details of how it was made up. It was capable of transporting the large numbers of tree trunks used to make up every platform and then to move the drilling rigs into position. Almost all the equipment was made from wood, which was in plentiful supply, and could be abandoned once an exploration well was completed.

The next major area of what might be termed "offshore development" was on Lake Maracaibo in Venezuela, where Shell discovered oil in 1917. More significantly a large field was discovered some way offshore in 1922, and within a few years exploration was taking place in a manner similar to that used on Lake Caddo. However there was one major drawback. This was the teredo, or shipworm, a bivalve clam which bores into any wood it comes across. The teredo was capable of reducing the piles which formed the base of the drilling rig to little more than a collection of holes, and as a result the whole structure might collapse into the lake without warning. This menace stimulated the search for alternative materials, and by 1927 concrete piles were being used instead of wooden ones, the piles being produced by the Raymond Concrete Pile Company, who had set up a factory on Toas Island.

By the mid 1930s the drillers on Lake Maracaibo had taken further major steps forward. Steel was now being used for the piles supporting the derrick itself, and floating barges, known as tenders, were used to provide all the services required for the drilling operation. The tender could be moved from one well to another, saving the cost of much of the construction and inadvertently providing the basis for the whole offshore drilling process.

During the 1920s exploration was also taking place in the bayous of Louisiana, although this was not a task taken on lightly. There was no gas bubbling to the surface, so there was a greater risk of dry holes, and this risk was combined with a much higher cost per well, because the drillers had either to build a road, or dig a canal to get their equipment to the well site. By 1930 some oil companies were using floating vessels to drill wells, so this meant that even though they might still have to dredge the canal to get to the well site, they did not need to unload the barge. Almost in spite of itself the industry was being propelled in the direction of the mobile offshore drilling unit.

Louis Giliasso and the Submersible

The use of these floating vessels prompted the next step, the submersible, first put into use by the Texas Company (later to become Texaco). Texaco were searching for a cheaper and more stable means of exploring for oil in the Louisiana bayous, and hit on the idea of the submersible. This was a barge which could be floated into position, and then sunk to the bottom of the swamp to provide a secure and solid work platform. However, they found that someone had already lodged a patent for the device.

Louis Giliasso, a former merchant ship master who had worked in the oil industry on Lake Maracaibo, invented the submersible drilling barge in 1928, but had been unable to persuade any of the oil companies then drilling that he had found a solution to one of their problems. Typically the oil companies had to go their own way, and find out for themselves that they needed Giliasso's invention. The Texas Company was initially unable to locate Louis, who by this time had become disillusioned and had given up inventing to become a bar owner in Panama, but they gained permission to build the craft from his lawyers and Giliasso himself was located in 1933. The first of these submersibles (appropriately named the 'Giliasso') entered service in that year.

Offshore At Last

What is considered by some to be the first offshore well was drilled in 1932 from a platform 100 metres off the coast of Louisiana in a water depth of 4 metres. Then in 1936, after some problems relating to ownership or authority over the offshore areas of the Gulf of Mexico between the federal and state governments, the State of Louisiana issued licences for exploration to Pure oil and Superior Oil. They decided to drill a well one mile off the coast, once more in extremely shallow water, and employed Brown and Root to build a platform 100 ft by 300 ft which would be resistant to wind and waves.

Although the platform was only one mile from the coast it was necessary to transport everything to do with the well from the port of Cameron, which was 13 miles away. The drilling equipment and supplies were transported mainly by tug and barge, and the personnel and smaller items were transported by fishing vessels. This may have been the first offshore location where marine logistics had to be considered. Hampered by lack of a radio, the offshore personnel had to rely on messages being passed by the boats running back and forth. Hence there was little opportunity for hotshots. However, the adventure paved the way for others and between 1937 and the end of the Second World War some 25 wells were drilling offshore in the Gulf of Mexico.

Possibly the next landmark event (if that is the correct term for something which happened at sea) was the construction by the Magnolia Petroleum Company of a platform five miles offshore in 1946. This platform was built to support all the drilling operations, including cementing and mud logging, and was provided with a radio shack. The crew worked their shift on the rig, and were then transported to a ship moored close to the shore for their off duty time. A couple of shrimpers provided the logistics support required for this operation.

The wreck of the Rip Tide, the second and visibly superior supply vessel built by Tidewater in 1955 at Alexander Shipyard as soon as the experimental Ebb Tide had been seen to be successful. Picture: Kenny Polson

Although Magnolia were unsuccessful in their search, their platform design pointed the way for Superior, who were already experienced in drilling over water. This company decided to drill a well 30 kilometres off the shore in 6 metres of water, and contracted J Ray McDermott to develop a platform design. The McDermott design consisted of a series of braced steel structures, or jackets, which would collectively support the work areas and the drilling derrick. The design had the merit of being very rapidly installed offshore, and being generally robust. The platform, installed in 1947, also for the first time provided accommodation for the workers. The offshore workforce had arrived.

All of this activity preceded the arrival on the scene of Kerr-McGee who, in partnership with Phillips Petroleum and Stanolind Oil And Gas, struck oil offshore at Ship Shoal, in the Gulf of Mexico, on 4 October 1947. The Kerr-McGee platform was installed by Brown and Root, and was quite different from the Superior platform. In order to minimise costs, the Brown and Root platform only supported the derrick itself, while all the services and accommodation for the work force were provided on a tender vessel, a converted war surplus Yard-Fighter (YF) barge. Kerr McGee had also purchased a Landing Ship - Tank (LST) which was intended to provide the supply service. The success of this small company caused many LSTs to be purchased and used for offshore purposes. For the first time a practical small ship was made available to be used principally for the carriage of cargo. In 1948 Humble Oil purchased 19 of these vessels and in order to more practically install the jackets J Ray McDermott built a 150-tonne heavy lift crane barge. The guidelines had been drawn up for oil exploration for the next few years, but even then the suitability of the LST as either a tender support vessel or a supply vessel was questioned. The open deck between the wing tanks was quite narrow, and there was poor visibility from the pilot house, and as anyone who has driven an LST will testify, they were pigs to handle, and only saved from being completely unmanageable by the distance between the twin screws, which enabled them to be turned short round with a degree of ease.

Exploration Drilling

During the post war years there was a gradual separation between exploration drilling and production, and in what would seem in hindsight a completely logical step, the fully-fledged mobile unit was developed. It became obvious that what was necessary was a rig which was capable of moving from place to place, carrying with it the derrick, all the machinery and all the necessary storage capability for the impedimenta necessary for the drilling operation. This resulted in the design and construction of the submersible Breton 20 for Barnsdall, essentially a barge on which were mounted a number of piles, in which in turn was mounted a deck supporting the drilling equipment.

The Breton 20 was bought in 1950 by Kerr McGee and renamed "Rig 40", and in this guise the unit was destined to continue working for a further 20 years. However there was always unease about aspects of its construction and stability. In 1953 a former marine superintendent for Kerr McGee, Alden J Laborde, founded the Ocean Drilling and Exploration Company (ODECO) and placed an order for the construction of 'Mr Charlie', an altogether more advanced submersible. This unit drilled its first well in 1954.

Like the Breton 20, Mr Charlie was a barge which could be sunk beneath the waves, leaving the working deck well clear of the sea, so that those engaged in the drilling operation could work safely. As well as drilling and storage, it also featured a crane fixed on either side of the main deck.

Following another principal altogether, the Magnolia Company had developed a drilling unit based on the Delong dock. These barges had been used successfully to build a temporary port to supply invasion forces subsequent to the D-Day landings, and consisted of a hull fitted with tubular legs. The hull could be towed into position and the legs extended until the barge was raised out of the water and cleared the waves. The Magnolia barge was known as Barge No 1.

In 1954 the newly formed Offshore Company also purchased a Delong barge. The hull of this unit could be elevated 40 feet above the waves, and the drilling was done through a slot in the side. It was called Rig 51.

Other developments included Mr Gus, the first mat supported jack-up, which was a hull which raised itself above the surface of the sea, and was supported on the seabed by a sort of large flat plate. A three-legged jack-up was also built to the Le Tourneau design, similar in principal to the Delong dock, but more stable.

It was easier for the sceptics to understand how a hull could be jacked up than how a hull could be sunk beneath the surface, and when Mr Charlie went out on its trials the news articles of the time reported that onlookers waited eagerly for the rig to turn over. But the trials were successful and Mr Charlie spudded its first well for Shell on 24th June 1954.

It may appear at this moment that we are about to embark on a history of the exploration rig, and while it is not intended that this be the case, during this period the development of the MODU is inexorably linked with the development of the supply vessel. Mr Charlie is also important because it was developed, at least in concept, by Alden J. "Doc" Laborde, who had refined the design of the Breton 20 as a result of his previous employment by Kerr-McGee.

From the point of view of marine support, the rigs could be towed into the appropriate position by tugs and then sunk to the seabed so that they could go to work.

Mr Charlie was not then the only mobile unit operating in 1954, but it was the only one designed by Doc Laborde who, having become the Chief Executive of ODECO, (the company formed to build and market the rig), turned his attention to providing a means of supporting the unit. It was possible for the craft doing the job to lie alongside the rig and for the crane on the deck to plumb the cargo, but even the most open decks used, those on the LSTs, were still surrounded by high bulkheads, and this resulted in the cargo snagging the sides. Doc Laborde therefore decided that something more appropriate was needed, and after having designed such a complex floating object as Mr Charlie, designing a "fit for purpose" ship was going to be pretty straightforward.

The First Supply Ship

What was required was a vessel with the maximum of available open deck commensurate with the size of the craft, and since all ships need a bow which, besides being pointed, must carry the windlass, anchors and cable stowage, it seemed a good idea to add the pilot house and accommodation. This resulted in a long open deck entirely uncluttered by the usual marine requirements such as rigging, masts, companionways and deck houses. It is tempting to add funnels to this list, but in fact there were two funnels which extended unobtrusively from the port and starboard bulwarks half way down the deck and stopped a few feet above the rail. After all, the ship was going to operate in the Gulf of Mexico and was only going to go to sea in fine weather.

Doc Laborde transferred his idea from his head to the back of an envelope and put it to Bill LeBlanc, then port captain for Kerr McGee, who felt that the design was impractical because it would "pound the crew unmercifully". It says something for Bill LeBlanc's immediate grasp of the vessel's potential qualities that no-one who has ever sailed on a supply vessel would be likely to dispute that statement.

High Tide, a second generation Tidewater supply vessel ordered a few months after the Ebb Tide from the Alexander Shipyard.
Picture: Tidewater Publicity

The Hercules, surely a Tidewater 136 foot supply vessel still at work in the Gulf of Mexico fifty years after it was built. It might even be the High Tide. Picture: Oddgeir Refvik

However, the designer was undeterred by any prospective limitations to crew comfort, and in the same month that the Mr Charlie commenced operations for Shell, he gathered a group of potential investors at the offices of the Alexander Shipyard in New Orleans. The result of this meeting was the formation of Tidewater Marine Services, and the company immediately commissioned the yard to build a ship along the lines of Doc's concept.

The yard refined the idea into formal drawings, which the board members criticised until everyone was satisfied, the result being a vessel 120 feet long, having a clear deck area aft of 90 feet, the only intrusion into this area being two squat funnels positioned at either side through which the engine exhaust gases were routed. This feature of supply ship design was not to change for nearly twenty years, until oil exploration began to take place in more hostile waters.

The other important dimensions were a deck width of 27 feet, a light draft of 5 feet and a loaded draft of 8 feet 6 inches. Twin GM diesels with a total of 600 bhp, provided second-hand by one of the board members, Don Durant, gave a top speed of 10 knots. The wheelhouse was also second hand, being scavenged from an old tug, the Navajo. The liquid capacities of the ship were 330 tons of ballast and 110 tons of fuel.

As was expected, before the ship was delivered to the owners it was chartered by Odeco, and at this point to avoid a conflict of interests Doc LaBorde withdrew from Tidewater. However, the company, learning that Shell was interested in chartering a similar ship, immediately ordered a second vessel.

On 25 March 1955 the *Ebb Tide* left the Alexander Shipyard and sailed down the Mississippi to Morgan City, presenting its distinctly un-nautical shape to public gaze for the first time. The Ebb Tide was rapidly followed by two sister ships, the Rip Tide and the Flood Tide, and this started a continuous process of building and development which continued from that date until today.

The World Turns

In terms of history there is no doubt that the decade from 1955 to 1965 is probably the most significant in the whole development of the supply vessel. The Ebb Tide made its debut voyage and further Tidewater vessels were built. From slightly less than promising beginnings the submersible, the three-legged jack-up and the semi-submersible were developing, the latter obviously only appearing because it was seen that there was a point between floating on the pontoons and being placed on the seabed when a submersible was afloat, but stable and so in reality it could be used where the water was too deep for it to rest on the seabed.

1955, year one for the supply vessel, was year three for the Zapata Corporation, whose president was George Bush the Elder. In Britain the population was still struggling with the aftermath of the Second World War. Rationing had only been terminated a couple of years earlier and in Germany the occupying British army had just built a new town for its headquarters staff on a greenfield site outside Mönchen Gladbach . The Americans still had large numbers of soldiers stationed at bases around West Germany, an occupation which now might be remembered more because Elvis Presley served with the military at Friedberg, than for any other reason. 1955 was also the year that the first McDonalds franchised restaurant opened in Des Plaines, Illinois although food historians will tell us that the first moves in the direction of the fast food hamburger store was made in 1949.

Oil exploration was continuing apace offshore in Lake Maracaibo, Venezuela, which had the advantage of being sheltered and shallow. American oil companies also ventured offshore in the Far East and the Middle East, particularly in the waters off Saudi Arabia, where Aramco was owned jointly by the Standard Oil Company , the Texas Oil Company and Socony Vacuum (later to become Mobil oil).

All of these areas were essentially benign environments and both the rigs and the ships were able to operate in precisely the same way as they had in the Gulf of Mexico.

Not to be totally left out, BP was operating in Abu Dhabi in an offshore exploration operation which started in 1953, and culminated in first production of the Zakum Field in 1958. Zakum was not an enormous offshore challenge, in some areas being only a few metres deep, and was fairly close to the port, but nevertheless it was at sea, in water which was deep enough to drown people. BP was also involved offshore in Trinidad. Shell was undertaking tentative activities in the Far East, offshore from Borneo, and it was from there that the company were to source their first North Sea jack-up. In all these areas the British construction company George Wimpey was the company which built the platforms similar to those being built by Brown and Root and J Ray McDermott in the Gulf of Mexico. The first platform built by Wimpey was for Shell in Brunei in 1947.

Elsewhere in the marine world the western maritime nations were building ships of all sorts to replace the tonnage sunk during the war. The Greeks, and others who could see that there was a profit to be made out of operating second-hand tonnage, were employing many of the more than 2,000 Liberty and Victory ships built in America for use on transatlantic convoys. Shipping in general was thriving, except in America itself, where it was virtually uneconomical to operate merchant ships without subsidy, this possibly the result of the Merchant Marine Act of 1920, known as the Jones Act.

American marine regulations used an entirely different means of determining the required levels of competence for its officers, having different standards for 25, 100, 200, 500 and 1600 gross tons. These requirements did not directly affect the Ebb Tide, which was in any case an extremely small vessel, but the regulations were to influence American supply design for most of the half-century which followed.

The Skill of Supply Ship Driving

The arrival of the first three-legged jack-up, the Scorpion, in 1956, ensured that all supply vessels would find a new technique for positioning themselves to discharge and load cargo, and effectively limited the operations of the remaining LSTs . It was now required that they let go an anchor and tie up stern to the rig in a type of Mediterranean Moor. Of course the positioning of the superstructure forward lent itself to this technique and in fact ensured that the design would continue in almost precisely that form for a further 50 years.

The technique of dropping an anchor forward, thrashing astern towards the rig and then trying to get into

The Sensor – originally the HBCarlton built in 1956 for Caldwell Well Services, powered by two 500 bhp engines which in their original form had to stop and operate in reverse. Picture: Bob Beegle

The controls of the HBCarlton, not the original but in any case give a good idea of what they used to be like. Throttles, thrusters direction and throttle, and steering tiller can be seen. Picture: Bob Beegle.

position despite wind and tide position is written about more easily than it was carried out, particularly in the early days One can imagine the early supply ship masters, stern on to the structure, shouting out of the front window of the wheelhouse to the mate, to drop the anchor, and then backing up looking over their shoulders, engines churning astern, and sweating as they got close.

Probably the crane would manage to drop a rope on the deck as the stern swung past, the deck-crew would leap to it and turn it down, and the vessel would be drawn up sharply to hang between the single rope and the anchor cable. They would then go through a process of shortening up the first rope, and then taking a second one, and finally tightening up on the anchor cable until the ship was secured and cargo could be worked over the stern. In benign environments they would then at least be in a position to shut down the engines and relax.

Design, Development and Construction

After the Ebb Tide, the Flood Tide and the Rip Tide, Tidewater constructed further ships of slightly larger dimensions but with the same size engines, 1000 bhp or less, these being considered absolutely adequate for the task. At the same time, other ship owners saw how effective the design was and began to construct vessels of their own. The first Chief Executive of Tidewater, John P LaBorde, (a close relative of "Doc") is quoted as saying, "At that time it would have been very difficult to find anybody who knew very much about this business, for not much knowledge existed. Anyone with any experience had to come from a fishing fleet or military sea service. As far as anyone really knowing a lot about the design and capabilities of our particular type of equipment, there was none. In fact the original investors didn't know much about this equipment. It was all experimental."

Shipyards on the Gulf coast, Halter Marine, Ingalls Shipyard, The Burton Shipbuilding Company, Trinity Marine and others - some famous, some not, enthusiastically took up the task of designing and building supply ships, although they were of variable specification and quality.

A Tidewater ship at an early jack-up in the Gulf of Mexico. The position held by a single rope indicates that possibly the technique of tying up stern to had yet to be developed. Picture: Tidewater Publicity.

For instance the 136 foot H.B. Carlton, built in 1956 for Caldwell Well Services (and later to become the Low Tide), was powered by two 500 BHP Enterprise diesels which were reversible. In other words, to get the ship to go astern the engines had to be stopped and then restarted in the other direction. More will be written later in this volume about the means used to control the ships in close proximity to oil rigs, but it is probably worth considering now the difficulty faced by the captain of the H.B. Carlton during the process of tying up to a LeTourneau jack-up.

First of all, the fact that the engines had to be stopped and reversed implies that the engineer had to be down in the engine room at the controls, and that the instructions from the bridge were passed down either using an engine telegraph, or more likely in such a small craft by voice pipe. If he adopted the technique of dropping the anchor and running in towards the rig forwards, he would get to a point where he would have to shout down to the engineer to stop one of the engines and put it astern, probably leaving the other engine driving the ship forward. The wait while this change of direction was carried out must have seemed interminable. The chain would still be rattling out of the chain locker and the ship, one engine ahead, would be pressing on towards the rig. It would not be until the other engine fired up that he could swing the wheel over and turn the ship, now minimising the power of the ahead engine and instructing the engineer to give him full power on the astern engine. It must have been a stressful experience.

The submersible Bluewater One built in 1957, but which was to become the first semi-submersible in 1960, when it was noticed that it was very stable under tow. Archive picture.

By the end of its first year in operation Tidewater was operating a fleet of eleven vessels. By 1957 the company was considering expansion, and was carrying out research into the prospects in Lake Maracaibo, which readers may recollect was already a developing area with many rigs built in the shallows on the edge of the water. In 1958 the company made its first acquisition, 'Semarca' an operator of small vessels and crew boats in the area.

By 1959 the offshore operators suffered the first downturn, but nevertheless Tidewater acquired a further 14 vessels to service its Venezuela operations. Tidewater were on the road to success, consolidated by the purchase of a rival, the Offshore Transportation Corporation.

This period of the offshore supply vessel industry is poorly documented and one gets the impression that there were numbers of tug, barge and ship-owners, as well as oil companies and rig-owners, having a go at being supply vessels owners, but the drawback for them all was that they had to build new ships. Many of these organisations seem to have totally disappeared, and it may indeed be the more cautious investors who waited and then bought the newly built tonnage at a discount who survived. The Humble Oil Company, who it will be remembered had been a big investor in LSTs, also had supply vessels built by Ingalls Shipyard, and the Humble CT and Humble CT 3 came into service in 1957. In the same year the Offshore Company also brought in to service the Offshore Orleans and the Offshore Jefferson.

There remains no trace however of Caldwell Well Services who had owned the H.B .Carlton. And although there are records of the building of two ships, the Tilman J and the Tilman J No 2, for Tilman Offshore as early as 1955, according to the Colton Company records, both the ships and the company which commissioned them appear to have sunk without trace, in the case of the ships literally. Tilman Offshore lasted long enough however to purchase the 1956-built High Tide from Tidewater. Humble Oil became Exxon, but doubtless dispensed with the ownership and operation of supply vessels as soon as they had established that there were others prepared to carry out the task. However, drilling companies have remained ship-owners on and off right through the existence of the offshore oil industry.

End Note

All in all it must have been with some enthusiasm that those who owned and operated supply vessels looked out over the Gulf of Mexico towards the distant structures sticking out of the sea. It must have seemed to them that here was a completely new shipping service. It still required ships and those who would go to sea in them, but they were not going to disappear for weeks at a time. It was an industry which in 1960 would appear to require special skills and as a result would offer considerable rewards for those who could offer them. A new world was at their feet.

Stirling Dee at the jack-up Noble Lynda Bossler carrying out a standard supply operation discharging a mini container. The ship is being held in position by joystick control. Picture: David Styles.

Chapter 3
SUPPLY WORK

The first task to be carried out by those who drove the ships working with oil rigs was that of supply, the carriage of all the commodities which needed to be moved from the shore to the offshore installation. Nearly everything carried out was in some way consumed.

The original requirement was that the deck should be long enough to carry a length of drill pipe, 30 feet. These 30-foot lengths are joined together to form the drill string on which the drill bit is affixed, all being rotated from the drill floor of the rig. As the drill bit cuts into the earth, the end of the drilling string gets near to the deck; another section is then added and the job continues. Hence, as the search for hydrocarbons has moved into deeper water, and the rigs have drilled deeper into the earth's crust, more pipe is needed. In the early days of the semi-submersible, and even today on some jack-ups, all the drill pipe has to be removed from the rig before it can be moved from one place to another. In addition to the drill pipe, other tubular sections, known as casing, have to be supplied. Casing is used to secure the hole and is supplied in diminishing sizes from thirty-two inch down to three and a bit inches. As the well gets deeper, smaller sizes of casing are inserted; the smallest size is that required to recover the oil to the surface.

The bulk chemicals carried include baryte, from which the drilling mud is mixed, and cement, used to fix the casing in place. While all these commodities were being used, the people on board the rig had to be fed and watered, so it is likely that every vessel visiting an offshore installation was carrying at least one container of stores.

In the Gulf of Mexico, the task of supply remained separate from the task of towing and anchor-handling for years, although they were combined in the North Sea virtually as soon as the semi- submersible arrived.

Using a Coaster

A little of the early history in the Gulf of Mexico was covered in the previous chapter; the manner in which the ships went to work changed as the objects they were supplying changed. Initially all that was required was the ability to put a ship alongside a jetty, the difference being that out at the rig, the jetty formed part of the structure.

In the North Sea, apart from a single attempt to build a drilling platform, all the early structures were jack-ups, which required the ships to drop an anchor and tie up to two of the legs. There was at least one coaster which had been altered to supply jack-ups in the southern North Sea, the modification amounting to the provision of an anchor and some cable at the stern. In order to position this vessel to discharge and backload cargo, the master would point the bow at the rig and start moving forward towards it. The mate would then let go the anchor at the stern. This takes some courage and an iron nerve on the part of the man on the windlass, who would be shielded from the rig by the accommodation and so would have very little idea of what was going on.

An early platform supply ship on its way out to the location with a cargo of fifty gallon barrels. If they actually arrived at the rig they would be discharged with barrel hooks. Picture: Peter Barker.

As the ship got close to the rig the mate would stop paying out the cable and the crew on the bow would attempt to tie the ship up. If they were successful the vessel would eventually be held in position by a rope from either bow to the legs of the rig, and the anchor out astern. Even without any direct knowledge, it is certain that the Captain was constantly worried by the fact that he was approaching the rig head-on, and it would not be until the bow was effectively between the legs of the jack-up that he could ease back the engine. Once the ropes were fast he might possibly breath a sigh of relief.

Tying Up

The pioneering approach, of using a vessel with the accommodation aft, was not to be repeated for many years, and in the meantime all the supply vessels constructed were similar, with the accommodation perched on the bow and an open deck aft. This construction required the supply vessels tied up stern to, in what the old-style shipmasters would have called a Mediterranean Moor. Using a technique which was not a million miles away from that used by the coaster Captain, it was necessary for the ship to drop an anchor and then back up to the rig until the stern was within reach of a rope hanging down from the crane.

In order to maintain direction and to ensure that the cable was laid straight, it became common practice for the master to take up a position at the appropriate distance from the rig, on the correct line, and then start moving slowly forward. He would then get the mate on the forecastle to let go the anchor and would increase speed a bit.

For the mate this was a particularly difficult time. The chain would appear to be screaming out of the cable locker, describing an arc in the air and then disappearing down the hawse pipe, and the instinct was to screw up the brake. To digress once more, on most vessels the windlass was held by a band-brake, which was tightened up on the brake drum by a screw. Braking was increased by turning the screw clockwise and decreased by turning the screw anticlockwise. It would be an automatic response by the mate to attempt to slow down the manic deployment of the cable, but it was a response which had to be resisted. If he stopped the cable running out he would either stop the ship or else pull the anchor in towards the rig, and in either case he would incur the wrath of the Captain.

When the ship was so close to the rig that it would seem to be possible to touch it, the Captain might give the signal to stop letting out the cable, and at the same time put one engine astern, the rudders hard over and the bow-thruster full sideways to swing the ship round so that the stern would now be facing the rig.

It would be pulled away a little by the cable, and it would now be necessary to push the controls astern to get the stern close enough for the crane to land a rope on the afterdeck. He manoeuvre the ship so as to get the quarter on which the rope had landed close up to the leg to which the rope was attached, until the crew had turned it down on the bitts. Then he would cross the engines in the other direction so that the stern swung across towards the other leg. The crane would land a second rope and the crew would make the ship fast.

The Captain would have the mate tighten up on the anchor chain, and if all was well the ship would be in position ready for the cargo to be discharged and loaded.

In order to make this task possible it became conventional to provide the ship with controls facing aft as well as a set facing forward. A complete set consisted of a combined throttle and directional control for the main propulsion and a direction and speed control for the bow thruster. There would also be a rudder control, which was usually a small stick, although at this time some ship-owners had been unable to dispense with the wheel, which would be positioned proudly in the forepart of the bridge, never to be touched.

This additional equipment naturally involved some rethinking on the part of the seafarers, and to actually drive the ship while facing aft needed considerable retraining, all of which was done 'on the job'. In after conning position, if the master pushed the engine control away from him, which at the forward end would be 'ahead' he would actually be going astern, or faster astern, and if he moved the rudder control towards his left, which would be to port at

The Star Vega tied up to the Pentagon 84 some time in the 1980s. The anchor has been laid well, and the anchor chain can be seen to be extremely tight, holding the ship in position. Picture George Craigen.

A supply ship tied up to the Pentagone 84. The pentagonal shape gave the ship masters the choice of the port or starboard bow to minimise adverse environmental forces.
Picture: Victor Gibson.

the forward controls, he would actually be applying starboard rudder. Additionally, since reversed rudder indicators were not then available, the after rudder indicator would show the rudder moving in the opposite direction to the direction of the control, unless the gauge had been installed upside down.

Personnel were recruited to operate these vessels from many sources. The Americans used tug-drivers, who were unused to operating more than a couple of hours from the base port, but who were generally very experienced in the somewhat obscure skill of "ship-handling" . On the other hand the British initially recruited former fishermen and officers from the coastal trades. All one could say about these guys was that they were used to being on small ships, used to frequent visits to ports and familiar with the generally horrible weather in the North Sea. For all of them, being presented with a variety of engine and rudder controls facing the wrong direction proved to be traumatic.

As the European deep-sea ship-owners became involved they naturally recruited officers from their deep-sea ships, both to be deck officers and engine-room officers. These officers had seldom been ship-masters, although many were qualified master mariners, and their sole experience of ship-handling was probably the manipulation of a wooden ship model during preparation for their oral examinations.

Deep sea mariners are also taught that it is a matter of concern to be close to any fixed objects, even the quayside in port, and for the latter task, a pilot would be employed. Hence approaching these objects sticking out of the water was frightening, and controlling the ship was a haphazard business.

Deep-sea marine qualification tended to concentrate on the safe operation of ships and the means of recovering from emergencies. Hence those taking certificates, both in the UK and internationally, learned how to navigate by the sun and stars, to keep out of the way of other ships, to check errors on the compass and how to load ships in a safe manner. Although they were soon to be required to develop special skills for loading, discharging and looking after oil cargoes, at that time even this level of specialism was not required.

It is traditional for officers joining specialist ships of all sorts to be taught how to operate them by those already there, and this proved to be the case offshore. Very well-qualified British officers generally drove very small ships very badly, and when it came to recovering and deploying anchors and towing oil rigs, they just did their best to learn the job as they went along. Their American counterparts on the other hand were much better at ship-handling, but had a tendency to get lost when out of sight of land.

Snatching

The after controls (or in the case of Smit-Lloyd the centre controls) and the bow thruster promoted the development of a technique known as snatching. As the name implies, this activity allowed the rig crane to pick up single urgent lifts without the supply vessel tying up, and in its earliest form consisted of the supply vessel drifting slowly past the structure while the deck crew quickly hooked on the lift before the crane was out of range.

The bow thruster allowed the master to apply forces with it, and the engines and rudders would keep the ship within range of the crane for longer periods, sometimes allowing complete deck cargoes to be discharged and loaded. It did however require a great deal of concentration on the part of the driver, since the crane booms were short, and the ship had to remain a few feet off the legs of the rig, even to allow cargo to be taken from and landed on the stern.

Towards the end of the 1970s virtually all supply vessels in Europe were being constructed with CP propellers, and control systems were becoming more sophisticated, and the supply vessel designers borrowed some technology from the diving ships which were now appearing in numbers.

The diving ships used computers to maintain station, operated by means of any one of a number of position-fixing systems, the most prominent being Artemis, a radar-type system involving stations positioned on the offshore installations, and taut wire, which as the name implies consisted of a wire with a weight on the end which was lowered to the seabed.

To allow these vessels to move easily and still take advantage of the computer installations they were fitted with a joystick, an omni-directional control which provided a facility for the ship to be moved by means of a single stick. It was the joystick and its associated computer which was taken up by the supply vessel operators, and the installation of this device allowed the supply vessel masters to snatch for extremely long periods in the close proximity of offshore installations.

The UT706 Far Grimshader in typical operating mode adjacent to a large jack-up. The position of the ship allows the access to virtually the whole of the deck.
Picture David Styles

The Highland Legend discharging riser to the Seaway Falcon. Small ships have been used for many years to support larger vessels. Picture: Oddgeir Refvik

The UT745 Maersk Feeder at an offshore installation. Modern platform ships can remain in position in weather which prevents the offshore cranes from operating. Picture: Victor Gibson.

Once confidence in the joystick grew, shipmasters began to operate beam on to the installations, giving the cranes access to much larger areas of the deck, and it was this development which allowed the pipe-carriers with their long decks and therefore higher carrying capacity to become platform supply vessels. This process did not carry over into the Gulf of Mexico, where the supply vessels were still being built with decks less than one hundred feet long, and where it was still normal for the ships to tie up. Even where the water was considered to be too deep for anchoring, the ships would still back up and tie up with two ropes, replacing the restraint of the anchor chain with a bit of ahead on the engines. Of course such a technique would have been almost impossible to carry out in places with strong tides or currents such as the southern North Sea and the waters of Trinidad.

The availability of the complete length of the deck to the crane caused a proliferation in the technique of "cherry picking", the management of the unit being serviced identifying individual containers in the stow. The deck crew would climb over the top of the stow and hook the required lifts on, and then stand back as the crane lifted them into the air. Of course there were dangers. The crew members could fall into the holes which had been left, or even over the side into the sea.

Carriage of Bulk

The oil industry had, and still has, an almost insatiable appetite for dry bulk, and its carriage was one of the challenges which faced the designers and builders of supply vessels for many years. Their success, or lack of it, was reflected in the time it took to pump up such cargoes to offshore installations. Ships were provided with vertical and horizontal hoppers. Some of the horizontal hoppers were fitted with a sort of belt system which propelled the powder towards an orifice at one end, down which the stuff would be blown towards the rig. Vertical hoppers were pressurized from the top and, assisted by gravity, the cement, baryte, or bentonite was forced out through the orifice in the centre of the cone at the bottom and propelled towards the rig through large diameter flexible pipes using compressed air as a carriage medium.

The hoses were connected to the ship's discharge systems by a variety of fittings, which required the well-managed ship to be provided with a number of connectors and converters. There was seldom any consideration given to the positioning of the connections on the ship, which were just aft of the forward housing, and so could only be connected when the ships were

The Northern Seeker, formerly a Bugge supply ship, in the conventional stern too mode at a floating production unit in the North Sea. Picture: Oddgeir Refvik

A typical manoeuvring setup at the forward end of an offshore support vessel with a large tunnel thrusters and a smaller azimuthing thruster almost immediately below it. Picture: Tony Poll.

A second generation North Sea supply ship pumping bulk. On deck there is a variety of oilfield equipment including a forty foot container, a pile of drill pipe and a number of downhole tools. Picture: Victor Gibson

tied up. In the early days the solid pipe on the ship was usually connected to the flexible pipe from the rig by 'Camlocks', which were used in the road transport industry, and which made an airtight connection by means of a lever operated cam on a female connector which acted against a groove on the male connector. The fact that the levers usually had to be tied in place with string generally spoilt the process for those with engineering mentalities, and as years passed hammer-tight unions used elsewhere in the oilfields became the connections of choice.

Once connection was made discharge could commence. This involved pressuring up the hoppers and bleeding air into the discharge system. A delicate balance would have to be achieved between pressure in the tank, throughput of the air in the pipe and the capacity of the compressed air system. If these were balanced in just the right way the pipe would be seen to be leaping all over the deck and a faint puff of powder would be visible at a vent somewhere under the rig. But even if things went well , the process took hours.

If things did not go well, and there were many reasons for them not to, discharge might be slow, or invisible. Sometimes an operative on the rig would fail to open the correct valve, or even shut a valve halfway through the job which would result in a plug of cement building up in the pipe. This was a total disaster, since there was no way of clearing it using the compressed air system. Often the pipe-work would have to be disconnected and each section shaken out while it was hanging from the crane, although the deck crew would always attempt to clear it by using big hammers. Even worse would be a blockage in the ship's fixed pipe-work, which would require the systematic removal of one section at a time until the blockage was found and rodded out.

The Carriage of Drill Cuttings

During the drilling operation the mud is returned to the surface carrying with it all the chips and bits from the drill bit. The returned mud from down the hole flows over mechanical devices called shale-shakers, which are large horizontal grids or screens mechanically agitated like a sort of giant garden sieve. The oil and the baryte which has to be retained in the mud percolates through the screens and the solids are channelled into a chute which in days gone by directed the cuttings over the side. This process resulted in piles of rock chippings accumulating on the sea floor adjacent to every well, some of them contaminated with oil based mud.

In many areas of the world where environmental concerns have become a means for governments to gain votes, it is necessary for the drill cuttings, if they are contaminated with any form of oil based mud, to be either re-injected into the substrata or else to be transported to the shore.

The aft controls of the UT705 Skandi Falcon. The driver has an uninterrupted view aft and can lay hand on any of the engine, thrusters and rudder contols as well as the joystick. Picture: Victor Gibson

Typically, in the UK in 1997 regulations came into force which limited the amount of oil on drill cuttings discharged to the sea to 10 grammes per kilogramme, so the operators were required to dispose of the cuttings in some other way, to clean them up or not to use oil-based drilling fluid.

At that time the way forward was seen as being the use of synthetic or pseudo oil-based muds, which would be as effective as the real stuff, but which would not limit the discharge of the cuttings to the sea, although even then there was an awareness that things would change, and indeed later in the same year it was necessary to similarly dispose of drill cuttings contaminated with synthetic drilling fluid.

For the semi-submersibles everywhere, the operators have opted for cuttings transportation by supply vessel, described most simply as 'ship and skip'. In Norway, where the legislation offers more options, the shipping may be done between one installation and another, suggesting that eventually one or more platforms in the Norwegian sector may be used purely for cuttings disposal. In the Gulf of Mexico it is possible to ship and skip with a limited number of containers and deck space due to distance.

The skip and ship technique seems to require a dedicated ship for each exploration rig. Also required are large numbers of small skips, since there must be some on the rig being filled with cuttings, some on the ship either on their way to the shore full or on their way back empty, and some in the cleaning plant. In addition the skips are sized for a rock with a high specific gravity, but usually the product is much lighter. This means that the skips could be bigger – some of the time. But of course they can't be bigger, just in case.

This is a logistic nightmare for the oil industry who, when it comes to materials handling, could learn a lot from the average do-it-yourself store. Research has resulted in an alternative technique for getting the cuttings ashore, which is to pipe it as a slurry into tanks on the deck of the supply vessel and then pump it ashore to a suitable facility.

RIGHT:
The Maersk Supplier built at Rolandwerft in 1967. It was the first of two platform ships which were followed by numerous anchor-handlers, all in one way or another setting a trend for others to follow. Picture: Maersk Publicity.

The Centurion Service built for Zapata Gulf Marine in 1964. Seen here entering Great Yarmouth when the American fleet dominated the North Sea. Picture: Paul Gowen

Chapter 4
THE SEMI-SUBMERSIBLE

Introduction

Every decade, and even every year, might be seen as a period of major development for the supply vessel, but it is perhaps the 1960s, involving as they did the development of the semi-submersible, which initiated the biggest evolutionary change in ship type. In addition to the invention of the semi-submersible, oil exploration migrated to the North Sea and for the first time faced a genuinely hostile marine environment. Hence, the changes were not just a matter of technical development, they were a reaction to the conditions in which those doing the job found themselves.

In the UK about 120 tons of oil a day was being produced at Eakring on the edge of Sherwood Forest. This discovery was made in 1939 by BP and was one of the better-kept secrets of the Second World War, the wells providing high-quality fuel for British aircraft. Later, in 1959 a huge land reservoir of natural gas was discovered by Shell-Esso at Groningen in Holland. The stage was therefore set for the move offshore in Europe.

By 1960 exploration and production was taking place in the shallow waters around many of the coasts of the world. They included the Gulf of Mexico, the coastlines of the United States, Mexico, and Venezuela in the form of Lake Maracaibo, In addition oil was also being recovered offshore in California. In the Arabian Gulf, then known of course as the Persian Gulf, oil was being recovered from the shallows adjacent to Kuwait, Saudi Arabia, Iran, Iraq and the Emirates and further afield Borneo, Australia and Nigeria were sources of hydrocarbons both onshore and offshore.

In 1962 a number of operators began to carry out seismic surveys in the North Sea and at that time a couple of slightly modified supply boats, the Clearwater and the Bayou Chico, were photographed in Great Yarmouth. Aberdeen Harbour records the first visit by an offshore vessel as being a survey ship in 1964. Surveying itself was in its infancy and George Craigen, subsequently a British supply ship master, remembers being on the Macduff golf course with his father when he was about 14. The group on the fifth tee could see over the Moray Firth where there was a small ship proceeding slowly eastwards towards the North Sea. Behind it at intervals there were loud explosions, and clearly visible waterspouts.

"What's that?" asked George. "Aye" said his dad, who was a former fishing boat owner "they're looking for oil. Won't find any though".

Anchor-Handling

In 1961 in the Gulf of Mexico, Shell converted a submersible into a semi-submersible. Now, rather than being positioned on the seabed, it had to be held on location by a number of anchors, and so the vessels supporting offshore operations gained a new task. The navies of the world had been installing moorings for their fleets for years in sheltered harbours such as Scapa Flow and Pearl Harbour, and both military and civilian authorities employed buoy-laying vessels which laid anchors in shallow waters, so it was natural that the offshore industry viewed these techniques and initially opted to have anchors lifted and laid by tugs provided with deploying equipment at the bow. The job was done in just the same way as the military did it.

However, in no time at all they realised that they had a suitable vessel for the task in the supply ship, which up to that time had been used solely for taking cargo to the offshore rigs and structures. And it required only the addition of an A-frame at the stern and the bolting on of a large (in relative terms) winch to the deck to convert the ships for anchor-handling operations. However the 1000 bhp which had been sufficient for the manoeuvring of a vessel to get it alongside a barge, or to anchor at a jack-up, was no longer sufficient, even though the winches had their own engines.

In 1963 Odeco returned to innovation and built the Ocean Driller, which was a multiple column v-shaped semi-submersible capable of drilling in more than 100 ft of water. Several tugs and supply ships were required to tow and locate it and the modern anchor-handling operation was born. However, an early photograph shows that the anchors were deployed only a few hundred feet from the rig. It may have been as far away as the ships could get them, but in adverse weather there would be quite a good chance of the anchors dragging. It was, like much of the early marine activity relating to the offshore industry, a process carried out more in hope than in anger, with little real expectation of success.

The new form of rig had only a little influence on the development of the supply vessel in the Gulf of Mexico. The numbers of jack-ups far exceeded the number of semi-submersibles, although the legs were getting longer, and so there was little incentive to modernise the ships. Even anchor-handling operations continued to be carried out by ships with the funnels half-way down the deck, and towing was carried out just as it had always been, by tugs.

North Sea Exploration Begins

So after almost ten years of supply ship operations the oil exploration circus finally arrived in the southern North Sea, and gas was soon discovered off the coast of Holland. In the middle of the year the Mr Cap became the first jack-up to commence drilling off the coast of the United Kingdom, and at the same time the jack-up Mr Louise commenced operation in the German sector. Mr Cap was initially serviced from Sunderland by the Hector Gannet, of which we will hear more, and the East Tide, which was the first Tidewater vessel to arrive in the area, having been built by Halter Marine in 1963. In the following May the first servicing of an offshore installation from Great Yarmouth took place.

Right from the start the oilmen found themselves having to deal with the legendary North Sea weather. Within weeks of the arrival of Mr Cap it was subjected to a 100-year storm, which could be considered to be bad luck. A one hundred-year storm, in meteorological terms, is a storm which is likely to occur, in the area where the activity is taking place, once every 100

North Shore sister ship of the South Shore, the first supply vessel to be built in the UK at J Samuel White's shipyard at Cowes in 1965.
Picture: Paul Gowen

years. And it is a generally accepted standard that rigs are designed to withstand a 100-year storm in the area where they intend to operate.

Of course they had dealt with bad weather before. Out in the Gulf of Mexico hurricanes had the capability to sink floating objects and to destroy the footings of jack-ups so that they disappeared beneath the waves in mud slides, but because the rigs were close to the coast, everyone would be taken off before the hurricane arrived.

In the Middle East it was necessary to forecast the approach of the 'shamal', which could blow for days and would prevent marine activities, although the hulls of the jack-ups remained safely above the waves. But the North Sea was different. When the oil men faced north on the Dogger Bank there was nothing between them and the Arctic and even in the summer deep depressions would roar in from the Atlantic, touch the tip of Scotland and unleash their full force down the North Sea. All in all, it was felt that the North Sea was no place for those who lacked the necessary level of courage - or recklessness.

Despite the fearsome reputation the region was gaining, the operators were undeterred and considered the misfortunes they were having as no more than opportunities for improvement. Hence, BP saw nothing wrong with adding ten legs to a barge and turning it into a jack-up. So, in May 1965 the BP drilling rig Sea Gem was towed out of Middlesbrough docks, and headed in the direction of its first location offshore. The drilling derrick had been brought from the BP onshore field at Eakring. This unlikely combination of hardware spudded in 40 miles of the Humber on 5th June 1965 and 104 days later, on 17th September, made the first discovery of hydrocarbons in the UK sector of the North Sea. Of course the initial discoveries were of gas, and there were still serious doubts as to whether there was any oil at all on the continental shelf, but exploration continued.

The difficulties suffered by the East Tide and the small American ships which followed did not deter people from setting up companies both in the UK and on the continent of Europe to own and operate supply vessels. However, the limitations of the Gulf of Mexico supply vessels

This ship was originally the Kent Shore built in 1967 for Offshore Marine, one of a number of sister ships powered by Lister Blackstone engines developing 1600 bhp. Picture: Paul Gowen

soon became evident, because of their difficulty in dealing with the weather conditions and their inability to run anchors and tow the new breed of semi-submersibles.

Hence a number of traditional British shipyards found themselves with these very unusual vessels on their order books. Charles Hill of Bristol and Bolson's of Poole, Cochrane's of Selby and J Samuel White of Cowes, Isle of Wight set to the task of metal bashing to fulfil the requirements of their clients. J Samuel White, a British shipbuilder who had once been known for manufacturing, in-house, every single component of the vessels they constructed, completed the first supply vessel to be built in the UK, the South Shore, for Offshore Marine.

Also typical of the vessels of the period was the Essex Shore, built in Rotterdam in 1967. Although the general shape was still that of the traditional Gulf of Mexico supply ship, it had a stern roller, to allow rig anchors to be lifted to the surface, and a winch to carry out the task. It was also capable of towing, having a bollard pull of 22.5 tons. While this figure seems ludicrous today, 40 years ago the Essex Shore was a powerful vessel, its two Lister Blackstone engines producing 2000 BHP.

She had further innovative features to help her tie up astern to the rigs. Forward she was fitted with a Gill Jet, a diesel driven 500 bhp omni-directional thruster, and on the bridge, she had a set of controls facing aft, so that the stern could be seen from the control position. The master could then drop the anchor and steer the ship astern using the bow-thruster until he was within range of the crane, and then manoeuvre the ship while the ropes were being attached.

While it appears that the Europeans were quick off the mark, Bryan Cooper and T. F. Gaskell writing in 1966 in their book "North Sea Oil – The Great Gamble" thought otherwise. They felt that it was public knowledge that the survey work had been going on for more than two years by the time the first rig arrived, and that the British could easily have anticipated the action and started earlier to build ships and rigs. Later, in 1975, pundits were still complaining about the lack of investment by UK companies.

Sea Quest built in Belfast for BP in 1966 to a Sedco design, was the first British semi-submersible. It is seen here during construction at Harland and Wolff in Belfast. Picture: BP Publicity.

The Sedco F Rig Design

In 1965 there were 75 drilling units worldwide and back in the Gulf of Mexico the Southeastern Drilling Company, Sedco, took delivery of the first triangular semi-submersible. This was a rig type which was to proliferate round the world and some of which are still at work today. It was designed by a Sedco subsidiary, "Earl and Wright", and was provided with nine anchors, three to each leg. In the same year BP started construction of a semi-submersible of the same design at Harland and Wolff in Belfast. This rig, the Sea Quest, was soon to venture out into the area now occupied by the Forties Field at a latitude only a little to the South of Aberdeen. As the quest for hydrocarbons moved northwards, Great Yarmouth ceased to be the only oil port. Aberdeen, then still a major fishing port, began to service offshore vessels, but many of the ports on the east coast were extremely tidal and the level of the water in the docks themselves was often maintained by locks.

A port which was unable to operate for 24 hours a day was anathema to the oil men, who were used to being able to dispatch a packet of sandwiches to an offshore installation at a moment's notice. It was the time of the "hot shot", a term to describe a service so urgent that no expense would be spared in its provision.

The Americans were used to this requirement and it was a feature of the engines supplied to the Gulf of Mexico vessels that it was normally possible to press the starter and to take off almost immediately for the field. The British-built ships on the other hand were normally provided with engines which needed to be warmed up and nursed into action, sometimes for an hour. This tended to be a source of irritation for the American management, who dominated the industry in those days.

In a number of places in the world oil ports began to develop. Morgan City and Fourchon in the Gulf of Mexico, Abidjan in the Ivory Coast and Warri in Nigeria, Raz Tanura in Saudi Arabia and Dubai in the Emirates. In Holland Den Helder provided the shelter and the facilities and in the UK Great Yarmouth and Aberdeen were the main ports, while BP uniquely made its base at Shed 16, Dundee, an extensive berth in the River Tay. Sometimes ports with large quayside areas were required, particularly after the arrival of the pipe-carriers, and this resulted in the development of Montrose in the North of Scotland and the return to business of Leith, the ancient marine gateway to the Scottish capital of Edinburgh.

The newly affluent workforce who arrived in the North Sea base ports after two weeks or more in a hostile and all-male offshore environment, appears to have caused a parallel development in the provision of personal services by the oldest profession, although this aspect of the offshore industry is only coyly alluded to in the various volumes written about the early days. The public houses along Regent Quay in Aberdeen were full of hard drinkers every night of the week, and even then it was possible for the alcoholically inclined to go from pub to pub from five o'clock in the morning until after midnight. The famous Steamboat in Leith was the focal point for the marine fraternity, and it was said that if anyone fancied some mixed company, all they had to do was bang on the pipe stacks as they passed, and young women would emerge from their cosy tubular sleeping places, ready to party. And it possibly should be remembered that the professional seafarers who manned the small offshore vessels had previously travelled all over the world in the world's deep sea fleets and were used to going ashore into environments

Berlinertor built in 1967 for OSA, its MAN diesels produced almost 2000 bhp. The company was to go on to own more than 100 vessels. Picture: Paul Gowen

where sex was routinely offered for sale, although this is not to infer that they availed themselves of such services.

Although the Europeans tended to employ mariners who had previously been manning the deep-sea fleets, the situation in America was not quite the same. Indeed nearly all the offshore fleets operated in Europe were owned by the traditional shipping companies, so where else were they going to find the marine staff to operate the ships. The mariners were attracted by the shorter trips and predictable lifestyle, although the weather tended to weed out the less resilient and the ship-handling requirements the less courageous.

The Americans, by dint of the rather tricky use of removable panels, managed to keep many of their ships under 200 gross tons. For the uninitiated, gross tonnage is a measurement of the total enclosed volume of the ship, so by ensuring that the time of measurement many spaces are not "enclosed" the very small tonnage is achieved.

This unrealistically low tonnage, as well as resulting in small port and canal dues, also results in a lower level of qualification being required to operate the ships. So, in the early days the American owners hired navigators to guide the ships across the Atlantic, since the actual ship captains might not have been qualified to work out of sight of land.

1965 Worldwide Developments

Although at this time the North Sea was seen as the sharp end, back in the Gulf of Mexico there was a level of maturity developing. By 1965 the Offshore Company, one of the leading drilling contractors, owned 16 drilling rigs, and in 1968 there were 200 platforms off the coast of Louisiana and Texas. Naturally large numbers of supply vessel were required to service all the marine structures, and virtually all these small ships were constructed in the gulf coast shipyards. Typically the "Atlantic Marine Corporation" (later to become part of the Halter Marine Group) built 78 supply vessels during the decade for a number of operators.

In the 1960s there was little sophistication in propulsion steering as can be seen from this picture of the underwater form of an anchor handler of the time. Picture: Victor Gibson

The Smit-Lloyd 1, the first of 18 identical anchor-handlers built between 1965 and 1969 all powered by two diesel engines developing 3000 bhp and providing 33 tonnes bollard pull. Picture: Paul Gowen

At this time there was a wide range of equipment and skills available to the oil companies in many parts of the world. Tidewater claimed in their brochure of the time to provide services In USA, Trinidad, Venezuela, Mexico, Nicaragua, Nigeria, Angola, The Red Sea and Persian Gulfs, Singapore, Australia and New Zealand. They remained the industry leaders and purchased a number of competitors. However Arthur Levy, The Zapata Corporation, State Boat Company, Otto Candies, and Edison Chouest all flourished.

As the years had passed the dimensions of the Gulf of Mexico supply vessel had gradually increased from the 120 ft of the Ebb Tide to 155 ft, and almost as soon as exploration commenced in the North Sea the Europeans got down to the task of building and operating supply ships, sometimes more out of ignorance than aptitude.

The first truly European supply ship was probably designed by the Dutch company Smit-Lloyd, who were incredibly innovative for 1965. They had a 60-metre ship built by Scheepswerf De Hoop of Lobith. This vessel had two tall funnels set just aft of the bridge, keeping them well clear of the sea. It was fitted with two 1500-bhp engines, making it extremely powerful. It was the Smit-Lloyd 1. The company continued to build identical ships until they got to the Smit-Lloyd 18 in 1969, and thereafter the first numeral of the name usually designated horsepower, so the next class when they were built started with the figure 4.

Curiously Smit-Lloyd never built a ship with two sets of controls. A single set of rudder, throttles and thruster controls were set on a console in the centre of the wheelhouse, and the Captain moved round it depending on the direction in which he wished to travel. By 1969 a number of the original 18 Smit-Lloyd ships were operating in Australia.

The major German ship-owners formed the Offshore Supply Association (OSA) and British ship-owners including P&O entered the field. P&O founded International Offshore Services (IOS) and had a number of ships built by Verolme in Holland and two by Hall Russells in Aberdeen. Offshore Marine, a subsidiary of Cunard, who were still operating the famous Atlantic liners, Queen Elizabeth and Queen Mary, commissioned the South Shore, which was, as previously

The Wimbrown 1 with sister ships Wimbrown 2 and Wimbrown 3 in Great Yarmouth. These vessels were famously slow in an age of rapid development. Picture: Peter Barker

stated, the first supply vessel to be completed in the UK.

We have already recorded the fact that the construction company George Wimpey had been involved with the British oil companies in the construction of the offshore platforms from which the drilling activities took place, but back in Britain they were better known as housebuilders. It was a surprise to some therefore when in 1965 they became the third British supply ship operator. Wimpey Marine Ltd took advantage of an association with the American engineering company Brown and Root. They took delivery of the soon to be infamous Wimbrown One and Wimbrown Two, a couple of vessels of indeterminate horsepower and limited capabilities, which could be overtaken by a fit man in a rowing boat. The Wimbrown Two was the first supply ship to be built by Appledore Shipbuilders in Devon, and was only the twelfth ship built by the yard. They were, however to continue building the ship type into the twenty first century.

In Denmark the Maersk Company entered the field with the imaginatively named the Maersk Supplier in 1967, to support the offshore activities of the DUC in Denmark. In line with the Smit-Lloyd designs, this ship was provided with two extremely tall funnels just aft of the bridge. In 1970, the Maersk Company were to go further, and commission eight anchor-handlers from the German yards Aarhus Flydedok and Rolandwerft GmbH. These ships were also provided with extremely tall funnels, which appear to have been the symbol of power in those days.

The Loss of the Hector Gannet

1968 was not a good year for oil exploration and development in the North Sea. In March the Ocean Prince was destroyed by high winds while drilling on the Dogger Bank, and because there was no loss of life there was no need to hold a public enquiry. However, from the somewhat disjointed reports in the journals of the time, it is possible to determine that the rig – a submersible – was actually resting on the seabed at the time, and one can easily imagine the damage which would result from it being lifted by huge waves to be dashed down again.

The Hector Gannet, one of the pioneer supply vessels in the North Sea, serviced the Hewett A Platform until it sank after colliding with the platform during a rescue operation. Picture: Ken Turrell.

On the 15th November there was a gas blow-out on the Hewett A, which was developing a field for Phillips. In those days the technique used was to carry out the exploration to map out the extent of the field, place a platform in the best location and then drill the wells from it. Hence it was usual for a platform to start producing as soon as the first well was complete, but for the drilling to continue sometimes for years.

The Hewett Platform is a spindly looking structure only 15 miles from the Norfolk coast. The derrick is set at one end with the accommodation at the other, and the production systems in between. Hence it is a rectangular shape with four supporting legs at either side, and at sea level on each of the legs, is a vertical girder sheathed in tyres. These girders therefore collectively form a sort of boat landing which might allow a vessel to lie alongside to be unloaded by the cranes set directly above. Those familiar with the conditions in the North Sea would doubt whether these boat landings had ever been used.

On the platform the crew feared that the gas would ignite, and so there was an immediate need to evacuate. A message was radioed to the Hector Gannet, and then the crew decided that they would throw scrambling nets over the side and climb down onto the vessel, already a veteran of the North Sea oilfields.

A graphic description in Bob Orrell's book "Blow-out" tells of the way the scrambling net was thrown over the side and how the Hector Gannet approached with the intention of picking up the men who were now hanging onto it waiting its arrival.

The Captain managed to put the stern under the net, but as he did so it was lifted by a large wave and dropped onto the edge of the boat landing, breaking the connection between the horizontal and the vertical girder. As the master held the ship in position to try to rescue two of the rig crew who were too afraid to jump, the stern landed heavily against the boat landing again, and the broken section of girder pierced the hull.

The two crew men were recovered to the deck of the rig and the Hector Gannet drifted away, and to the horror of the men on the rig, visibly began to list. Within a few minutes the ship was on its side where it remained for long enough to allow the survivors to climb onto the hull to await rescue and to be photographed in that situation. Then the ship rolled over and sank, depositing most of the crew and the rescued personnel from the Hewett A into the water.

The Boston Hornet, a Boston Putford standby vessel was close enough to start picking up survivors almost immediately, in the end rescuing all but three of the Hector Gannet's crew. Two of them were picked up from the sea but unfortunately had perished and the second engineer was never found. He had, it was assumed, gone down with the ship.

The sinking of the Hector Gannet was the first loss of an offshore support vessel in the North Sea.

The Lady Margaret was a typical example of an IOS vessel, well designed and constructed and capable of doing most of what was asked of it. Its funnels are just visible aft of the accommodation. Picture: Paul Gowen

Ekofisk

On October 25th 1969 The Ocean Viking, working for Phillips in the Norwegian sector, struck viable quantities of oil at Ekofisk. It was the culmination of a long campaign and the Ocean Viking had on one occasion broken adrift from its moorings and had to be recovered. It was becoming evident by this time that mooring semi-submersibles was a fairly technical business, and that there was a constant requirement to walk the line between what was possible and what was required. While it might have been ideal to have the anchors laid three-quarters of a mile away from the rig, using three-inch chain, which would probably guarantee that it would stay in position in all circumstances, this requirement had to be set against the capabilities of the vessels, which would probably have some difficulty in pulling 2" chain out half a mile. Hence the possibility of mooring failure was never far from the minds of those in control of the semi-submersibles of the time. Chain sizes are, by the way, described in terms of the diameter of the steel bar used to make the links, so 2" chain uses bar 2" in diameter, 3" chain 3" bar, and so on.

The Ocean Traveler, sister rig to the Ocean Viking, also working in the Norwegian sector, was similarly put in danger by the adverse conditions, and possibly the difficulty of marine support. The rig was being supported by one of the earliest of the Smit-Lloyd vessels, and this ship was being discharged when it was overcome by the current and hit the rig, holing it in several places. The rig healed over until one of the pontoons was visible even though it was at drilling draft, but fortunately the ship remained virtually undamaged and was able to pick up the majority of the crew who evacuated by shinning down the anchor chains. The five men left on board managed to ballast the rig upright and it was towed to shallow water for repair. Distressingly for the relatives of those on board, a news broadcast was made by both Norwegian and British radio saying the Ocean Traveler had capsized.

The Maersk Company

Just as Tidewater might be considered to be the most influential supply vessel company in the United States, Maersk hold the same position in Europe. By the end of the 1960s Smit-Lloyd and OSA might also have been contestants for the position, but only the Maersk Company has continued over the years to set new standards, to which other companies have aspired. Of course Maersk has become a major player in other shipping sectors, as shipbuilders and in the oil industry, and even have their own airline, and it is rumoured that they have considerable influence on the economy of Denmark.

They were already a successful shipping company when they commissioned their first supply vessel in 1967, and almost immediately they detected the need for effective anchor-handlers, as the ships of the day struggled with the moorings of the semi-submersibles in the North Sea They immediately ordered eight anchor-handlers, billed as supply and towing vessels for worldwide operations.

In order to fulfil the capability for operating world-wide, the new ships had the latest of every sort of equipment. The winch was diesel powered and provided with multiple gears, giving it a maximum pull of 100 tons. And the two MAK main engines offered 3800 bhp, giving a healthy bollard pull of 45 short tons. A slightly unusual feature of these ships was the positions of the main engines almost directly under the winch space forward of the cement room. This was a contrast to the American designs of the time which always positioned the engines as close to the stern as possible, so that they usually occupied the best of the cargo space. The Maersk ships were 172 feet long, with a 90 foot clear deck. They could carry 235 cubic metres of fuel and 430 cubic metres of water and had bulk tanks for a total of 122 cubic metres of dry bulk.

Another advertised feature was a large stern roller, indicating that the designers were already getting the idea that the stern roller was an important feature for an anchor-handler if they were no longer to use the A-frame.

1969 The BA and VA Islander

At the end of the sixties, by which time one would have thought the business would have been settling down, the British were still having unusual ideas about supplying oil rigs, and about the provision of standby vessels. Typical of this entrepreneurial approach was the story of the BJ Islander and the VA Islander, two former Dutch minesweepers which served as supply and standby vessels at the Hewett Platform in the early seventies.

These vessels were wooden hulled and were generally equipped with very expensive bronze and stainless steel equipment to ward off the risks of magnetic mines; even the two 450 bhp GM diesels were mostly alloy. When the two ships were converted for use in the North Sea, a wooden housing was built over the open bridge, with a kitchen door purchased from a DIY store at the aft end. When backing up to a platform, the master would operate the wheel and the engine controls while bending double in order to see out of the kitchen door, latched in the open position.

To start with they would drop an anchor and tie up rather as has been described earlier in these pages, but the anchors, which were stowed in a very naval way on a sort of launching platform either side of the bow, proved difficult to recover and the ships were soon backing up and tying up to a single rope from the platform and hanging from that down-tide. In this position

BA Islander a former minesweeper converted into a supply vessel employed to service the Hewitt Platform and othr adjacent facilities at the turn of the decade. Picture: David Bland

they would discharge and load cargo and embark and disembark passengers, who they moved from one platform in the field to another. They would watch more conventionally motivated ship-masters try to tie up by lining up at right angles to the platform, dropping the anchor and then attempting to back up to tie up the ropes. These efforts were usually unsuccessful. Unless the anchor cable was kept absolutely slack, so that the stern could be put into the tide, the anchor would hold the bow up, and the vessel would be swept down-tide, ending up in an entirely different position to that intended.

On the Islanders, in the position which had formerly been occupied by the minesweeper's sweep gear, a 25-ton water tank had been fitted and the ships routinely discharged its contents to the platforms. Dave Bland, who was mate of the BJ Islander, remembers the process. When it was time to discharge the water one of the crew would be dispatched to the steering gear, entering through a submarine hatch at the stern. Once under deck he would make his way forward through a void space until he arrived at a point below the water tank where there was a small diesel powered pump. On being given the instruction to pump by the platform, the message would be relayed down the deck to a sailor who stood at the open hatch and shouted down "start the pump". The intrepid pump operator would then pull the string wound round the starting pulley and hope that the machine would burst into life. On the instruction to stop pumping the operator would decompress the engine.

The rather ad-hoc manner in which the ships were run resulted in more professional seafarers making their way to a more secure part of the industry, Dave Bland for instance joining the embryo Harrisons (Clyde) offshore arm, Stirling Supply Ships. Finally the company running the two ex-minesweepers went bankrupt and the ships were broken up in Portsmouth.

Down in the Engine Room

By the end of the decade there were signs that the Europeans were taking the supply vessel forward in a way which had not been necessary in the Gulf of Mexico, or in other sheltered seas round the world, and the greater distances travelled from the shore meant that there was a tendency for the oil companies to want to use the same ships for different tasks. Hence, while there were many more supply ships than anchor-handlers in the Gulf of Mexico, the opposite was becoming true in Europe.

The European ships were being built with more of everything. More deck area, more liquid-carrying capacity, more powder-carrying capacity, more horsepower, more winch power and more wire-storage capacity, and last but not least, more height on the funnels. All these factors, except for the last, have remained the key factors against which vessels are measured.

Engine power remained a problem. While the American car market was just coming to the end of an era, with the 1970 incarnation of the Plymouth Barracuda, whose V8 developed 500 horsepower, marine diesels small enough to fit under the deck of a supply vessel did not develop much more. The British pressed into service engines which had been developed for the railway industry, and other diesels which had been built to power generators. But the problem of all of them was the fact that they had been built to operate at a constant speed, and although this meant that they were fine when the ships were on passage, they became much less reliable when they were being cycled from tick-over to maximum power, sometimes within seconds.

By this time the man at the controls was no longer relying on voice pipe communication, or the engine room telegraph, as a means of transmitting the requirements for the speed and direction of the propellers. He was actually operating the throttles himself, and almost universally at the time the transition from forward to astern was a function of this control. From ahead the throttle would be returned to upright and the engine would declutch; it would then be possible to put the engine astern by pulling the throttle back. This may seem to the reader to be a perfectly logical, but it is worth bearing in mind that there were still at the time a variety of means by which engines on small craft could be controlled, most commonly there would be one lever which changed the direction of the propeller and another to control the power. While this was seldom the case for main engines, it was common for the single bow thrusters usually fitted at the time, to have one lever for the direction of thrust and one for the application of power.

Of course, with the single combined directional control and throttle, to the horror of all chief engineers, it would be possible for the unthinking, the uncaring or the extremely frightened to pull the stick right back without waiting for the de-clutch and re-clutch operation. The resulting churning of gears and revving of engines, accompanied by clouds of black smoke from the funnels, would indicate that there was a good chance of the abused machinery failing later.

The approach taken by the Norwegians to overcome this problem was the controllable pitch propeller and the approach taken by the Americans was to make the "de-clutch clutch" operation faster, and to get Detroit diesels to be more responsive to requirements of the industry. Those who drove the later productions from Halter Marine and others could not help but be impressed by the speed with which the movement from ahead to astern could be achieved, and by the flexibility of the engines which could be coaxed to go from tick over to full ahead or full astern in moments.

Endnote

By the end of the 1960s the Americans were under the impression that they were part of a mature industry, and the British were thinking that they were at the edge of a whole new marine activity. In the North Sea ships were being built and people hired to drive them by ship managers who had little idea of what either the craft themselves, or the mariners on board them, were actually going to do. They were not a million miles away from the situation described by John P LaBorde in Chapter 2.

A story is told of a British supply ship sent out to an offshore installation but unable to discharge its cargo due to the inability of the master to go through the tying up operation. In typical oil patch fashion the errant vessel was recalled, and another carrying an identical cargo sent out. Unfortunately the newly dispatched vessel collided with the returning vessel, and so the whole operation was aborted.

It gradually began to dawn on the companies operating the ships that many things were required of its crews. They had to be tolerant of very modest accommodation, capable of enduring lengthy periods of adverse weather, at all levels to be good seamen, and most of all to be extremely courageous. Hence, in a process which was completely alien to almost all British ship-owners, they had to offer conditions of service and salaries, which would be sufficiently attractive to professional seafarers to prise them out of less challenging working environments.

An OSA pipe-carrier in the River Dee. The Offshore Supply Association built 10 of these small vessels capable of carrying two tiers of pipe between 1974 and 1976. They proved to be of very limited use. Picture: Victor Gibson

Chapter 5
THE NORTH SEA

European and American Newbuilds

In the early 1970s the Norwegian designers and shipbuilders completed their own versions of what they saw as being the North Sea supply ship, and also built one or two ships for both the British and the Americans. Some Norwegian companies, unexpectedly in retrospect, ordered ships from American yards. Wilhelmsen Offshore Supply had three ships built by the Mangone Shipbuilding Co of Houston, all powered by EMDs with a conservative output of 2500 bhp and Bugge Supply Ships had the Sea Explorer built by the same yard in 1971.

But regardless of new production in Norway, Holland, Germany and UK, American yards were still building the majority of the supply ships entering service. The American Marine Corporation built 50 ships for a variety of owners, including Tidewater, Bo-Truc Rentals, Zapata and the Gulf Fleet. Offshore Trawlers of Bayou La Battre built 34 ships all for one owner, Seacor. Halter Moss Point built an amazing 123 vessels for some of the same companies as well as Jackson Marine, Seahorse Inc and State Boat. They also built Gulf Fleet 1, and so was born yet another major American supply ship owner. As usual the Americans were thinking big in terms of numbers, but were at that time less than innovative when it came to design.

Back in Europe more British ship-owners were eyeing up the prospects offshore, as their deep-sea fleets began to contract under the assault of the container ship. The largest British ship-owner, P&O, was already in the business with International Offshore Services and the best known, Cunard, who were still operating transatlantic passenger ships, owned Offshore Marine.

In 1972 Ocean Fleets, commercially known as Blue Funnel, entered into a partnership with the Inchcape Group to operate a supply vessel company to be known as Ocean Inchcape Ltd or O.I.L . While Ocean Fleets had no previous experience in the field, the Inchcape Group had been the owners of a single supply ship, the San Pedro Gulf out in Australia, and later had formed an alliance with the Straits Steamship Company, which became the Borneo Straits Offshore (Pty) BSO. This company had built three ships to support Shell's activities off Borneo.

The Inchcape experience was put to use in the design of the first eight of the company's ships, built at a number of yards in Holland, the company being unable to find any UK yards which would deliver this number of vessels, on time. We should remember here that it was not possible to find one yard to build eight small ships – two a year – when Halter Moss Point was averaging 12.3 ships a year over the decade.

In any case, from a number of yards in Holland the four OIL Mark Ones were delivered in 1972. They were the Oil Producer, the Oil Prospector, Oil Supplier and Oil Explorer. They were followed in 1973 by two further vessels, though by now OIL had learned that the low bridge structures of the first four were vulnerable to the sea, and put in an extra deck. These two vessels

The Maersk Trimmer one of the "T" class built in Norway between 1971 and 1974. The MAK engines produced 6100 bhp and gave them a bollard pull of 65 tonnes.
Picture: Maersk Publicity

were called Oil Venturer and Oil Discoverer, and finally another two ships were brought into service in 1974, the Oil Mariner and the Oil Driller. The fleet became progressively more powerful, starting at about 4000 bhp and finishing at over 6000 bhp.

In 1972 yet another British company, Seaforth Maritime, was to join the ranks of North Sea ship-owners, although they might have seen themselves as "Scottish" ship-owners. The principle shareholders were Lyle Shipping, Hogarth Shipping, Sidlaw Industries, North Sea Assets and the Bank of Scotland, and this group recruited the well known Scottish entrepreneur Ian Noble as Chairman.

Seaforth immediately contracted Drypool Engineering (Cochrane & Sons) of Selby to construct three anchor-handlers and the first to enter service was the Seaforth Hero, followed by the Seaforth Prince and the Seaforth Chieftain. These vessel were powered by two Mirrlees Blackstone engines each developing 2500 bhp, the total power delivering 60 tonnes bollard pull. Unusually for British supply vessels of the period they were provided with CP propellers, and in common with several UK-based ships of the time they were provided with a White Gill Jet multi-directional thruster.

Anchor-handling capability was provided by a double-drum hydraulic winch, the anchor-handling drum having a capacity of 620 metres (2000 ft) of 52mm wire. British companies were really following the lead of the Americans and engaging yards experienced in building fishing vessels to construct the small supply vessels of the day, and the interior of the Seaforth Hero and its sisters was not unlike the interior of a deep sea trawler of the same period, with narrow dark alleyways and steep companionways with narrow stair treads.

The Seaforth Hero went to work with the early OIL ships on the Forties field development, moving the semi-submersible Sea Quest about as they attempted to determine the extent of the field.

Oil and Offshore Marine were building almost identical ships during this time, and they could hardly have been further away from the Americans, whose funnels remained halfway down the deck, and most of which still had the Smatco winch bolted down to the deck before being dispatched to do an anchor job.

Two of the OIL ships were particularly innovative for the time, being provided with a hydraulically operated moving deck. In 1973 all ships were still tying up with two ropes to offshore installations, but the problem was that the cranes could not often reach the forward end of the deck, hence by having a moving deck, once the after end of the ship had been discharged the second half of the cargo could be trundled aft. The deck itself was on rails and was pulled into position by large chains on hydraulic motors.

This curious innovation was also adopted by two Zapata platform ships. These vessels, the Royal Service and the Regal Service were extremely large, and the moving deck was probably seen as an essential accessory for ship which, if aligned at ninety degrees to the side of a platform or rig would place the forward end of the deck far out of reach of the crane.

The Shetland Service, originally Shetland Shore, built in 1973 at Richards of Lowestoft. Lengthened in the early 1990s for its role as a standby vessel, but still defining the style of the British supply ship.
Picture: Victor Gibson

First Ships Built at Ulstein Hatlo

In Denmark the Maersk Company continued to expand its fleet and built seven anchor-handlers of 4600 bhp in 1971 and 1972. These were the original S Class and H class vessels. Maersk still use the same names, only the ships have been changed. And, more importantly for the industry as a whole, they placed an order for two ships with the Norwegian shipyard Ulstein Hatlo, who up to that time had been building fishing vessels. These vessels entered service as the Maersk Tender and Maersk Topper. They were 191 feet (58.5 m) long and had 6,400 bhp available.

In 1974, in what was to be a rather limited attempt to break into the European market, Tidewater commissioned the Mammoth Tide and Goliath Tide from the Ulstein yard. They were 218 ft long and total horsepower was 7800 bhp, provided by four engines. These ships were fitted with a gantry crane which ran back and forth on rails down the deck, apparently in order to deliver cargo from the forward end of the deck to the aft end, and to lift and carry anchors forward.

Rather interestingly, the Senior Vice-President of Tidewater, Damon B Bankston, said at the naming ceremony:

"One of the more dramatic ways of pointing out how the size of the marine equipment in this industry has changed over the past 25 years is that the Ebb Tide would easily fit onto the back deck of one of the largest vessels we have now. The total horsepower in the engine room of the Ebb Tide would not match the bow-thruster power of one of our largest vessels", and he added helpfully "A bow-thruster simply helps to move a vessel's bow laterally for easier positioning".

After this speech Mrs Brankston christened the Mammoth Tide, and Mrs William E Bright, wife of the Tidewater Senior Vice-President in charge of worldwide operations, christened the Goliath Tide. The Mammoth Tide and the Goliath Tide were at that time the most powerful supply vessels in the world, a title which moved between nations almost on a monthly basis at that time. However, it might be worth saying that at the time Tidewater and its subsidiaries operated a number of extremely powerful tugs which were used in the offshore industry.

These two vessels also have a possible claim to fame in that there are some who believe that they were the inspiration for the Ulstein UT 704, although others believe that the inspiration might have been the British ship Seaforth Victor, which was an early "largest" in the British Seaforth fleet.

The UT704 appeared in 1975, possibly as a result of Ulstein's experience with the Tidewater vessels. The design was a real milestone in the development of the type. It was, for its time, extremely large, with over 100 ft of clear deck space and very powerful with a minimum of 7040 bhp available usually provided by two Nohab engines. The UT704 became the basic workhorse of the industry worldwide, except in America, being built under license in the Far East, India, Yugoslavia and Spain, and was only superseded by more advanced designs ten years later as the industry was beginning to move into recession.

The UT704

The UT704 almost deserves a chapter of its own. It is the most prolific supply vessel type ever built, and may only be exceeded in numbers as a ship type by the American Liberty and Victory ships built during and after the Second World War, a total of ninety-one having been built all over the world between 1975 and 1987.

Between the appearance of the first 704 in 1975, and the end of 1976, nineteen ships had been built all for Norwegian owners, and all but two operated under the Norwegian flag. These vessels allowed the Norwegians to become a major force in the British sector, which as we saw in the previous chapter, had up to that time been dominated by traditional British shipowners.

The UT704 was a quantum leap forward. The first vessel to enter service was the Skaustream built in Finland by Oy Laivarteolisuus, who also built three further vessels in the same year. It was powered by two Nohab diesels giving 7040 BHP, and was provided with a single 500bhp bow-thruster. In this configuration bollard pulls of between 90 and 100 tons were claimed for the design.

Accommodation was spartan by today's standards, the winch being set well forward between the funnels, giving a clear deck area of 124ft by 36ft.

It seemed to have combined all the possible requirements for offshore anchor handling and supply operations in a single vessel without sacrificing anything. Some of the Smit-Lloyd and

The UT704 revolutionised the design of the anchor-handler with its large roller and rounded quarters. For twenty years it was to be the workhorse of the North Sea. Picture: Victor Gibson.

OSA ships of the period were superior in engine power, but invariably they had less available deck space, and in the case of the Smit-Lloyd vessels the master was still required to stand at the controls. The majority of the British ships of the period were dimensionally smaller, and generally lighter in construction. Indeed all these companies seemed wedded to their designs, which in a way is not surprising since they were generally subsidiaries of deep-sea ship owners whose trademarks were often the actual shape of the ships. It was therefore against their whole philosophy to accept a standard type with no sign of their personal imprint.

In the years which followed most of the British, Dutch and German supply-ship owners persisted with modifications to their earlier ship-types, and painted them in their traditional colour schemes. The Norwegians on the other hand bought UT704s off the shelf, and usually painted them orange - orange hull, orange upper-works and orange deck, the only distinguishing feature being the funnels and the names.

The design was the first to incorporate rounded quarters to allow the tow wire free movement during turns. Up to that time naval architects had attempted to emulate the stern of a traditional tug in the towing mode, while providing a roller for decking the anchors during rig shifts. This necessitated the closing of a gate under the tow wire to provide free movement, and required a certain amount of dexterity on the part of the deck crews, who had to make the initial connection with the gate open, and then close it under the wire.

However the moulded quarters required the provision of some means of restricting the movement of the wires during anchor handling, and for this purpose the 704s were provided with hydraulic pins which rose out of the deck and trapped the wire, almost incidentally making the operation 100% safer.

The design also moved the winch controls from a deck-house ahead of the winch to a position on the bridge. This, at a stroke, improved communication between the master and the chief engineer, who operated the winch, improved visibility and kept the Chief warm. Later the master was also given much improved visibility while manoeuvring, the vessel being provided with a full-length window at the after end, although in the earliest ships the funnels restricted vision on the quarters. This problem was solved by reducing the funnel height and extending the exhausts from the top.

After the initial flurry of vessels in 1975 and 1976 there was a reduction in construction generally, due to the inevitable boom and bust cycles of the industry. However, three vessels were constructed by Ultsteins for the Russians in 1977 and two ships constructed in Spain in 1978. One of these ships, the Dee Service went to work for Shell in the southern North Sea.

In 1979, with the North Sea still in something of an over-supply situation, two ships were constructed in Canada and two in Finland for Huawei Offshore of Hongkong, and in 1980 a further four of the type were built, two in Poland for Petrobaltic and two in Korea which Danish ship-owners AP Moller purchased while they were under construction, for operation in the Far East.

The two Maersk vessels were unique in being provided with wire-operated controls rather than the air controls which were generally being used at the time. The reason for this specification is lost in the mists of time, but doubtless the two ships are still active somewhere in the world, and it will still be a requirement that the masters engage in a prolonged period of weight training before taking command.

Improvements in Control

One of the features of the UT704 much envied by the drivers of the British ships of the time was the controllable pitch propeller, which resulted in much greater control of the propeller thrust, and a reduction in the time taken to get the propellers from ahead to astern.

Prior to the arrival of the CP propeller ship-masters would place their ships roughly where they needed to be and then put one engine ahead and one astern, countering the tendency of the vessel to turn by putting the rudders over in the opposite direction and using the bow-thruster to hold the bow in position. This technique was apparently similar to that used by helicopter pilots to neutralise the tendency of their aircraft to spin in the opposite direction to the main rotor blades by using the tail rotor.

The CP propellers also allowed the engines to maintain a constant speed and so one of the reliability problems was solved.

Star Offshore and the Forties Field

In March 1974 yet another British ship-owner became involved in the offshore industry. Star Offshore Services was a joint venture between Blue Star and United Towing. At the time Blue Star was a wholly owned component of the Vesty Group, Britain's largest wholesale and retail butchers. The company's deep-sea ships were typical British liners, with their grey hulls and extremely large red funnels decorated with a blue band around the top and a large blue star on the side . United Towing were a successful towing and salvage company whose activities up until then had not been adversely affected by the oil industry.

Star immediately ordered 13 vessels, the first one of which, the Star Taurus, was delivered in April 1975. The Taurus was built in Bolsones by Verft of Molde, Norway and was 59 metres long, powered by two Nohab engines developing the standard 7040 bhp giving a bollard pull of 90 tons. Star leaned towards the Norwegians in colour scheme, the Taurus having white upper-works and a red hull. A white funnel embossed with a restrained blue star and two blue bars, symbolizing the amalgamation of the two companies, was a tasteful contrast to the rather brash Blue Star funnels.

The Oil Mariner built in Holland in 1974, powered, like many ships of the period with two English Electric diesels originally intended to power railway engines. Picture: Victor Gibson

The Star Taurus was a state of the art anchor-handler in 1975. Seen here in Peterhead Bay. Picture: George Craigen.

The Star Taurus and its sister ship the Star Aquarius got their first charter in the same year. They were hired to assist the Navy in the Cod War, but immediately proved unequal to the task and were replaced by the United Towing tugs, Statesman and Lloydsman.

Also in 1974 the Forties Alpha jacket in the form of Graythorpe 1, and the Forties Charlie jacket in the form of Highland 1 were installed, and the following year the first oil from the North Sea was produced by the Hamilton Brothers floating production unit Transworld 58. The Graythorpe jackets were built at Hartlepool and the Highland jackets at Nigg. They were floated out on the larger of their legs and then set upright at the location. The scale of these structures was amazing, and would still be amazing today. It is probable that the American refusal to accept any limitation was a major factor in their construction. They looked like primordial skeletons lying dead on the surface of a small planet when they were under construction, dwarfing all structures in their near vicinity.

When upright and in position they were ready to receive the many modules it would take to make them complete, and the task occupied numbers of support vessels of various sizes for two years.

The Transworld 58 on the Argyll Field was, on the other hand, a straightforward transfer of systems from the onshore to the offshore environment. Hamiltons set up the TW58, a conventional but already ageing semi-submersible, to which was added the hardware it would take to carry out the initial separation of the crude oil from the water and gas. The product was piped to a loading buoy, where a tanker would swing round for two or three weeks while it was filled with oil.

By 1976 ships had been servicing oil rigs and platforms for twenty years and the offshore oil industry could be said to be achieving a degree of maturity. By now there were many ship-owners operating vessels, enormous numbers of platforms in the Gulf of Mexico and the middle east and numerous mobile units drilling holes in the seabed all over the world. However, the Americans saw no real benefit in modernising their fleets to do anything other than they had been doing since the beginning, and although the industry was moving into deeper water there was in the beginning no real change in the approach. They still expected to tie up to discharge and load and still expected to struggle with the process of moving rigs.

Proven in the North Sea

In 1974, Jane's Book of Ocean Technology catalogued 63 supply ship operators working in the Gulf of Mexico. They ranged in size from Tidewater, even then an enormous company, to B & L Boat rentals, catalogued as owning two ships. In the middle were companies like Theriot, an old-style tug company which had taken on the role of supply ship owner, and Zapata Marine Services, who owned twenty-six supply vessels and who were originally rig owners.

There were upstarts who had no history whatsoever, such as Arcadian Marine Service Inc, who in the mid 1970s owned six ships all built since 1973 and claimed in their publicity literature to be "proven in the North Sea". These ships were known by the owners as the 'Freedom class' and according to them represented the 'second generation' of oilfield marine transportation equipment. Typical of American companies both of the time and even of the present day, they made claims not unlike those made by the makers of rejuvenation creams and potions.

They claimed that the ships were so advanced that they would deliver cargo "in one third less time in all weather condition short of hurricane." Like the claims made by the purveyors of the perfumes and potions, there was little anyone could do to verify these assertions.

Most of these companies have since disappeared or been absorbed by others, but some survive. Otto Candies Inc of Des Allemands, who owned a very large fleet of assorted vessels and Cheramie Bros, who owned fourteen ships, are still operating today in one form or another.

The reality was that by the latter part of the 1970s the American influence in the North Sea was beginning to wane, although they were by now hiring Europeans to man the vessels. Taking on local labour was probably how they viewed it. British merchant navy officers generally preferred the more traditional employment processes offered by the British ship-owners. At that time the Americans typically hired officers by the day in dollars and expected them to find their own reliefs if they wanted time off.

Gulf Backer 1, originally the Njord built in 1975 for Heerema mainly for barge moving and towing, one of the many powerful compact anchor handling tugs built in the 1970s. Picture: Wullie Bremner

British ship-owners accepted the influence of the Merchant Navy and Airline Officers Association on their employees, and were prepared to negotiate with the union for terms of employment. This union influence resulted in the crews on board British ships gaining one-for-one agreements. One day's work for a day's leave. This after all was the condition under which the crews on the rigs and platforms worked, and it was a condition which resulted in a continuous supply of well-qualified marine personnel being available, who in general made up an experienced and loyal workforce.

Despite this evidence the Americans continued in their old way. Typical was the experience of Theriot Inc, who sent six identical brand-new ships over from the Gulf of Mexico in 1976. They worked for the first summer and then in the autumn the ships were laid up in Leith and the crews paid off. In the spring of 1977 they re-activated the ships but were unable to get anyone to work for them in what might today be called a tight labour market. The vessels were sold and became the Scotoil 1 to 6.

New Semi-submersible Designs

One of the offshore periodicals of 1975 listed the rigs in service as being 19 submersibles (In this case a type of oil rig rather than a type of submarine), 64 semi-submersibles, 62 drill ships, 134 jack-ups and 56 tender rigs. Amazingly that year there were 69 semi-submersibles, 60 jack-ups and 47 drill ships on order. The industry was going for it big time, possibly due to the massive increase in oil price due to the middle-east oil embargo.

The increase in oil price may also have spurred on the designers. First came the Pacesetter in the form of the Western Pacesetter 6, which was a straightforward design with two pontoons and six rather robust legs. This rig was followed by the Aker H-3, in the form of the Deep Sea Driller, possibly the most important semi-submersible design after the Ocean Driller. This simple eight-legged design proved to be universally popular with European rig owners, who now included the Scandinavian ship-owners Stena and Fred Olsen, the British ship-owners Ben Line and Salvesens, the French company Forex Neptune, and the German company Transocean.

The American companies, who still owned the majority of the tonnage, favoured home-based products, which included the Sedco 700 series designed by Earl and Wright, the Pacesetter designed by Freide and Goldman and the Ocean Victory designs, developed at the end of the previous decade as the first multi-hull semi-submersible. The Pentagon, designed by Neptune, also at the end of the previous decade, was not provided with hulls as such; its five legs were supported by cylindrical tanks at the bottom. There were now Americans, Norwegians, Japanese and French designing rigs and Americans, British, Norwegians, Danes and Germans designing supply ships.

The increase in activity offshore, particularly in the construction sector, required that the ships be better cargo carriers. In the late 1970s anchor-handlers were used for all purposes including the supply of materials to the platforms which were under construction. They were therefore carrying all the requirements for drilling and in addition everything necessary to keep a marine unit functioning for months, and sometimes years, offshore.

They had to have deck capacity for drill pipe, drilling tools, scaffolding, helicopter fuel tanks, chemicals, food and maintenance equipment. Under deck they had to be able to carry cement in bulk, barytes, bentonite, gas-oil, fresh water, brine and oil-based mud. In the 1970s builders of North Sea supply vessels were still hampered in their efforts to provide under-deck capacity by the necessity of having large ballast tanks available to ensure that the ships remained

The Wimpey Seafox, in 1975 briefly the most powerful anchor handler in the world with an available 8480 bhp. The class has a marked similarity to the Smit-Lloyd ships of the time. Picture: Press.

stable at all stages of loading and discharge.

Also during the early seventies it became obvious that another type of supply vessel was going to be required, as the oil companies began to contract for the laying of pipelines from the fields being constructed in the Shetland basin to the mainland and to the Orkneys and Shetland.

The pipe-carriers needed to have decks capable of carrying either two or three lengths of pipe, and both types of craft were constructed in Norway, Denmark, Germany and UK. This phase also saw the emergence of a couple of standard types: the UT705 and the ME202, designed by Ulsteins and Maritime Engineering respectively. The Maersk Company characteristically went out on their own and built a pipe-carrier unique to themselves, as did OSA, who constructed large numbers of small vessels capable of carrying two lengths of pipe. Star Offshore initiated construction of three pipe-carriers, two of which were eventually to become diving ships, since typically in the supply vessel market, the pipe-carrier requirement was quickly over-tonnaged.

OIL also built a single pipe-carrier the Oil Challenger, which was the only supply vessel to be built with aft accommodation, up to that time. This vessel was specifically constructed to supply the pipe-barge Viking Piper, but when it started work it was found that when the Oil Challenger was lying alongside the pipe-barge it was doing so much damage that it was quickly taken out of service and spent the duration of its contract lying at anchor in the River Tay.

The process of pipe-laying was, like most offshore activities, easy to say but more difficult to do. The pipe-layer was a large barge, or ship shape, in some cases a semi-submersible like the Viking Piper. This vessel and the ETPM 1601 entered service in 1976, both of them capable of laying pipe in more than 1000 feet of water. They were provided with 12 anchors and a "stinger", which was a ramp suspended over the stern down which the pipe was guided. Initially the Viking Piper had winch problems which necessitated a visit to dock in Holland for repairs, but it soon returned and went to work for Chevron at the Ninian Field.

The pipe was carried out to the pipe-layer by the pipe carriers. They would tie up

*The Gulf Rambler. A typical Gulf of Mexico anchor handling tug built at Halter Marine in 1974. Its two EMDs developed 5750 bhp, making a powerful vessel for the time.
Picture: Ron Jansen.*

alongside protected from impact by very large Yokohama fenders, and the pipe would be discharged to the deck. This process was problematical in the North Sea, particularly as the ships got larger, and by the early 1980s a number of British and Norwegian companies had large ships in service which would only just fit alongside some of the pipe-layers. This might not have been a problem if the leads for the anchor wires had been anywhere else but straight out from the sides of the vessel, requiring the ships to ease in between wires, in some cases at the same level as the top of the hull or even the bridge.

Because of the comparable lengths of the vessels, the lack of well-designed leads, and the weight of the ropes, it was seldom possible to tighten up the moorings, leaving the poor shipmaster having to hold the ship alongside without much assistance from the ropes.

On deck there would be a production line, a number of 40-foot lengths of pipe being laid end to end and welded up by the welding crew. When a set of pipes were welded together a whistle would sound, everyone would stand back and the pipe-layer would be pulled forward one hundred and twenty feet on the moorings. It was a mobile production line. If the ships had failed to get the moorings tight, as was usually the case, the master would have to attempt to match the speed of movement forward with the ship's propulsion, and then of course stop at the same time. This took strong nerves and good judgement.

*Highland Champion built at Ulsteinvik in 1979, an early UT705 constructed to haul pipe but quickly turned into a versatile platform ship.
Picture: Victor Gibson*

The development of the pipe-layer also resulted in the development of the European anchor-handling tug, which was derived from the anchor-handler rather than the offshore tug.

In the mid-seventies the Americans continued to service the pipe-laying operation with traditional tugs, such as the second Navajo and El Leon Grande, which were owned by Tidewater, and the Godfather and True Grit, which were owned by Jackson Marine.

The task which they carried out was that of moving the anchors of the pipe-layers forward on a continuous basis for 24 hours a day. Often there would be a tug assigned to each side of the barge, and they would continuously lift anchors, move them forward and lower them to the seabed again. The forward anchors only needed to be lifted and moved directly forward, as did the after anchors. But the anchors nearer the beam had to be recovered towards the barge and then run out again, a process which required considerable skill on the part of the ship-handler due to the speed with which the winch driver on board the pipe-layer would reel in the anchor, and equally the speed with which the ship would be expected to redeploy the mooring.

The American tugs, many of which had rounded sterns, were unable to deck anchors and had a limited capacity when it came to recovering the buoys. When moving the barge anchors they were only required to hook a loop of wire on top of the buoy, which by means of a tube through the buoy was connected directly to the anchor. Hence they could pull the anchor off the bottom without having to bring the buoy on deck.

The Europeans decided to build a more flexible vessel, so Maersk, OSA and others constructed what looked like miniature anchor-handlers. Best known were the Maersk B class built between 1976 and 1977, which with 8400 bhp available and a consequent high bollard pull, were the envy of the North Sea. The working decks were large enough to allow for the storage of a couple of anchors and anchor-buoys and still leave room to work, but they were short enough to ease the sometimes difficult process of pulling the work wires down to the stern roller ready for the next anchor.

In addition to the Maersk ships, OSA put a number of small grey vessels into the field,

The Tempest built in 1977 with an available 8500 bhp. It and sister ship the Typhoon were generally considered to be the ultimate anchor-handling tugs. Picture: Oddgeir Refvik

the type manifested in the Magnitor, built in 1974, which had 5400 bhp available, and a single larger unit, the Hirtenturm, with 7000 bhp and 95 tons of bollard pull available in 1977.

Also in 1975 Wimpey Marine, whose construction up to that time had been cautious and not overwhelmingly successful, took delivery of the Wimpey Seafox, claimed by the June 1975 edition of the offshore magazine "Ocean Energy" to be the most powerful supply ship in the world. It and its sister ship the Wimpey Seatiger looked just like the Smit-Lloyd ships of the time, and for a while it was rumoured that Smit-Lloyd were going to sue Wimpeys for stealing their design. Well, it was true that the ships were built in Holland.

They were powered by two 16 cylinder B&W engines developing 8480 bhp, which gave them a bollard pull of 112 tonnes. The winch was capable of pulling over 100 tonnes, and the specification indicates that the ship could anchor in 300 metres, over 1000 feet, of water.

Worldwide Developments

In 1975 the Chinese showed interest in expanding their offshore operations, having purchased a Japanese 1969 built jack-up. In that year it was also rumoured that the they had built two drill ships and that a number of semi-submersibles had been contracted to be built in Europe. What was not in dispute was their order for offshore support vessels. Eight anchor-handlers were ordered from Aarhus Flydok in Denmark and five ships from the Sanyo Shipping Company. The first ship to be delivered from Denmark was the Weco Supplier 1 and the first from Japan the Unit 222. The ship and its sister had an outward similarity to the Maersk ships built by the same yard. The ships were powered by MaK 8M452 engines developing 3800 bhp, which was similar to the American built ships of the time. This gave a service speed of 13 knots and an bollard pull of 40 tonnes.

It was felt by the commentators of the time that these ships would therefore be unsuited to shifting semi-submersibles, but they would still be adequate for jack-up moving. It was also uncommon for any vessel built during the decade to be built without a winch, no matter what it was intended to do.

The imaginatively named Unit 222 the second of a fleet of eight anchor handlers built for China at the Sanyo shipyard in Japan in 1975.

The Norwegians meanwhile made inroads into the North Sea operations in their own country and in the UK. Ulstein, having designed the UT704, developed the UT708 and UT712, as well as the UT705 for the developing pipe-carrier market. Other Norwegian designers began to have influence, particularly Vik-Sandvik and Maritime Engineering, and the more forward-thinking British companies began to buy Norwegian-designed ships, if only to be able to compete with the Norwegian ship-owners.

At the time the Norwegian tax system allowed individuals to invest in ships at an advantageous rate, and seafarers to work on board the ships at lower rates of income tax. The result seemed to be a continuous supply of wonderfully modern ships manned by very experienced and courageous crews.

Elsewhere in the world the well known Far Eastern conglomerate Swire's formed Swire Pacific and began to build ships in Japan, mainly for operation in the Arabian Gulf. Swire's were traditional ship-owners in the British Hong-Kong tradition, and also had access to an experienced English speaking workforce, although their officers tended to work on a two-for-one basis. The advantage in this case was a tax-free salary and more benign conditions.

Meanwhile, as oil exploration began to move into more hostile waters, the requirements for anchor-handling and towing were becoming more onerous, and bollard pull was beginning to become the measure of efficiency in this sector of the market. In response to this requirement the Maersk Company initiated the construction of six very powerful anchor handlers, the Maersk R class. The first of these vessels, the Maersk Retriever, entered service in 1979. This vessel was powered by four Mak engines developing a total of 13,000 BHP, giving a bollard pull of 146 tons continuously and a maximum of 160 tons. She was also fitted with two bow-thrusters and a stern thruster for maximum manoeuvrability, and a winch capable of lifting 260 tons and twin tow drums each capable of holding 1200 metres of 72 mm wire.

In common with later Maersk anchor-handlers they were also fitted with effective remotely operated fire monitors capable of spraying a burning offshore structure with over 2000 m^3 per hour.

The Sinking of the Ocean Express

Of the many sinkings of jack-ups under tow which have taken place since their inception, the loss of the Ocean Express remains one of the most tragic, and one which still has lessons for the industry. On 15th April 1976 the rig sank in 167 feet of water in the Gulf of Mexico while under tow. Almost all the crew evacuated from the unit in two Whittaker capsules moments before it disappeared beneath the waves. Subsequently one of the capsules capsized and sank with the loss of 13 lives. In hindsight it appears that the findings of the court of enquiry were extraordinarily predictive, but despite them the tragedy set a pattern which was to be repeated on many occasions in subsequent years. The only lesson learnt has been that these objects, which are normally elevated on stilts above the waves, become unacceptably vulnerable when afloat, and that therefore when things go wrong the best thing to do is to call for help. A number of vessels were involved in both the disaster and the recovery of survivors, principally the three tugs owned by the Gulf Mississippi Marine Corp.

The tugs were all about 100 feet long, and ranged in power from the Gulf Explorer at 3600 bhp to the Gulf Knight at 2400 bhp. The third tug was the Gulf Viking. A survey vessel, the Nicole Martin rescued survivors from the sea. Also briefly involved was the supply vessel M L

Levy which was used to transport six offshore workers to the rig when it was under way, in readiness, one assumes, for the next job. Four of the six were to lose their lives when the survival capsule, in which they had evacuated from the rig, capsized.

The Ocean Express was owned by Odeco, a name which was to appear again in the annals of offshore accidents, and the rig move was carried out more or less under the control of an Odeco barge-mover. Also involved in the management of the unit was a Marathon Oil company representative and the tool-pusher for Odeco, who had been in charge of the rig when it was jacked up on the previous well and was to be in charge again when it reached its new location, which was only 33 miles away.

The Ocean Express was a mat supported unit not unlike the first rig of the type, the Mr Gus, described in Chapter 2. It was designed to operate on the level soft mud of which much of the seabed of the Gulf of Mexico is composed. When in its drilling position the mat, a rectangular structure with a slot in the after part, which mirrored the slot in the hull of the rig itself, was lowered to the seabed on the three tubular legs. When the mat was on the bottom, the hull could be elevated above the sea surface, and in this position drilling could be carried out.

The mat was of cellular construction, composed partly from tanks which were filled with water, and partly from tanks which remained buoyant. Since the mat contributed to the buoyancy when mated with the hull, as it was lowered towards the seabed the stability of the unit would be reduced.

On the morning of 14th April 1976 the hull was lowered into the water and the mat recovered until it became essentially part of the hull. The most powerful tug, the Gulf Explorer was designated as lead tug. The rig was rectangular and the points where the towing gear was attached forward were small triangular areas on the port and starboard sides, approached through doors from the deck structures. The Gulf Viking and the Gulf Knight were attached to the towing point on the port bow and the Gulf Explorer to the towing point on the starboard bow, and in this configuration the 33-mile tow was accomplished.

About one mile from the new location, at about 2300 on 14th, the Gulf Knight was relocated from the starboard bow to the port quarter and the Gulf Explorer from the starboard bow to the starboard quarter. The Gulf Viking remained on the port bow. The rig was now positioned with the stern towards the location but was being held bow to the weather by the Gulf Viking, and in this position the mat was lowered until it was 148 feet below the hull.

During the lowering operation the weather had deteriorated and so the relocation was not completed. Instead the rig was held in position by the ships. At 0630 on the following morning the seas had increased in height to 10 to 12 feet and the wind was correspondingly stronger. Obviously there was no alarm at this point because the supply vessel M. L .Levy arrived and discharged the six Offshore Hammer employees by personnel basket. One assumes that at that time it was still dark, and almost certainly the rig was pitching and rolling and moving randomly in the seaway. It must have therefore taken considerable bravery and skill on behalf of both the Ocean Express crane driver and the M. L. Levy captain to accomplish the task, although, in view of how things were to turn out, it would have been better if they had been unsuccessful.

Mid-morning on 15th the weather was really getting up, spray was blowing across the deck of the rig and seas were occasionally boarding. There had been concerns about the freeboard of the unit, which should have been between seven and eight feet, but the rig had a natural list to port which required counter-flooding, and the derrick was not positioned as far forward as was possible so ballasting forward had probably taken place, reducing the freeboard to as little and five and a half feet. At this time the barge-mover instructed the tugs on the aft corners to head forward to hold the rig in location. Some water was entering through apertures in the deck, and uncomfortably for those in the accommodation, this resulted in leaks into the living quarters through the light fittings. Other spaces on the rig were also filling up, particularly the mud pits.

If one accepted that water dripping out of the light fittings is more or less normal, the first sign that things were seriously going wrong was the loss of one of the engines of the Gulf Knight. The barge-mover asked the ship if it wanted to recover its tow wire and return to port, but the master opted to remain attached and to continue to hold the rig up to the weather. At this moment the tugs on the port and starboard quarters were steaming in the same direction as the rig was facing, the tow wires angled outwards from the sides.

Despite the optimism of the Gulf Knight's master, he was unable to hold the ship head to wind with only one engine and he dropped back until he became part of the tow rather than one of the ships doing the towing. The Gulf Viking was now taking the weight on the port bow, with the most powerful tug, the Gulf Explorer doing what it could to assist from the starboard quarter.

The weather continued to get worse so that there was no question of the mat being put on the bottom. By late afternoon the tugs and tow were experiencing wave heights of up to 25 feet and wind speeds of up to 50 knots, far in excess of the relatively benign conditions which would be required to land the mat and elevate the rig.

At 1930 the tow line of the Gulf Viking parted, and although the Gulf Explorer was still attached, the rig wallowed in the seaway while the deck crew attempted to re-attach the tow line. The break had occurred in the towing spring, and the three men on the tiny deck area found it impossible to recover the heavy nylon. The seas which kept swamping the space knocked the men down, and flooded the welder's shop from which access to the area was gained, and eventually they gave up the unequal struggle and retreated. Shortly thereafter some of the pipe on the deck shifted, causing the rig to list, and efforts to re-secure it were soon abandoned due the danger to the crew.

At this time some-one sounded the general alarm without instruction from the person in charge, who was, depending on one's viewpoint, either the barge-mover, the tool-pusher or the Marathon company man. The barge-mover also asked the tool-pusher to drop the anchor but this was not done, so the rig continued to be at the mercy of the weather, the deck being under water for most of the time, the pipe on the main deck rolling from side to side and various compartments gradually filling up. After the sounding of the alarm most of the crew gathered on the upper deck wearing their lifejackets and waited for instructions.

At about 2115 the derrick shifted to starboard, increasing the starboard list, and immediately the tool-pusher gave the instruction to abandon the rig using the Whittaker capsules on the starboard side. The capsule on the port side had already been washed away. The two capsules got away from the rig, leaving the barge-mover on board. He gave the Gulf Explorer and the Gulf Knight instructions to release their tow lines and was rescued by helicopter from the helideck at about 2120. Very soon afterwards the rig, continuing the list over to starboard, disappeared beneath the waves.

Surprisingly, as the emergency developed during the early evening the M. L. Levy was lying at anchor, and after the crew had eaten supper they got under way. This was at about 1900. At this time they were told that the port capsule from the rig had been washed overboard and they were instructed to keep an eye on it. When the coastguard cutter Point Baker asked for the position of the stricken rig, the Captain of the M. L. Levy provided it.

Whittaker capsules were, and still are more or less circular lifeboats whose principal advantage is the ease of launching. The makers also claim that they are easy to manoeuvre due to their shape. Inside there are seats around the periphery and seats around the centre so the majority of the people are seated facing inwards from the outside, and a small number face outwards from the centre. Each of the capsules on the Ocean Express had a capacity of 28 and once inside it was necessary for the passenger to do up seat belts for stability purposes.

There were 14 men in No 1 capsule, which motored away from the location, lookouts keeping an eye out for lights, but after a while those inside were assailed by paint fumes as the engine overheated, or appeared to. And during a period of stopping and starting the engine the capsule landed heavily against the side of the survey vessel Nicole Martin. This capsule was tied on to the survey ship by light lines from various points and despite the extremely rough weather, which resulted in the capsule landing heavily against the ship at times and in variations in height of up to ten feet, all the survivors in the capsule were successfully transferred to the survey ship.

There were problems releasing No 3 capsule from the falls, but eventually it got away from the side of the rig and motored downwind until the smell of paint and hot exhaust began to nauseate the crew. After about twenty minutes the Gulf Viking closed with the capsule and over time, with some difficulty, ropes were attached. However there was considerable vertical motion between the vessels and in a confused exchange between the survivors in the capsule and the crew on deck it was decided that the tug would tow the capsule to calmer waters. One of the ropes was released and unavoidably the second rope gradually slid through the fingers of the one crewman who was trying to hold on to it, until finally it disappeared over the stern. At the time when the capsule was alongside several people released their seat belts, and shortly after the line was lost the capsule flipped over.

After this the tug backed up to the capsule and efforts were made to right it. These were unsuccessful and it appears that the efforts made by the tug's crew increased the rate at which the water was entering the inverted capsule. At any rate, after some minutes the confusion in the capsule resulted in some of the survivors being propelled through the doors which up to that time had been held shut by two men. The Captain of the Gulf Viking radioed for assistance and the Gulf Knight responded, picking the last two survivors from the sea. The remaining thirteen men were drowned.

A late participant in this drama was the aircraft carrier the USS Lexington, which arrived on the location at about 0230 on 16th, in time to assist with the recovery of the capsules.

The board of enquiry found much wrong with the manner in which the rig had been operated, both in general and on that particular occasion, aspects singled out for mention being the difficulties of making the tow fast on the tiny triangular decks, and the lack of information contained in the stability book. There was also considerable discussion as to what constituted a "field move" and what might constitute a "short move", which would be amusing but for the tragedy which resulted from the confusion created by such distinctions. The board had something to say about the qualifications of the tug's personnel, suggesting that offshore tugs should be subject to the same regulations as other vessels of a similar type, and that the chosen language to be used at such time should be English – the Louisiana tug crews tended to speak French. In all, this disaster should have resulted in changes which would in the future make the moving of jack-ups safer, whether it did or not remains debatable.

Endnote

By the end of the 1970s the American fleets had virtually disappeared from the North Sea. They had failed to modernise and so were unable to compete with the Norwegians, the Dutch, the Germans and even the British, who by now were having most of their ships built in Norway.

The decade came to an end with the revolution in Iran. Although the full influence of this political upheaval in one of the major oil-producing countries of the world was not immediately felt, there was an immediate increase in the oil price. It is one of those economic realities that any major political unrest in an oil producing country will be no bad thing for the companies supporting oil exploration, and if the unrest is in a country where the means of recovering oil are fairly easy, it becomes necessary for those the majors to look for the stuff somewhere where both exploration and production will be more difficult, and so require more expertise, more hardware and more time.

Once more the supply ship owners looked out to sea, this time towards the ocean deeps, and rubbed their hands. Good times were coming.

North Prince built in 1978 as the Faldentor for OSA. Like all OSA ships of the period the design was unique to the owners and so robust that all the remaining vessels of the class are still in use today. Picture: Victor Gibson

*The KMAR404 Ray J Hope towing a rig in the Southern Ocean. Despite the fact that good weather is preferred for rig shifts, sometimes there is no choice.
Picture: James McLellan*

Chapter 6
RIG SHIFTING

Introduction

To what extent the designers of the Ocean Driller had actually worked out how the rig would be moored is unknown, but doubtless they had confidence that the masters of the then quite extensive and varied fleet of offshore support vessels would work out how to do it. They knew that warships were routinely attached to moorings that had been pre-laid by special craft, so surely it could not be that difficult. At the same time anchoring a ship is very straightforward. The anchor is housed near the bow, and is connected to a chain which is piled up in a chain locker, somewhere close. It is therefore just a matter of releasing the anchor at the appropriate moment and allowing the chain to run out until the person in charge can be reasonably confident that the anchor will "hold". Hopefully the anchor will be lying on the seabed with the flukes embedded in the sand and the chain will be leading in a straight line for some distance before it curves upwards to the bow of the ship.

All being well, despite any movement of the ship, particularly vertically, the chain will extend far enough so that there will be no uplift of the shank of the anchor, and therefore the flukes will not be pulled out of the sand. Of course this does not prevent the ship moving with the wind or tide, and a ship which is moored to a single anchor will take up a new position, probably 180 degrees away from the previous one, on change of tide. It will have taken up the new position and dragged the whole length of the chain with it, so that the radius of the swing will be the length of the chain, plus the length of the ship.

If this circle is too large the Captain may decide to lay two anchors, and having released the first, the ship will proceed under power towards a point when the second anchor can be laid, while all the while the winch driver is ensuring that the chain is laid across the seabed. When the second anchor is dropped to the seabed, the second chain will be paid out while that attached to the first anchor will be recovered, until the ship is half way between the two. Now, when the tide turns, the bow of the ship will remain in virtually the same position while the stern swings round – a much smaller radius. The downside of the latter technique is the possibility that the ship may turn right round – possibly more than once – over a number of tides and twist the cables together. However this is the starting point for anchoring a rig – and it is now obvious to us, as it must have been to the designers of the Ocean Driller, that there was no way in which the rig could lay enough anchors for it to be held in precisely the correct position, without some help from attendant vessels.

It may also be worth remembering that the process just described is the procedure which uses the modern stockless anchor and the self-stowing cable locker. The stockless anchor was developed because the old admiralty pattern anchor was very awkward to stow, with its stock at ninety degrees to the flukes, and the self-stowing cable locker was just a locker which was sufficiently large to be able to take in all the cable without members of the crew having to enter the lockers to flake it down. So in 1961 the semi-submersible designer had at his disposal mooring systems which had already been developed to the point where they were easy to use. They just had to be adapted.

The Star Polaris working at the Pentagon 84. Its wire moorings and LWT anchors often necessitated the addition of piggy backs. Picture: George Craigen.

Anchor-Handling

On a modern anchor-handler, which is engaged in mooring a semi-submersible, the engineer driving the winch and the deck officer driving the ship sit side by side in similar seats, the ship's driver with all the ship's controls available and the winch driver with all the winch controls to hand. Usually the seats are placed on runners so that the operators can be positioned close to the large aft facing windows. From this position they have a very good view of the deck, and it is normal for the funnel or funnels to be placed forward of them so that they can see the installation they are servicing, even if it is on the ship's beam. In the dark the whole area is illuminated by a number of extremely bright lights, usually installed above and below the aft side part of the bridge.

Often there is survey equipment on the bridge, sometimes with an operator, and this equipment allows the team to see exactly where the ship is in relation to the intended track and anchor position as they run out with the anchor and chain.

The job of running an anchor, one of the basic tasks for the ship, starts when the master or the chief mate backs up the stern of the vessel close to one of the corner legs of the rig. A pennant is passed down to the deck and the end of it secured in what is often known as a "shark's jaw", and which is actually a hydraulic stopper which captures the end of the wire. The crew then secure this wire to a winch and heave it up the deck until the shark's jaw can be lowered out of the way and the crane released. The other end of the wire is secured to what is known as a chasing collar, a large steel loop which encircles the anchor-chain.

At this point the ship will usually move away from the leg and the anchor-winch driver on the rig will lower away the anchor. The engineer on the ship will heave up on his winch until the anchor – still attached to the rig of course - is very close to the stern of the ship. Once in this position the ship's driver will align the vessel on the required heading, and when everyone is ready, will move out in the direction of the anchor position. This sounds like a complex operation, and it is. There is very little room for error on board. If the driver makes an error he may contact the leg of the rig, or drift away causing panic in the crane-driver's cab if the crane wire is still attached. If the deck crew make any mistakes they risk being bruised, having limbs broken or being crushed.

However, all being well the ship will be able to make steady progress towards the anchoring position and when the surveyor says they have arrived, the anchor can be lowered down onto the seabed. Once this has been done the rig will tension up on the wire and the ship will run the collar back along the chain until the crew are able to return the wire to the rig. One anchor may take several hours to run if the water is deep.

The stern of an anchor handler showing the kort nozzles and the cut away hull which ensure the maximum bollard pull for a given horsepower. Picture: Darren Green.

Early Anchor Jobs

What has just been described is the technique which is used for running anchors now, but it was not always so. It was probably not until the early 1970s that the semblance of a routine was developed, but even then the operation was seldom carried out without difficulty. Lacking the advanced survey systems available today it was necessary to dispatch a survey ship to the proposed rig location to lay small buoys. This vessel would be equipped with the position fixing system, in those days probably Decca Hifix.

This ship would be provided with a chart on which was inscribed the proposed position

Men working on deck at a Sedco rig in the far east a chasing collar and the towing pins can be seen on the deck. Picture: Wullie Bremner.

of the rig, and the positions of all the anchors. It would also show a direction of approach. Following the positions on the chart, a buoy would then be laid by the survey ship at each of the anchor locations, and at the position of the centreline forward end of the rig. Two buoys would also be laid a distance away from the final position on the line of approach; these were known as 'the gates'.

The rig, usually towed by two anchor-handlers, one on the forward port anchor chain and one on the forward starboard anchor chain, would then approach the position through the gate and would head for the buoy locating the bow. A third anchor-handler would back up astern of the now slowly moving rig and take the pennant for the first stern anchor down onto the deck and connect the buoy.

This part of the job was particularly exciting, requiring as it did a very close approach to the rig, which at that time was moving forward. The Enhanced Pacesetters were provided with a crane at the centre-line aft, which made the job just a little easier, as were the Pentagones, but the latter with their curious five-legged design required a particularly high standard of ship-handling.

When taking the first anchor pennant from a Pentagone the ship had to insert itself between the two aft circular buoyancy units. It would then be caught in the eddies swirling around the structure and would be pulled along virtually without the assistance of the engines. This was a heart stopping moment even for the most experienced ship-handlers, who would adjust the controls with only a moderate level of success while the aft crane on the rig would pass down the buoy and then the pennant. When the pennant was landed on the deck the crew on the deck would pass a wire through the eye and pull it forward with a tugger winch, then they would pull the pelican hook across and secure the wire in it. This took place with the crane still attached to the pennant and therefore to the ship, but once the pelican hook was closed and the pennant secured, the crane could be released and the ship allowed to drift aft until it was clear of the legs.

The rig would lower away the anchor and once the first pennant had been connected to the pennant string on the work-drum, the ship would also be able to lower away, and eventually the anchor would be on the bottom and the ship would cease to move forward. The

The work drums of the Normand Drott. Two work wires can be seen in the foreground and the tow drum is behind. The design changed little for twenty years. Picture: Victor Gibson

buoy could be attached to the last pennant and then released, freeing the ship to carry out its next task.

Once the first anchor was in position it was used as a brake and the rig would be eased into place with the bow marker buoy just ahead. The tug attached to the mooring diagonally opposite the first anchor then ran out towards the anchor position buoy, and when it got as close as it could the anchor was lowered to the bottom and buoyed off. The aft anchor handler ran out the second after mooring and the other vessel forward was dispatched towards its anchor buoy, and within a fairly short space of time the rig would be secured in position by four anchors. This of course was only the starting point.

As well as being secured in position during the relatively benign conditions under which the anchor job was taking place, it also had to remain there when the weather worsened, and the ability of the rig to do this was determined by cross-tensioning the moorings. Even without cross-tensioning, the mariners in charge of these operations knew that it was necessary to get the anchors out to the position of the buoys, but the ships were seldom powerful enough to achieve this.

Typically the anchor-handler would back up to the leg, receive the pennant on board and connect it up to the winch. They would then, in co-ordination with the windlass driver on the rig, get the anchor to the stern, just below the roller. Then on the word, the master would put the sticks down and the vessel would power away from the rig as the windlass driver released the brake. The latter was faced with the task of just letting out sufficient chain to ensure that the ship would not be held up, without allowing it to pile up on the bottom. Despite the fact that during this process the engine room was full of smoke, the fire alarms were going off and the engineers had to retreat to the deck, either of these actions would stop the ship dead. If this happened they would have to go back to the beginning and start again.

Some-times the location buoy was missing and so the survey vessel was given the job of hovering in the correct position while the anchor-handler steamed out at full speed towards it. Since the anchor-handler would be unable to get the anchor out to the correct distance, it was not in much danger, but nevertheless it must have been a frightening experience for the crews.

Once the eight, nine, ten or twelve moorings were in place the task of tensioning up was undertaken, and if an anchor moved remedial action was taken, the precise sort depending on the tow-master and the available back-up equipment.

In virtually all cases the anchors used on the rigs were LWTs, solid traditional navy anchors which could be laid either way up; it really depended as much as anything on their 15-ton weight to achieve holding power. If they dragged under tension the first action might be to lay them again, but this was seldom successful and so further back-up anchors or "piggy-backs" would be laid.

In the early 70s and before, a vessel would recover the main anchor and attach a second pennant to the crown, then pass this to another vessel which had the back-up on deck. They would both then lower their respective anchors to the sea-bed at the same time. This sounds easy. However it takes great courage and skill to manoeuvre one vessel within heaving line distance of another, even in what passes for calm weather in the North Sea, and doing this as a matter of routine filled the log books of the early anchor-handlers with long reports on contact damage.

As time passed it became evident that a single ship could recover the anchor-buoy to the deck, take it off, connect the piggy-back to the end of the pennant string and then lay it in the same line as the original mooring. Some-times fabricated anchors were added to achieve holding power which was not directly related to the weight and sometimes big bits of metal were added, theoretically to prevent anchor uplift, but in reality just adding to the sheer weight of stuff on the seabed.

Although the whole of this activity can be described in a paragraph, in reality many hours, sometimes days, were spent laying these moorings. The ships were often damaged, and on occasions holed, and always the crews were completely exhausted by the time the work was finished. However, none of this seemed to deter the European ship-owners from the desire to be in the business.

With the passing of time the guys on the deck have gained the assistance of substantial cranes which ease their task. This one is on the Far Scout. Picture: Keith Ricketts.

Chasing

One of the problems associated with the operation of semi-submersibles was the presence of eight or more anchor buoys distributed round the unit at a range of about three-quarters of a mile. Even those who knew they were there would still approach with caution, particularly in the dark, when the obligatory searchlight would be played on the sea ahead. Those who had no idea they were there sometimes ran into them at full speed, occasionally damaging their vessels and always sinking the buoy.

The first improvement was to change the steel buoys for GRP and elastomar foam ones, and this modification solved the problem of damage and sinking. However these buoys were fragile and unless they were launched with care, chunks would be ripped out of them by any protuberances on the after decks of the anchor-handlers, and of course the problem of them drifting off in rough weather was not solved despite more and more elaborate ground tackle connecting them to the crown of the anchor.

An early attempt to overcome there problems was the use of acoustic buoys, connected to the end of the pennant string by a small diameter line, and which lay on the seabed until they received a signal to release themselves from their bottom weight and rise to the surface. Of course these technically sophisticated devices did not immediately make life easy. Firstly they did not always release when asked, and secondly no-one knew exactly where they were, so the vessel sending the signal was at risk.

During the development of the Forties Field one of the OIL Mark 1 supply vessels sent the signal to a submerged acoustic buoy and it released itself and came up under the engine room of the ship. Every point under the engine room was protected by a double bottom tank except for the areas under the main engine flywheels. This point was of course the place where the buoy hit, and unfortunately made a small hole.

The engineers tried to prevent the engine-room filling up. They were unsuccessful in their attempts to block up the hole and so they fired up the bilge pumps, while the Captain literally headed for the beach, eventually running the ship aground close to Bass Rock. The tide went out. The guys blocked up the hole and at high water the ship was floated off and resumed its job.

When the buoys were sunk or drifted away, or the acoustic buoy failed to release, it was down to a supply ship to go fishing, usually using a shepherd's crook or J-Hook. There was no other way of recovering the anchor. The J-hook is a very large steel hook weighing several tons. It was shackled onto the end of the work-wire and eased over the stern. The master then chose a depth at which to suspend it and then steered the ship across the possible position of the anchor chain close to the rig, while some-one on the deck of the rig provided information about what was happening over the stern.

This person could see when the wire was touching the chain and tell the Captain of the ship. He then began to move the ship away from the rig or across the chain, hoping that eventually the hook would attach itself to the mooring. This was and remains something of a haphazard business, but with experience the connection between the mooring and the ship can be achieved.

Triplex gear, the most complex system for recovering and securing the wire or chain in a position to allow it to be worked on by the deck crew. Picture: Victor Gibson

The Highland Endurance towing a semi-submersible. Modern anchor handlers may be assigned to towing semis or jack-ups regardless of size and horsepower. Picture: Tim Roberts.

Working Rigs with Chain Chasers

Possibly due to experience with this process someone invented what was initially known as the chasing collar. This device was a ring round the mooring attached to a pennant which was secured at the rail of the rig when it was not being used. When the ship was going to recover the anchor, the end of the pennant was passed down and secured on the deck, and then the crane released and the pennant attached to the work wire. This was a wire, supplied by the charterer, of a suitable length for doing the job, ideally at the time one and a half times the water depth. Hence it does not take a very complicated mathematical calculation to see that while a pennant string with a buoy on the end only required a work drum capable of storing a length of wire a little longer that the water depth, to use the chasing system the work drum would have to be 50% bigger.

Hence in the late 70s and early 80s deep water operations still used buoy systems but shallower water operations sometimes used chasing systems. As usual the equipment was installed on the rigs and the guys on the ships were faced with the problem of working out how to use it, although there were a variety of publications, some from the manufacturers and some from the rig-owners and the oil companies, showing pictures of small ships attached to collars, with arrows showing the direction of travel.

In the late 70s ships usually had a drum full of wire when the collar was at the stern, and an empty drum when they were making their way down the mooring towards what they thought might be the position of the anchor. At this time there was absolutely no guarantee that the anchor would be where it was supposed to be, so the ship was moving along using nearly all the five or six thousand horsepower available and feeling the collar moving over the links of the chain, and seeing the wire leaping up and down on the deck. Suddenly the movement would cease and the ship stop moving, and it was natural to assume that the collar was on the anchor and that they could now lift it to the surface.

The winch was cranked into action and on most ships, after a distressingly long time, the collar would come over the stern with or without the anchor, but with a length of chain which could be seen to disappear over the stern at either quarter. Of course there would be no way of telling which end went towards the anchor and which end towards the rig, so the unwise spent hours trying to work this out, and then trying to move the chain through the collar, still on the deck, in the right direction. It was a better move to let the whole lot go back over the stern and to ask the rig to tighten up the mooring.

Laying the anchor was equally fraught with difficulty. The collar on the shank of the anchor was pulled up to the stern and the ship then went through precisely the same process as it had done with the buoy and pennant systems until the anchor was on the seabed. But getting the chaser back to the rig was the problem. Since the diagrams in the manuals showed the ship spinning round, this is what was done, before starting back towards the rig, but the crew often found that they were dragging the anchor back as well. Sometimes the collar was successfully released from the anchor, but progress ceased when it got caught in a loop of chain. If the rig was unable to straighten the chain by tensioning up on its winches, the chaser might have to be buoyed off where it was, the battle to be resumed when it came to the time to move the rig again.

The chasing system together with the move into deeper water spurred the ship-owners and designers into producing ships with more wire storage space, and spelt the end of the road for the bolt-on Smatco winch.

Working on the Deck

Some might say that only a very brave man or a fool would have worked on the deck of an anchor-handler in the early days of rig moving. The job might go on for days, in many parts of the world the weather was uncertain, and everyone would have a good chance of getting very wet. However, sailing on deep-sea ships was regulated by outdated legislation and was at best unpredictable. It was possible at that time to sail from Europe on an apparently known voyage and not to return for two years. Added to this, on British ships, the articles of agreement generally offered 90 days leave within a year, but gave the ship-owner the right to substitute cash for 30 days of them if he wished. The deep-sea working conditions made any form of short sea trade attractive. Even so, a particular level of pragmatism was required for anyone to sail on a supply vessel out to the North east of Aberdeen and Peterhead.

In the North Sea, the masters of the ships often kept them heavily ballasted by the stern to make it easier to get the anchors on board, to reduce windage and, so they thought, to improve the manoeuvring capabilities of the craft. It is doubtful whether the philosophy actually achieved any of the intended results, but it made the deck of the ships extremely wet, so that the crew usually went out clad in oilskins and sea-boots, with gaffer tape round the tops of the boots to stop the water running in.

When the anchors were buoyed off, the first job was to get the buoy onto the deck. To do this, the work wire, or possibly the tow wire if the crew were thinking well, was pulled down the deck and a long pennant shackled by its ends to it. This was called the lasso. Two crew members stood, one either side of the roller holding the sides of the lasso, waiting, while the master at the controls backed up to the buoy. Even this simple task could take an age in the 1970s as inexperienced masters used too much power to back up, overran the buoy and then had to move forward again. As they moved forward the wash from the screws could drive the buoy away and the whole process would have to be started again. Masters who were able to ease the ship up to the buoy in a single action usually gained the approval of the team on the deck; the others would be conscious of glares from the stern of the ship, and the sight of disconsolate figures with slumped shoulders and bowed heads.

At some point the buoy was close up to the stern and the lasso was thrown outwards, to drop over the buoy or at least the crucifix on the top. The crew then ran forward making rotating gestures with their right hands, and the Chief Engineer on the winch started to heave up on the winch. The Chief was also required to be

As time has passed the equipment provided on the deck of the anchor handler has allowed the crew to engage in more and more complex tasks. This is the Far Senior at Visund. Picture: Gier Jarnes.

The fabricated anchor has made the job of anchor-handling a little more difficult but of making sure that the anchors hold easier. Picture: Victor Gibson

patient, and in some cases well wrapped up. The early British anchor-handlers left the poor fellow out on the deck aft of the accommodation, with a couple of levers and a big wheel. Later the Dutch put him in a little cabin on the aft end of the deckhouse, and finally, due to the influence of the Norwegians he found himself on the bridge in a seat next to the Captain, with his own set of controls and television screens.

The winch ground away slowly, and the buoy was heaved up over the roller and onto the deck. When it was judged to be far enough away from the stern the crew gestured to the Chief to stop heaving and pulled the pelican hook across under the buoy pennant and close it up.

Means of stopping off the wires were borrowed from conventional marine or naval anchoring and towing systems of the time, finally focusing on Smit brackets and pelican hooks. Using Smit brackets the wires centred themselves on the deck, which was useful, but finally the industry took the pelican hook to its bosom, despite the dangers when connecting and releasing it. The purpose of the securing system is to allow the crew to work on the wire in a situation of relative safety, despite the fact that almost inevitably, the weight of the ship will be exerted on the pennant string as it is allowed to drift downwind or down-tide.

With the pelican hook latched over the first pennant next to the talurit splice, the chief slacked back on the work-drum and allowed the pelican hook on the end of its wire to take the weight. The pennant string moved over towards the side of the ship until it came up against the edge of the gate, and then the crew stepped forward with their wrenches, hammers and marlin spikes to disconnect the buoy. Often the threads on the shackles were damaged, which resulted in the use of the very large wrench, or possible the oxy-acetylene cutting gear, the 'gas axe' as it was known.

With the passing of time marine equipment manufacturers put their minds to improving on the pelican hook, and as a result a number of hydraulically operated systems were made available. They all incorporate a pair of hydraulic posts which lift from the deck and trap the wire between them, some of these having plates on the top which turn inwards, preventing the wire from escape. The posts are known as "towing pins" or "pop ups", and the plates on the top as "elephant's feet."

The three commonest forms of securing system are the Ulstein "Shark's Jaw", the

Karmfork and "Triplex Gear". In all cases the wire is first of all trapped between the towing pins, then, in the case of the Shark's Jaw the operator, standing behind the crash barrier, raises the jaw and captures the wire, then closes the jaw. Once this has been done the wire is slackened off and the ferrule on the first splice comes up against the face of the jaw. The wire can then be worked on.

Karmforks consist of a pair of slotted tubes which are positioned one in line with each "pop-up". Therefore as long as the incoming wire is positioned against the post it will be picked up by the Karmfork which rises out of the deck and collects it in a slot in the top. The wire enters the slot and when fully in position passes a latch which will only be released if the fork is retracted into the deck.

The system is therefore very simple and, when weather conditions allow good manoeuvring, one fork can be set up for wire and the other for chain. The drawback of the early versions of system was that in the event of hydraulic failure the forks would gradually retract into the deck, opening the latch and eventually releasing the wire. Today a member of the deck crew inserts a pin into the top so that even if the hydraulics fail, the mooring will not get away.

Triplex gear is probably the most elaborate of the systems and consists of two triangular plates, set into the deck, which hinge forward hydraulically, creating a vertical slot in which the wire or chain is trapped. The big advantage of this equipment is that it will gather the wire into the slot no matter where it lies between the pop-ups.

But on with the anchor job. Once the topmost pennant of the string was connected to the work-wire the chief heaved away and everyone would see the weight gradually coming onto the wire and the tension in the gauges increasing. Sensing rather than seeing it, it was evident to everyone that the ship was gradually being pulled back over the anchor; then when the wire was leading directly up and down the weight was suddenly reduced, indicating that the anchor had been pulled out of the seabed, and was now hanging by its crown under the ship, as far beneath it as the depth of water on the chart.

The winch would grind away again and eventually the crown of the anchor would appear against the roller, although the mate might be the only person to see it, from a point at the aft quarter. If he gestured with a thumbs up then the anchor was clear and the master could tell the rig to start heaving in. If it was thumbs down then a whole new saga would begin.

It was expected that things would go wrong during this work and one of those things was a damaged or fouled anchor. Sometimes the chief heaved up on the winch and only the shank of the anchor appeared over the roller, sometimes a shank with other bits attached, sometimes a complete anchor on the verge of falling apart due to the failure of securing welds and the loss of wedges. At other times the anchor was pulled onto the deck in the middle of a ball of wire, and since as a minimum it was two and a half inches in diameter, this caused considerable distress.

One way or another the anchor was fixed, sometimes over a period of hours, and allowed to return to the sea over the stern-roller. If luck was out the flukes might tear up the wooden deck of the ship, making it close to impossible to recover any further anchors. Over time the ship-owners got fed up with replacing the wood, and carried out a modification in the form of a steel plate welded over the wood. New ships were built with a steel apron the width of the roller extending about a third of the length of the deck. Here there was a need to compromise, since both containers and anchors would slide about dangerously on the steel as the ship moved, whereas they would remain stationary in all but the most adverse weather on the wood.

As the water got deeper the job became more difficult. More pennants had to be recovered onto the work-drums and on occasions the crew were faced with the problem of stripping the pennant string off the drum and flaking it down on the deck, while the anchor still dangled beneath the ship, then reeling the rest of the pennants onto the drum.

As time has passed the task has become better planned and in some respects easier, and for some time there has been the expectation that the operation will be carried out successfully, within an acceptable timeframe. The anchor job has become a routine not a risk.

The heavy lift vessel is carrying out many long distance moves of mobile units. The Jack Bates being returned to the sea off the coast of Australia. Picture: Charles Baker.

Moving Jack-ups

The task of moving jack-ups had not changed over the years, and since most of the mobile units in the world are jack-ups the traditional Gulf of Mexico designs remain pretty effective.

However, despite the fact that smaller ships may be used for moving jack-ups, and even though moving jack-ups over long distances is not as glamorous as towing semi-submersibles, it would certainly appear to be more dangerous. Many jack-ups have been lost while afloat. In at least one case one sunk when the distance to be travelled was less than 40 miles. During some tows, even if the rig has not been lost it has shed bits, particularly legs.

Jack-ups are not really marine structures. They are most secure when they are standing on the seabed with the hull fifty feet or so above the waves, looking a bit like triangular coffee tables. Making the change from being a secure structure, impervious to the effects of wind and waves to being a marine object – now an upside down coffee-table with the legs sticking up hundreds of feet into the air – is difficult. Particularly difficult is the actual moment of transition

*The Pike a 1980s built Halter Marine 180 footer, a ship type still used in many places of the world for moving jack-ups.
Picture: Fergus Mack.*

and the Operations Manuals of these objects always specify the environmental criteria under which it can take place. Wave heights of more than one metre are normally unacceptable. In addition the warranty surveyors will normally only give towing approval if the weather conditions for the whole tow were acceptable.

In addition to the problems of ocean towing created by the configuration and the low freeboard of jack-ups, which is really a whole subject on its own, there are numerous operational difficulties which those moving jack-ups routinely faced.

Oilfields in benign shallow water environments such as the Arabian and Mexican Gulfs consist of numerous individual wells each with its own small unmanned platform complete with helideck. Pipelines are run on the seabed from each of the small platforms to a large central platform where the oil from the field is processed and then pumped onwards to the shore. Much of the work in these areas is related to work-overs where the rig has to make a close approach to the platform, jack up until it is above it, and then slide the drilling package out on the cantilever so that the well can be re-entered.

Jack-ups are often required to work in shallow waters, most extremely off the coast of the Indian subcontinent, in 'drying heights'. In these areas the location was approached on a rising tide and the work completed before the tide fell to the point where the vessels carrying out the move would go aground. Off the coast of Saudi Arabia there are complete oilfields consisting of fifty-odd small platforms all in water depths varying between a maximum of 10 meters and a minimum of two or three meters. Jack-ups which are specially selected for their minimal draft are deployed in these fields and they are put in position and supplied by support vessels with similarly low drafts.

Commonly a small anchor-handler will be attached to each of the corners of the jack-up and the platform approached with a single ship at the bow and two others being towed along on the aft corners. The derrick of course is at the centre of the aft end of the unit, usually on a

Even jack-ups use moorings to stabilize their positions and to winch themselves alongside platforms. Picture: Victor Gibson.

cantilever which can be moved out over the platform. This means that the vessel on the bow will pull the rig past the platform, diagonally across the face, and once it has passed it will slow down and the after ship closest to the platform will take off across the face at which the rig is to be located.

The rig is now being pulled at the bow and the stern across the original direction of travel with the third ship offering a slight braking effect. Eventually there will be a ship pulling the rig astern on either side of the platform and the one on the bow acting as a brake. When the rig had been pulled within a few metres of the platform, the rig will have its legs extended downward until they are just touching the seabed, and then the ships will pull the rig the final distance until the aft end is only a few feet from the platform. The rig can then be jacked up and the derrick cantilevered out over the platform.

Development in the construction of rigs has resulted in extremely large jack-ups being made available to the industry, probably due to the modern leg designs, which are of lighter construction and sometimes more than 500 ft long. This has curiously resulted in the requirement for those in control of aircraft movements to be told of intended rig moves, to prevent aircraft colliding with the elevated legs. Sometimes the tops can be in the clouds while the rig itself is in clear air.

The size of the rigs and the length of the legs have also resulted in larger vessels being required to move them, and with the availability of large ships so the specification of those required for jack-up rig moves has increased, although in some cases for good reason. One of these jack-ups with its legs lowered twenty metres or so to limit movement may have a maximum towing speed of about two knots, even if the towing vessel has 150 tonnes of bollard pull available.

In the North Sea it is normal for an anchor-handler to lay anchors from the corners of the rig if it is to be located alongside a platform, and then as well as having a ship on each corner it is winched into position. This is normally done with the ships and the rig using survey equipment connected to the worldwide GPS system. As the platform is approached the principle system becomes laser range-finding. This more precise technique makes it possible to locate a rig within a few inches of the desired position.

During the operation each of the anchor-handlers is provided with a computer, a transmission system and a screen which allows everyone to see what is going on. The ships appear on the screens as a ship shapes of the correct size, with a pointed bow and a squared off stern and the rig appears as a precise shape which has been measured and which is to scale. More importantly, on the computer screen, the platform at which the rig is to work is shown, as is any undersea construction such as pipelines and flow-lines.

Even the most modern jack-up is not provided with much in the way of, for want of a better name, a Pilot House. After all they spend nearly the whole of their lives perched on top of the legs, up to 90 feet above the waves, and so the need for a good viewpoint is seldom seen as being necessary. Hence, when the ships are connected up it is left to the lead tug to keep a lookout and to control the movement of the tugs and the tow. Of course, if the tow-master is sufficiently enthusiastic he can stand on the helideck and keep a look-out, but this is seldom thought to be necessary.

The UT704 Invincible Tide. 8160 bhp. Built at Kristiansund in 1981. The UT704 was to continue to dominate much of the offshore industry during the early part of the 1980s. Picture: James McLellan.

Chapter 7
DEEP WATER

The Worldwide State

Offshore oil exploration and production does not simply move from one place to another; it spreads like a rash. Once the oil circus has arrived, it never goes away again, and by the beginning of the 1980s supply ship ownership was no longer limited to the Americans and the Europeans. The Offerpace book 'Offshore Supply and Support Vessels – Worldwide', published in 1985 contained entries for 309 companies owning and operating supply vessels and other craft in support of the offshore oil industry, and listed over 3000 vessels in all.

Countries in which their owners were domiciled, or from which ships were operated, included Norway, UK, Abu Dhabi, Panama, Italy, Dubai, Kuwait, Saudi Arabia, Bahrain, Argentina, USA, Canada, Malaysia, Brazil, India, Denmark, Yugoslavia, Sharjah, Singapore, China, Brunei, Spain, Holland, Australia, Bahamas, Egypt, Japan, South Korea, Romania, Hong Kong and the Philippines. Many of these countries have strong maritime cultures, and the process was little more than a diversification from more traditional shipping activities.

Noteworthy operations at the beginning of the eighties included the Canadian exploration off the coast of Newfoundland, where in addition to rough seas, the ships were having to deal with the enveloping Grand Banks fogs and during the winter, drifting ice. They were also active in the Beaufort Sea where ice rather than water was the predominant element. The China Sea was looking like a potential source of hydrocarbons, and in the Gulf of Mexico and the Arabian Gulf continuous exploration and development was taking place.

Internationally the Iran/Iraq war was considerably influencing activities in the Arabian Gulf. Tankers making their way towards the most northerly Gulf ports were often the subject of missile attack and there was much money to be made by the more entrepreneurial marine companies with a few tugs, fire fighting vessels and supply ships. At least one supply vessel was destroyed with the loss of all hands, but generally the small craft were left alone.

Due to the war the oil price reached a level far above even the heights reached in 1973, and in the rest of the world the search for oil went on with a whole new level of enthusiasm.

The American Scene

By the early 1980s there were two genuine sources of design, the Gulf of Mexico and the North Sea. American designs continued to be conservative, simple and moderate in size, and these vessels had applications in areas of the world where shallow waters and calm seas provided a reasonable working environment. North Sea designs could be found anywhere where conditions made life difficult; the penalty for using these ships was the greater technical back-up required to ensure that their complex operating systems and technically advanced hardware remained operational.

The Hatch Tide. Built in 1982 at Halter Lockport. The enlarged funnels alone cannot hide the lines of the standard Halter Marine design. The towing gate is still in use. Picture: Ron Jansen.

The Trafalgar Service. Built in 1983 by Halter Marine. The engine exhausts still rise out of the afterdeck and are plumbed forward to the " North Sea Stacks". Photo: Sandy Stewart.

The American ships continued to be successful in their traditional areas of operation, virtually the only concession to North Sea developments being the placing of the funnels in the area immediately aft of the wheelhouse. Otherwise they were mostly still fitted with fixed-pitch propellers and were seldom more than 5000 BHP. They were much cheaper to construct, and were therefore able to trade at lower rates.

Indeed it is just a bit difficult to believe that while the Norwegians were designing the ME303 the Americans were sticking to the Halter Marine 180 footer, and there were brand new companies still springing up in Louisiana and Texas, commissioning small fleets of small vessels and going to work. Just as in the 1970s Arcadia Marine built a number of ships and advertised that they had been blooded in the North Sea, so one or two of these new companies did just the same thing.

The oil industry itself was in its usual state of boom or bust. In 1981 the price of crude oil reached a level which was not repeated until 2004, and as the 1999 Marcon International report states "Shipyards could not turn out new vessels fast enough. Offshore Trawlers in Bayou La Battre, Alabama were delivering supply and utility boats at the rate of one every other week. It was almost as if hulls were being built by the mile and just cut off at the appropriate lengths".

There are records of the construction at Offshore Trawlers available, and between 1980 and 1985 this yard turned out 35 offshore vessels of various sizes, all for Seacor. The American Marine Corporation, on the other hand, did not built any offshore support vessels, probably because Tidewater had been their best customer, and it appears that this company had turned to other yards. Incidentally, Seacor does not appear anywhere as a ship-owner in the conventional sense, so one assumes that they were building and leasing ships to people who thought they could make money out of operating them. Unfortunately as anyone who has done it will tell you, bareboating ships is not a really successful activity.

Another major American supply vessel builder, Halter Moss Point, built 17 vessel in 1980 alone, many of them for Tidewater, and 53 in all during the decade. However, it is notable that at Moss Point production of supply vessels ceased altogether in May 1983.

Companies who sprang up during this short boom period included Petromar of Rockport Texas, who built seventeen ships between 1981 and 1982, all of then under 300 gross tons and about 4000 bhp. These ships were advertised as being able to operate in the North Sea, despite their moderate size, their 40 tonnes bollard pull and their 136 ton Smatco winch. The winches were at least permanently installed.

PBR Offshore of Morgan City built 24 ships, all of them under 300 gross tons in 1981 and 1982. Marsea Marine of New Orleans built 17 ships at the same time. And so the list goes on. However, these companies have, in the main, been absorbed into more resilient organisations. Some of the Petromar ships for instance were sold to Fish, the French supply ship owners, who were in turn bought by Seacor. And by the mid 1990s several of them could be found operating out of the ports of Saudi Arabia, bareboated by companies native to that part of the world.

While these ships were seldom used for moving semi-submersibles in the North Sea, they were still well used all over the world for moving and supplying jack-ups.

The Smit-Lloyd 121, one of the last of the Smit-Lloyd anchor handlers. The design had hardly changed from the beginning. Built in Holland in 1983. Picture: Tony Poll.

The 704 – the Continuing Saga

By 1981 there was a general increase in offshore exploration activity worldwide, and as a result 14 UT704s were built, the spread of builders and owners illustrating the worldwide popularity of the design. Two were built in Australia for Australian owners, two by Ulsteins for Huawei Offshore of Hong Kong, four in other Norwegian yards for Norwegian owners, two in Norway for the Russians and four in Italy for SNAM/AGIP

1982 saw the brief ascendancy of the Norwegian shipping magnate Parli Augusonn who by the end of 1983 had become owner or manager of ten newly built UT704s, and it might have been eleven had not British tug Operator Alexander Towing purchased one of the two being constructed at Tangen Verft in 1983.

This vessel went on to become one of the best known 704s in the British sector, since as well as operating as an oil rig support vessel, it also undertook long-range towing activities. In 1989 it towed the barge Goliath Atlantic, on which was loaded the jack-up Zapata Heritage, from the Gulf of Mexico to Singapore, a distance of some 13,500 miles. This was the longest tow ever undertaken by Alexander Towing.

1983 also saw the construction of five 704s in the Yugoslavian yard of Totovo. These vessels were intended for operation with the Yugoslav National Oil Company but did not enter service, three of them being purchased by Smit-Lloyd, at last acknowledging the qualities of the design, and two being bareboated to British support company BUE, being named British Forties and British Auk.

Two of the Smit-Lloyd vessels were dispatched to the North Sea, and the third was immediately chartered long-term by Conoco Egypt, and Smit-Lloyd offered the wife of Conoco Egypt's Chief Executive the privilege of naming the vessel. This did not prove possible during its service in the Red Sea, and so it was decided to carry out the ceremony when she returned to Europe.

However in the days immediately before the ceremony was due to take place, the ship sustained bottom damage in the Shetlands. Any other company would probably have called the whole thing off, but Smit-Lloyd, commendably image conscious, still steamed the ship to Aberdeen, where the oil industry assembled under a marquee on the afterdeck to watch the champagne being cracked over a suitably ceremonial anvil.

It is still remembered by a few of the guests that it was difficult to hear themselves speak over the noise of fixed and portable pumps in the bowels of the ship, and that there was a distinct lack of the usual liquid hospitality before everyone was hustled down the gangway to allow the craft to steam rapidly to Hall Russell's dry-dock.

1982 and 1983 also saw four ships built for Tidewater (this was the next major step they took in order to compete with the Europeans) at the Kristiansund yard of Sterkoder Mek Verstad, though only one of these vessels, the Majestic Tide, went to work in the North Sea.

This may have been a sign of the times - finally the 704 was no longer the ultimate in support vessels. By this time Vik Sandvik and Maritime Engineering, both Norwegian designers, were designing ships, and Johannes Ostensjo of Haugesund was having a unique class of platform ships constructed.

The Star Sirius. 1985. UT734. 9100 bhp. 65m long. Possibly the ultimate iteration of the UT704. The Sirius and sister the Star Spica were Shell's AHTS of choice in the North Sea for more than 10 years. Picture: Victor Gibson.

The Olympic Supplier 13312 bhp. One of the first of Maritime Engineering's ME303s, built in Germany in 1984. Seen here working with a semi-submersible pipe-layer. Picture: Jaques Carney

The First of the Super Ships

Back in Europe the Maersk Company of UK and its parent Maersk Supply of Denmark had become a well-established organisation and were now operating over 30 ships. However, in a spate of crystal-ball gazing, the management determined that a larger and higher powered vessel was required to carry out anchor-handling duties, and so the first of the Maersk "R" class, Maersk Ranger and Maersk Retriever, were commissioned and built at the Odense shipyard. These ships were 12,800 BHP, so were possibly the most powerful in the world at the time. They were shortly followed by the second two of the class, the Maersk Rider and Maersk Rover, and although they looked identical to the first two they were even more powerful, at 14,400 bhp. This phase in the long and distinguished Maersk Supply history was completed with the appearance of the Maersk Cutter in 1983, which was not quite one of the R class, although it had obviously come from the same mould, and was provided with the same engines as the previous two.

Probably within days of the arrival on the scene of the first of the Maersk R class the Norwegian designers were sharpening their pencils to see what they could do with a larger hull and four big engines. Ulsteins drew the UT708 and the Maritime Engineering developed the ME303. Seaforth Maritime, who might always have been the most innovative of the British companies commissioned UT708s from Norway and ME303s from Korea, and while the former entered service almost seamlessly and without fuss or notice, the Korean-built ships arrived with something of a fanfare, and rumours of building problems and difficulties with the equipment echoed round the bars on Aberdeen's Regent Quay.

One thing that everyone understood as soon as they saw the new ships was that the ME303 was extremely large, almost a different type of ship from its forebears, and while the DNA of the 704 could be seen in the 708, the Seaforth Crusader and the Seaforth Centurion were altogether the result of blue-sky thinking. The 14,000 bhp was not that different from that available to the last of the Maersk Rs, and the winch was made up of one tow drum and one work drum, both of moderate size. But the accommodation seemed to be vast, and the bridge, with its sofas, sinks, tea-making spaces and toilets, took the watch-keeping areas to a whole new level of luxury.

Visitors to these ships looked down from the bridge onto the after deck and had to strain their eyes to see what was going on, it was so far down, but Maersk had solved this problem by providing the Maersk R class with lots of closed-circuit television cameras and several monitors within sight of the ship driving and winch-driving positions.

A Korean contemporary of the Seaforth ME303s, the Edda Sun, was never accepted by the owners and was bought by Star Offshore a couple of years later. This ship contained all the faults which had been rumoured to be in the Seaforth vessels, and was a good example of how things could go wrong with a bit of shoddy design and even more shoddy construction. This ship and doubtless the others had to be well ballasted down in order to remain stable and as a result the deck was always very wet in the North Sea, regardless of the weather conditions. The winch, which was operated on the principle of high pressure rather than low-pressure hydraulics, failed frequently, the controls were so widely spaced that the master could not reach them all without getting up from the driver's seat and the intercom operated on the basis of an increase in noise level, so as a result all the stations were active all of the time. But the sofas were nice.

The Falklands War

In 1982 the Falklands War tested the British merchant fleet, numerous ships being "Taken up from Trade" . The most famous of these was the Canberra and the most unfortunate the Atlantic Conveyor . Vessels taken up from the offshore industry included the Stena Seaspread, which had been a diving and ROV vessel assigned to the Thistle platform, and the Wimpey Seahorse, the latest and largest of the Wimpey fleet.

The British Navy were so impressed with the performance of these vessels that they ordered a diving ship of their own, and purchased a couple of old Seaforth ships to train the deck officers in ship handing.

During this decade the North Sea became the testing ground for offshore surface ships, systems and equipment. It was felt that if they could work in this extremely hostile environment they would work anywhere in the world (although the seas off Newfoundland were possibly even more testing for the mariner and the units operating in the marine environment).

Sealion Shipping

While the American supply ship industry was by now in a state of consolidation, in both Norway and UK new companies were springing up. In 1983, Sealion Shipping, which was at the time operating a small fleet of chemical tankers, was purchased by TNT, the courier and transport company, which resulted in the departure of the chemical tankers and the building of four offshore vessels. These ships, known as the Lion Class, were constructed by Richard Dunstan of Hessle, the company having purchased the designs from Cochranes just up the river, who where at the time building two of the same class for Harrison's Clyde. The four ships entered service as the TNT Leopard, TNT Lion, TNT Panther and TNT Tiger. They were 61 meters long, had 3500 BHP available and were assisted in their efforts to manoeuvre by an azimuthing thruster under the bow. This layout had been traditional for British designed vessels since the early seventies, the azimuthing thruster compensating to a degree for the limitations of fixed pitch propellers. These small ships traded in the North Sea, at times venturing as far as the most northerly platform of the time, the Magnus platform.

Two Chinese-built vessels soon followed, the TNT Cougar, which was an anchor-handler, and the TNT Gryphon, which was a platform supply vessel, although both looked identical from the outside. They were muscular looking ships, but of limited bollard pull, being powered by four 1000 bhp MAN engines.

Over the next few years the fleet was augmented by second-hand tonnage including the Seagair, which had been BP's multi-role support vessel, and the Balder Baffin, which had been a platform ship or ROV support vessel. They became TNT Sentinel and TNT Mariner.

Most of these developments took place as the oil industry and all the support services were being rocked by the recession, which was at its worst in 1987 and 1988, and even ships recently brought into service were being laid up to wait for an improvement in day rates. It may have been these years of sparse returns which determined the future for TNT, who were probably more used to the steadier trade resulting from the delivery of newspapers, and so sold the company to Gregory Callimanopolous.

Beaudril

The Beaufort Sea may be one of the most hostile areas in the world where offshore drilling has been undertaken. For the majority of the year the area is completely frozen, and for some of the time in the spring and the autumn the ice is on the move, and possibly even more dangerous than at other times. There are Inuit, polar bears and seals, not to mention numbers of species of whales the presence of all of which ensure that the area is considered to be environmentally sensitive, and because of the polar bears, a bit dangerous.

Nevertheless Beaudril of Calgary went to work there in 1983, bringing into service two innovative mobile drilling rigs. One, the Kulluk, was a conical floating unit, with the 12 moorings being led through the bottom. This rig was built to operate throughout the summer, with the added capability of resisting the drifting ice which occurs in spring and autumn, in order to extend the drilling season. It was billed as being capable of withstanding ice up to four feet thick without the support of an icebreaker.

The second rig, the Molikpaq, was what we might call a submersible, but what Beaudril called 'a mobile arctic caisson'. The rig, roughly 111 metres in diameter, would be sunk onto a previously levelled area of seabed using the ballast system, and then the centre area would be filled with sand using dredgers. In this state it was supposed to accept ice loading of 100,000 tons. It fairly illustrates the lengths to which the oil industry will go to find hydrocarbons.

In support of these rigs, Beaudril also required ships, and so they had two designed by Robert Allen of Vancouver and two designed by German and Milne. The Robert Allen ships, Ikaluk and Miscaroo, were 79 metres long and their four Wartsila diesels produced nearly 15000 bhp. They might have briefly been the most powerful supply ships in the world, until the arrival of the other two Beaudril ships the Kalvik and the Terry Fox. These vessels were powered by four Stork Werkspoor diesels producing 23,200 bhp and giving a bollard pull of over 200 tonnes and were an impressive 88 metres long. They were only matched in power at the time by the South African tugs the John Ross and the Wolraad Woltemade, which also had a bollard pull of over 200 tonnes. The German and Milne ships were provided with much larger and more powerful winches than the Robert Allen ships, but had a deck area of only 443 square metres. All were given Inuit names except for the Terry Fox, which was named after a young man who died of cancer in the early 1980s but took part in a number of marathons and other distance events to raise money for charity. At the time he was voted the best known Canadian ever. Although his name may have faded from the memories of many Canadians, the Terry Fox is still at work and acting as a fitting memorial to his courage.

The VS469 Viking Queen. At 75 metres long, probably the first offering by the Norwegian designers Vik Sandvik to make a real impression on the offshore industry. Picture: Victor Gibson

The 80s Downturn

By the middle of the 1980s every supply vessel which had ever been constructed was probably still in service, and the ones which had been ordered at the beginning of the decade, sometimes in large numbers, were all beginning to be available for work. It was rumoured that even the Ebb Tide was still in operation in the Bahamas. This happy situation was interrupted when the oil price plummeted and the oil industry went into hibernation.

In America in 1986 the oil price slumped to $9 per barrel and the reaction there was to lay up large numbers of vessels and to sell others. In what might be seen by the Europeans as a curious reversal of roles the Alaskan fishing industry was beginning to take off, and large numbers of supply ships were purchased for conversion into fishing vessels. Others turned to commercial towing, and the Canadians living within sight of the waters off British Colombia became used to seeing the unmistakable supply ship silhouette towing rafts of logs up and down the coast. It is important to note that at this time the American designs were very much as they had been a decade earlier. Virtually all the ships working in the Gulf of Mexico and other benign areas of the world were 180 feet long and about 4000 bhp, and only a few American-owned ships of larger dimensions were in operation. American companies were not to resume building for ten years and as will be seen later, they had a lot of catching up to do in the late 1990s.

In Europe, despite the fact that ship-owners were much less prone to laying up ships than their Gulf of Mexico counterparts, numbers of ships were taken into Dundee and similar little-used Dutch and German ports and their doors welded up, to await better days. Many older British and Norwegian ships were subsequently sold off into other industries where they became anti-pollution craft, survey vessels, port control ships and standby vessels.

Despite the trauma experienced throughout the industry, this weeding-out process was considered by many to be long overdue, since supply vessels are solidly constructed, and so well-maintained that they will seldom cease to be operational due to age alone.

The oil companies operating in Europe trimmed their activities to a minimum, and kept their reduced operations supplied with the least possible number of ships. Some operated with no long-term vessels at all, picking up one of the many modern ships available on the spot market whenever they needed one. Operators with several platforms would use a single ship, which would meander from one to another delivering the odd food container and pumping up a little water.

At the time there was still a number of British ship-owners who operated their vessels as traditional merchant ships, and this included union representation of their officers by NUMAST, the British Merchant Navy Union. Because the employees were part of British companies, the ship-owners would be liable to pay redundancy payments in the event that they laid off the crews of the ships. This meant that they would be cautious in their approach. Most companies therefore tried to keep their fleets working even if this resulted in them sustaining small losses. However, there was a feeling that it might be possible to reduce the conditions of employment, particularly the work leave ratio. Officers on deep sea ships still, after all, worked for two days to receive one day's leave.

At the end of 1986 Star Offshore decided to change the conditions of work for its officers and announced that the work leave ratio would be reduced from one day on, one day off, to two days on, one day off. Almost immediately the union called a strike, and on December 1st all the ships in port were unable to move. Striking is difficult and just a little convoluted for mariners. The rules were that the ship had to be in port - any port - and of course the master remained the owner's representative and therefore could not strike.

Within days the managers of the British northeast ports were refusing entry to Star Offshore vessels, because they knew that once alongside the ships would not be moving again and over a few days the Company assembled most of its fleet at the anchorage just to the North of Aberdeen harbour. The strike was short-lived, and in the end the officers were able to retain their conditions of service, but accepted a reduction in pay. All the crews of the other British ships operated by other owners were grateful to the Star Offshore fleet; without their stand all their conditions of service would have been changed.

As a result of the downturn the only newbuildings were those commissioned by the Maersk Company, some said because they had to find something for their in-house shipyard to do. In 1986 they took delivery of the very unusual anchor-handlers, the Maersk Master and the Maersk Mariner.

Maersk Chieftain. Built in 1985 as the Storfonn at Orskov shipyard. The VS473 was the immediate successor to the VS469, and was similarly hampered by a small winch. Picture: Tony Poll.

These craft were over 80 meters long, with a large open working deck aft and a cover hatch on the foredeck. They had 15,000 BHP available, the thrust being provided by a single large screw flanked by two azimuthing thrusters, thereby providing what would appear to be the best of all worlds.

This was a time of many changes in ownership of both ships and companies, but if one was to make an attempt to chronicle them all, this volume would make very dull reading. However, the sale and purchase of ships would appear to be the best way of making money from them. Operating them would seem to be a better way of owning them than keeping then in lay-up until someone wants them. This would certainly seem to be the way in which some operators view ownership; one or two Norwegian companies have invested money in ships when times are hard, operated them and then sold off the whole fleet when times got better.

Sometimes these changes were forced on owners by their change in fortunes, and as a result of day rates which did not even cover crew costs many small companies were forced to the edge of bankruptcy. Investors who had put up money for ships when times had been good, now called in their loans and as a result became ship-owners themselves. The whole Norwegian process of investment in ships began to be called into question as the banks and small groups of dentists and doctors who had taken advantage of the tax breaks offered by what was known as KS schemes, saw their investments tied up in lay-up berths in Stavanger and Kristiansund, rather than being out on the high seas earning them money.

Some of the better-known sales and purchases were the Kongsaard, a VS473 anchor-hander to OIL, which became the Oil Champion and became the third VS473 to be operated by Oil, but owned by banking interests, and the Kongstein, an ME303 formerly operated by the

The supership Maersk Master. Built at Odense shipyard in 1986, with many unusual features, including a hatch forward. It and sister ship Maersk Mariner were much used for deep water work. Picture: Victor Gibson

same Norwegian owner, Brodrene Olsen A/S. A spokesman for the former Norwegian owners blamed British protectionist policies for its failure, and meanwhile a spokesman for OIL said "We are sure we will soon find contracts in the North Sea because there is still a market for that type of anchor-handler".

As the downturn persisted into 1987 it seemed that the British and Norwegian ship-owners who were still trading had turned to politics instead of ship management. Lloyds List reported that a British group were setting up a study to look at the possible rationalisation of the North Sea fleet. This was an idea floated by Seaforth and Wimpey Marine and was intended to suggest means by which the UK companies could be sustained by a series of mergers. In what would seem in hindsight to be an extremely negative view, Peter Gibson, then Chief Executive of Seaforth said " We have to accept that levels of support vessel employment will never be the same in the North Sea as they were in the early 1980s, even if there is a significant rise in the oil price, Seaforth and Wimpey want BOSVA members to give financial support to a study into the rationalisation of the industry".

In 1987 a group of Norwegian ship-owners got together to protest at what it perceived to be British discrimination against their vessels. Some well-known shipping family names were present. Johannes Solstad and Lauritz Eidesvik suggested that British industry as a whole was earning large sums from the Norwegian continental shelf while the only means of revenue available to the Norwegians in the UK was ship operating, and they were being prevented from competing on equal terms. Meetings had taken place between BOSVA, the British Offshore Supply Vessel Association, and the supply ship arm of the Norwegian Ship-owners Association, but to no avail.

There were claims by the Norwegians that they had reduced protectionism on their oil patch, but the British had suggested that this was of little account since they had enough to do in the British sector. In reality neither of these views were likely to have been true. Although it was in theory possible for British ships to work on the Norwegian continental shelf, in the event of a marine accident operators felt that the employment of a foreign ship would have required justification, and so it just was not worth the hassle. And for the British to suggest that they had no interest in expanding their sphere of operations in this time of famine seems at best naïve.

Maersk Launcher. 1988. 12000 bhp. The Maersk L class were a groundbreaking design, although due to their moderate size have received little attention. Here the ship is servicing the crane barge Hermon. Picture: Wim Kosten.

There were also dark rumours that the Norwegian ship-owners were being investigated by Norway's fair trading authorities for price fixing, and the British owners were being investigated by the UK Office of Fair Trading for the activities of the so-called "coffee club", which it was rumoured unofficially set minimum day rates.

The whole situation was of course the very opposite of what quality management in its broadest terms is all about, and one which was to be repeated in later years. The oil industry appears to go through inevitable cycles which relate to the price of the commodity. When the price is high then activity in the oilfield goes up, and when it goes down then everyone pulls their horns in, and inevitably the rates for ships and rigs, and indeed all other services, go up and down in response. There is therefore no love lost between the charterers and the chartered, and rates will be as low as anyone can tolerate, or as high as can be negotiated, depending on availability. At times of low activity oil companies will hire ships at rates which are lower than the operating cost, and still expect to get a first-class service. It is natural for the owners to want to get their own back when times change. But back in 1987 the owners obviously felt that things would never change.

American companies seem to go through constant consolidation, the smaller operators being picked up by larger ones, and this activity becomes more intense at times of famine. By the middle of the 1980s Zapata had become owners of Jackson Marine, and many other small operations ended up being consolidated into larger groups. Towards the end of the decade Tidewater, surely the original predator, became the target of a take-over bid itself as Irwin Jacobs, a major US investor, offered $200 million for the whole company, which had consistently been making large losses over the previous few years. However no agreement was reached, and Tidewater continued to operate and to wait for better times.

Curiously, as the decade drew to a close the bust started to boom, and charter rates began to rise. By this time there had been numbers of take-overs, mergers, sales and disposals which had, in one way or another, reduced the size of the available fleet, resulting in a headline in Lloyds List which read "Best hire rates ever in North Sea", and in the article that followed the Star Polaris, last of the UT704s and the Takapu, a Canadian owned UT708 achieved rates of £9500 a day. Predictably, orders for new ships began to be placed as investors multiplied £9500 by 365 and came up with a number which might have no relation to the likely annual return on a ship when it emerged from the builders in 1992.

Moving into Deeper Waters

The eighties saw further moves away from the shallows, this time in the Gulf of Mexico and mostly in the coasts offshore from Brazil. The Brazilians needed to be in deep water if they were going to recover any oil and so they made all the running, sending ships out into the South Atlantic and leaving it to them to work out how to do the job. They were the first to try to develop an underwater habitat for carrying out field control operations, and in the early part of the 1990s had a large supply vessel employed as a floating production unit.

In most parts of the world, where semi-submersibles were in use, the water depth had traditionally been limited to about 1500 feet as an absolute maximum. This would usually be the limit for the storage of the moorings in the chain lockers, although by now the ships were powerful enough to drag the chain across the seabed until they got to the maximum distance. But in order to service this new frontier, rigs with wire moorings were being constructed, or even chain and wire combinations so that the first thousand feet or so of the mooring was chain and then the rest was made up of wire. This system would allow rigs to be moored in several thousand feet of water.

However, regardless of the capabilities of the rigs, it is necessary for the supporting vessels to be capable of carrying out the tasks, and although many anchor-handlers of the period had the power to drag the moorings out, not many of them had the necessary drum size to store sufficient wire to do their part of the job. Even though chasing collars were now common, much more wire than the water depth was required if the ships were to chase out to the anchors, and so during the gradual movement into deeper water it was more common for the moorings to be supported in the traditional manner by buoys and pennants.

So getting back to the Maersk Mariner and Maersk Master, they had been provided with very large work drums which could store most of the wire which was required for deep-water work. Smaller ships could sometimes manage a couple of pennant strings and a few could store three or four. There was much business generated for those who owned large powered storage reels. These were employed to remove the tow wires and spare tow wires from anchor-handlers and to reel on the sets of pennants which it was going to take to moor the rigs.

It should be noted that at this time most of the moves into deeper water were being taken at the Atlantic margin of the North Sea and at the outer edge of the Campos Basin. There had also been a little activity offshore Nigeria and Captain Cliff Roberts, who worked for many years for Tidewater and its subsidiaries, remembered a Tidewater approach to deep water which involved bolting a Smatco winch to the afterdeck of his ship in the traditional manner.

People kept telling him that he was not going to have a problem, and despite his protests he was sent out to recover a mooring in 1000 feet of water. In the traditionally manner he backed up to the buoy, his team lassoed it, and the buoy was heaved on board and the pennant to which it was connected secured. The pennant was then connected to the winch work-wire. At this point the ship was virtually moored by the pennant and the anchor to which the pennant was connected was still on the seabed connected to the mooring chain. The only weight on the system was the weight of the wire.

The Chief Engineer started to heave away on the winch and the pennant began to be reeled in onto the drum. The anchor – one assumes – was lifted from the seabed and began to rise towards the surface and of course the chain was connected to the end of the shank. The effect of this process was that as the mooring was recovered the weight on the winch got heavier as more of the chain hung below the anchor.

At a point in this process the bolts holding down the winch gave up the unequal struggle and the winch careered down the deck rounding up against the posts.

The Piper Alpha Disaster

Of all the accidents which have occurred offshore since the 1950s, the Piper Alpha disaster is probably the one which has had the greatest influence on the manner in which safety is approached all over the world. For the installations operating within the UK sector came the requirement for the "Safety Case", an approach which by 2007 is gradually beginning to migrate to the whole of the offshore environment worldwide. It also influenced the development of the standby vessel in the UK sector. It is therefore essential that at least the activities of the support vessels during the event be summarised in this book.

The disaster occurred on the evening of 6th July 1988 when an operator fired up a pumping system from which a valve had been removed, resulting in the escape and ignition of gas in one of the processing modules. The failure of the Tartan and Claymore platforms to register the scale of the emergency, and therefore to stop pumping, resulted in the ignition of further gas inventories, and the only people to escape from the platform were those who jumped into the sea, some from the helideck.

Wick radio received a Mayday message from the platform at 2204 describing the scale of the event, and this was followed by several further messages up to 2208 when the radio room was abandoned.

The standby vessel assigned to the Piper Alpha at the time of the disaster was the converted trawler Silver Pit . Also on location was the Tharos, a semi-submersible of the Sedco 700 type, but capable of DP operations and provided with construction and fire-fighting capability, rather than a drilling derrick. Today it would be termed a "Life of Field Support Vessel". The Tharos had its own anchor-handler the Maersk Cutter on location and in addition the Lowland Cavalier was carrying out trenching operations 25 metres off the southwest corner of the platform.

The Piper Alpha was sited close to the shipping route between the Shetland Basin and the north-east coast of Scotland and within an area of continuing offshore exploration and development. As a result a number of other vessels were to be involved in the rescue operations. The Sandhaven, a former supply vessel, was assigned to a Santa Fe mobile unit 4.5 miles away, the Loch Carron was on its way to the Brae Field and the Loch Shuna was on its way to the Kingsnorth UK. Both the latter vessels were platform supply vessels.

Within a few minutes of the initial explosion the FRC from the Silver Pit and the workboat from the Lowland Cavalier had been launched, and were picking up survivors who had found their way to the lowest points on the platform. The Tharos winched itself towards the platform until it was able to operate its fire-fighting monitors, which to some extent protected the crews of the FRCs working in extreme heat close to the burning structure.

The Maersk Cutter also took up the role of fire-fighting vessel and within 10 minutes was using its fire monitors to attempt to control the blaze at drill floor level. With three of its four monitors operating the estimated rate of discharge was 7500 tonnes per hour.

The ignition of the MCP-01 riser at 2250, caused an explosion at a time when the FRC from the Sandhaven had just rescued a number of people who had shinned down ropes on the south-west corner of the platform. The explosion destroyed the FRC and killed all its occupants except for one, and partially engulfed the Tharos which was forced to move away from the platform. A later explosion damaged the FRC from the Silver Pit, and the occupants were rescued by the Maersk Cutter after it had ceased fire-fighting.

A little after 2300 two further Maersk vessels, the Maersk Leader and the Maersk Logger, were on location and were also rescuing survivors from the sea with their FRCs and now transferring them to the Tharos. The Tharos was able to recover personnel from the support vessels with its crane and was by now the recipient of medical teams, who had arrived by helicopter.

By 0400 there were 45 vessels at the location, all fire-fighting activities had ceased and the activity was now one of search and rescue, and by 0815 63 people had been rescued. Of the 61 survivors of the Piper Alpha, 29 had been picked up by the FRC from the Silver Pit and 8 by the vessel itself. Nine who had been picked up by various FRCs were taken directly to the Tharos and seven to other vessels, particularly the Maersk Logger. The search for further survivors continued until 2245 on the same day.

Inevitably the investigation into the disaster found failings in the manner in which the rescue efforts were carried out, citing in particular the chaotic communications, the tendency for FRCs to break down and the manoeuvring difficulties suffered by the Silver Pit. This book has identified the loss of the Sea Gem as being the trigger which instituted the requirement for a standby vessel, but witnesses to Lord Cullen's enquiry reflected an industry view that the craft were nothing more than "a necessary evil" and "a token gesture". The Silver Pit itself was provided with a single screw, hand steering and a temperamental bow-thruster, which failed after five minutes in operation. Lord Cullen said "I am entirely satisfied that in the above respects (manoeuvring capability) the Silver Pit was essentially unsuitable for the purpose of effecting the rescue of survivors". The Silver Pit was found deficient in many other respects, some due to poor maintenance and some due to the inadequacy of the regulations under which standby vessels in general were operated and equipped.

The Tharos also came in for criticism during the enquiry. Its operators, Occidental, had claimed that it would effectively deal with many emergencies including fires, but in the event it had been late to get alongside the platform due to the length of time it had taken to heave in its anchor cables, and it had been slow to operate its fire monitors. Some survivors suggested that if it had operated properly it would have been able to extend its gangway under protection of its fire monitors and would have therefore been able to rescue people directly from the platform. The vessel was referred to by some as "the most expensive white elephant in the North Sea". The report states specifically that there can be no criticism levelled at the master of the Tharos for his decisions and for the exercise of his responsibility, but it remains difficult to say whether the lack of effectiveness of its hardware has had a long-term effect on such vessels. The Tharos and Shell's equivalent vessel the Stadive are now both drilling rigs, and the Iolair, the BP emergency and diving semi-submersible, is now an accommodation unit in the Gulf of Mexico.

By the end of the enquiry converted trawlers in general, rather than the Silver Pit in particular, were becoming the recipients of fairly extensive criticism. At that time 162 of the possible 187 standby vessels were former fishing vessels, and even though the enquiry itself had only considered the Silver Pit, Lord Cullen recommended extensive changes to the standby vessel code, which effectively made most fishing vessels unsuitable for further service.

The recommendations resulted in the development of a code by the industry itself. This book is about ships rather than safety, but the manner in which offshore activities continue to be conducted, in the UK and elsewhere, remain a subject of some discussion by professional mariners all over the world.

OIL Purchase of OSA

The purchase of OSA by OIL was one of the more surprising events of the decade, and definitely the most surprising of 1988. Everyone looked back to the mid 1970s when the OSA fleet had seemed to be in the ascendant, in the same way as the Maersk fleet was to become at the turn of the century. When the business needed anchor-handlers OSA would turn out a few and when it needed pipe-carriers, no problem, there they were occupying most of the berths alongside in Aberdeen.

During the previous decade the OSA anchor-handlers had lain in the River Tay, grey, glamorous and menacing as they swung round their anchors for weeks at a time waiting for the day rates to rise to a point where someone could afford them. To the crews of the smaller ships, and at that time that was everyone else, they were known as "the Grand Fleet".

OSA (just to remind the reader - OSA stands for the 'Offshore Supply Association'), had a tendency to build parallel ships for their main partners, some of them ending in the letters "turm" and others in the letters "tor". Hence the group of 9000 bhp anchor-handlers which entered service in the mid 1970s were the Schepelsturm, the Schnoorturm, the Werdertor, the Herdentor, and the extremely large and efficient platform ships were the Huntetor, the Faldentor, the Kaubturm, and the Kreuzturm. Some of these vessels still formed the backbone of the OSA fleet when OIL made the purchase, and large numbers of small pipe-carriers were also included in the deal.

OIL were very proud of the acquisition and were able to continue their operations as a worldwide service provider. The deal was done for £28 million and it enhanced OIL's increasing reputation as a successful fire-sale bidder.

GulfMark

If some of the names and titles in this narrative look just a little strange, like 'GulfMark' for instance, it is because this is the way these organisations like their names to be presented, and in some cases the names make no sense anyway.

In 1989 Lehman Brothers, the merchant bank, purchased the Lafayette-based supply vessel company Offshore Logistics. They bought the remainder of a large and diverse fleet which had been best known in the North Sea for their ownership of the American-built anchor-handlers Magnus Sea, Maureen Sea et al, originally the Theriot One to Six, which you may remember were brought over to Scotland in about 1975. These six ships, with 7200 Bhp available, were the most powerful Offshore Logistics ever owned.

In 1990 GulfMark, as Gulf Offshore, expanded into the North Sea, purchasing two small platform ships, the Highland Sprite and the Highland Legend, and building two large PSVs, the Highland Pride and Highland Star. The latter were two of the last and best of the UT705s, constructed before the inception of the UT745. The company set up an office in Aberdeen to administer the fleet, but like all small operators found that the provision of proper onshore support used a disproportionate amount of revenue, and if the support was set at an appropriate financial

The Highland Star, one of the last of the UT705s and the first ship built for GulfMark in Norway. Picture: Victor Gibson.

level the service to the ships and the clients was less than adequate.

Their search for an answer to this problem coincided with British Petroleum's effort to reduce its peripheral activities and GulfMark purchased BP Shipping's small fleet of offshore vessels, which comprised both owned and managed ships and a complete support service. The ships which became part of the GulfMark fleet included the Balblair (renamed Highland Champion), and the Northern Fortress (renamed Highland Fortress); both Ulstein designed platform ships.

Internationally GulfMark, despite its American origins, had made a policy decision to trade in what an annual report described as areas with "higher barriers to entry", which in their view resulted in lower levels of competition and less volatile day rates. This approach was in direct contrast to that of all other American ship-owners which was, effectively, "anything for an easy life", but as we will see that state of affairs was shortly to change,

The UT745 Maersk Fighter 1993. The 745 followed the 705 as the platform ship of choice, and was claimed by the designers to be capable of working beyond the limits of offshore cranes. Picture: Derek Mackay

Chapter 8
THE AMERICAN REVIVAL

Toughing out the Downturn

During the first Iraq war in 1990 there was a resurgence of the oil price, but the improvement was temporary, and later the price fell back, causing consternation amongst the European ship-owners. In America it had become normal practice for ships to be laid up and in some cases driven aground when they were not required and for the crews to be sent home to await better times. In addition many take-overs took place. However in Europe some ship-owners could see that there was still work to be done for the right sort of ship.

The first defined necessity was seen to be a number of pipe-carriers to service the pipe barges for several new lines to be laid in 1991 and 1992, particularly since all the existing pipe-carriers had become platform ships, and so numbers of UT705s were ordered in Norway. It could also be seen that there might be a demand for large anchor-handlers, and so the Norwegian companies Sverr Farstad and Viking Supply Ships placed orders for a number of large anchor-handlers to be built in Norway and Singapore. These were all Maritime Engineering ME303 Mk II designs.

Elsewhere Zapata Gulf Marine ordered a number of vessels for service in the Gulf of Mexico, to be built in Singapore, and the best-known American supply ship builder, Halter Marine, also received orders for new tonnage. In addition Trinity Marine built a number of vessels 220 feet long for Oil & Gas Rentals. This order may have been the first major change in the design of US Gulf supply vessel for 20 years, which effectively doubled its capacity.

The Farstad ME303 Mk IIs were ordered from Sigjorn Iverson at Flekkefjord. These ships had four engines, developing 14,400 bhp. The Farstad group thought that "the orders were based on the expectations of a continued market uplift for modern high capacity anchor-handlers in 1991/92, based on the planned increase in North Sea offshore activity in construction and exploration" (these words are taken from a press release from that company issued by Farstad executive Thor Flademark).

However, market conditions in Europe were not great and the supply ship-owners continued to be troubled by the boom and bust cycle. One of the difficulties appeared to be that when a boom was taking place everyone ordered new ships, but they did not appear on the market until the next bust, making the situation even worse. Indeed, in the middle of 1991 a group calling themselves the "International Support Vessel Owner's Association" held a meeting at which they urged its member companies "not to indulge in speculative newbuildings and to withdraw older vessels".

The president of this newly-formed group was the same Thor Flademark who had been involved in the ordering of the four ME303s the previous year, and is reported to have said "It is pleasing to note that ISOA members did not order a single new vessel during the first quarter of 1991".

Manta. One of the migratory Russians, this one is a survey ship rather than a supply vessel, which might be a better use for it. Picture Victor Gibson

A Russian Supply Ship in the North Sea

To make matters worse in an already depressed market, a Russian supply vessel, with the tops of its funnels removed and the mast lying on the deck, made its way with the aid of two tugs, up the Volga from the Caspian Sea and through the inland canal system to the Baltic.

It was a three-week journey from its base at Baku in Azerbaijan to the Baltic, and a further few days from there to Aberdeen, and in making the voyage it completely changed its working environment and many of its working practices.

The ship, the Neftegaz-62, arrived in Aberdeen due to a commercial initiative from BUE, the Leith-based support vessel operator, who had seen that there might be a market for Russian vessels, and felt that with their management expertise such ships might be able to operate out of British ports. The association with the Russians was later to result in BUE becoming the main operator of support vessels in the Caspian.

BUE made their initial approach to Sofrac, who were able to put the British company in touch with KasperNeftflot, who operated the majority of Soviet supply vessels out of Baku. During a period of protracted negotiations BUE made a commercial agreement with the ship-owners that they would charter and manage the ship, and once they had made this agreement they found a client in Amoco, who initially hired the ship on a month-by-month basis.

The incentive to the oil company was that the ship was relatively cheap to hire and was extremely large, at 80 meters long, although this dimension belied the available deck space, since much of the forward end was taken up with accommodation. However size is synonymous with the provision of a stable work platform, allowing the ship to continue working in marginal conditions.

To help the Russians with the transition from the Caspian to the North Sea, BUE provided the ship with four of its own staff, a master, a chief engineer, a mate and a boatswain. In this way all the ship's functions were covered by British seafarers.

It was not that the Russian supply ship crew were not competent seafarers, it was just that they were unfamiliar with the pace, efficiency and weather conditions of the North Sea supply operation.

The Russian shipmasters who had been working in the Caspian had never done anything other than tie up to the installations, while once in the North Sea they were faced with installations which were not even fitted with ropes, requiring them to snatch for hours at a time. The British shipmaster was able to assist the Russian master with this rather unusual form of ship-handling as well as ensuring that communications with the rigs were correctly interpreted. The presence of the mate and the boatswain similarly ensured that the cargo was stowed and discharged in the usual North Sea manner, and meanwhile the Chief Engineer was able to assist in the running of the machinery and the discharge and loading of bulk cargoes.

Carl Rolaston, managing director of BUE, accepted from the inception of the scheme that British seafarers would need to be assigned to the Russian ships to shorten the learning curve of the crews, especially since the oil companies had over the years come to expect a very high level of efficiency from their supply vessels.

It was also accepted that the Russians would have to become familiar with the commercial environment. In the Caspian Sea the Russian shipmasters had been accustomed to what amounted to overall control of the cargo operations, so the change of status needed some familiarisation, and here the British masters were particularly useful.

When the Amoco charter commenced in May 1990 the Russian crew consisted of 23 men, all of whom were expected to remain on board the ship for twelve months. This manning was based on the sort of deep-sea towing operations in which other Russian anchor-handlers were engaged. Not only was the ship provided with a standard three watch system, this was backed up with a number of cooks and stewards, providing a level of comfort which used to be common to British deep-sea ships during the 1950s.

The first UT722 the Far Grip, built at Ulsteinvik in 1993. A wonderfully practical vessel setting the tone for most designs which were to follow. Picture Hayden Brown.

THE AMERICAN REVIVAL

BUE prevailed upon the owners to consider changes. Firstly they felt that the ship did not really need twenty-three men, and secondly that the crews should be changed more often than once a year; so the owners gradually moved to a conventional North Sea work/leave ratio of eight weeks on and eight weeks off.

The ship itself was also operating to some extent outside its normal environment. It was constructed in Poland in 1989 as an AHTS with 7500 bhp provided by twin Sulzer diesels available for anchor-handling and towing, and a 150-ton winch. It was one of the largest anchor-handlers built by the Russians and on arrival in Aberdeen the crew expected it to be the largest ship in the harbour. Consequently they were amazed when confronted with a VS473 operated by OIL and the many ME303s working out of the port.

From the outset it was decided that the winch would not be up to North Sea anchor-handling and so the ship was chartered in a supply role. The 500 BHP bow-thruster also proved to be unable to hold the bow in position against the massive windage of the accommodation block so this was replaced with a larger 1000 bhp unit.

In October 1990 a second Russian supply ship, the Rioni, started work for BUE and this vessel was also chartered to Amoco. This vessel, built by Warstsila in Helsinki, had been laid up in the Baltic prior to the commencement of her North Sea operations.

The exhausts of the Far Fosna setting a trend which continues to today. It appears that the larger and more sculptural the exhausts, the more powerful the ship. Picture: Victor Gibson

The Loss of the Vulcan Service

The sinking of the Vulcan Service on Christmas day 1990 raised some questions relating to the operation of supply vessels and the inherent safety of the structures with which they worked.

The circumstances of the misfortune, in which fortunately no lives were lost, were and still are fairly typical of many supply vessel operations and relate to many of the day-to-day activities in the industry. The weather was poor and the Vulcan Service was working with a jack-up in the southern North Sea. The ship was old enough to lack a complete double set of tanks round the hull, being single skinned in the area of the forward cement room.

The rig had a small quantity of cargo to be dispatched to the shore, and despite the unfavourable weather asked the ship whether she would be prepared to work. It was obvious to all concerned that if she took the lifts she would then be dispatched to the shore and would be able to have Boxing Day lying alongside in Great Yarmouth. There was therefore an inducement to carry out the service.

The jack-up itself was of modern construction, and used a means of raising itself which can best be described as "rack and pinion", the pinion being on board the rig and the rack extending down the edges of each leg. A ship making contact with the leg would be thrust against the teeth of the rack, and be opened up like a tin can.

The Vulcan Service came alongside the rig and was pushed up against one of the legs by the weather, and it was ultimately unfortunate that the contact was in the area of the cement room. The teeth on the leg cut through the hull, opening the cement room to the sea. The compartment gradually filled with water, and three hours later the ship sank.

This event and others like it resulted in modern designs of supply vessel having no part of their hull which is not double skinned, and therefore such contact, though it would result in damage, would not sink the ship. However no corresponding changes have been made to the designs of jack-ups, and it is probable that the racks are still opening up the sides of supply vessels on a fairly regular basis.

The Standby Vessel Codes

By 1991 the first of the recommendations from Lord Cullen's enquiry into the Piper Alpha Disaster were beginning to make an impression on the UK shipping industry, and the standby vessel owners who had been operating fleets of old trawlers were now faced with the task of updating their fleets in line with the new code. Standby vessels, remember, were an almost entirely European and Canadian phenomenon, these countries being prompted to the regulations by the loss of, respectively, the Sea Gem and the Ocean Ranger.

Ahead of any legislation the industry itself was producing a code of practice which seemed to be constantly under review, and by the spring of 1991 five drafts had already been produced. The document was known as "Code for the Assessment of Suitability of Standby Vessels for Attending Offshore Installations".

As each draft of the document appeared the standby vessel industry revised its ideas as to what is required to provide effective marine safety cover for oil rigs and platforms throughout the North Sea, and it became evident that there was little likelihood of many of the old deep-sea trawler fleet surviving the change.

The code said that all standby vessels would require at least two sources of motive power, together with considerable upgrading of treatment rooms and emergency spaces, and their crews will have to be more highly trained than was previously necessary.

Even though standby vessel operators had started to update their fleets by purchasing old supply vessels, and in some cases purchasing purpose-built craft from Norway, the crewing requirements had not changed, and they were now faced with the prospect of not only spending large sums on capital equipment, but in addition expending time, organization, energy and money on crew training.

Companies like Farstad UK and BP Shipping offered standby boats which were capable of carrying cargo on deck and in tanks, so that their voyages to and from location would not be wasted, and in addition they would be capable of holding or transferring cargo on location, within the limits of the legislation when it was in place.

These companies also offered supply vessels capable of relieving the standby vessels, so both vessels would be enhanced by additional capability. They thought the oil industry could afford the cost, because it would reduce the total number of vessels on hire.

A similar approach was being taken by a company called Stavanger Tank in Norway, who ordered six specialised standby/supply vessels to be built to a new Ulstein design. Although the ships survived, Stavanger Tank did not.

Meanwhile, the naval architects with standby vessels on their drawing boards attempted to produce at least the minimum which legislation required, at a price which someone might be able to afford. Designs were put forward by Fergusons on the Clyde, A&P Appledore Aberdeen (formerly Hall Russells) and Yard of Holland, none of which were built.

The traditional standby vessel owners, having managed for years to fill the needs of the industry at a price it was willing to pay, and having geared their companies to the extremes of budgetary restraint to remain in business, suddenly found that no price was too high to pay for safety, and that much more sophisticated management techniques were instantly required.

Ulstein PSV Developments

After the many years of success with the UT705 there were rumours that a new, larger and more powerful platform ship was to be brought into service, the first of the class to be operated by Maersk. In any history of the supply ship the Maersk Company is extremely important, just as they are important in every other area of shipping, and if it comes to that, in the country of Denmark. It is rumoured that some years ago the parent company AP Moller threatened to leave, and there was consternation in government circles. Maersk's brand new thing was the Maersk Fighter, the first UT745 in 1992.

The 745 was designed to do everything the 705 did but better. The Maersk Fighter had over 7000 bhp available and four transverse thrusters. It was claimed to be able to hold station in a force 9. This was a crucial point in ship specifications because the usual wind speed at which the offshore cranes have to be housed is 45 knots – a force 9. The ships now appeared to be in a position to remain working up to the point where the rigs would have to give up, and therefore would possibly initiate something of a change to the process and to the pressure points in the industry, since up to that time the decision as to whether the work was to be done lay with the shipmaster. Now it might lie with the crane driver. Of course we are still talking about the North Sea. Elsewhere ships were still tying up.

While Maersk were ordering platform ships from Ulsteins they were also developing a new range of anchor-handlers with Maritime Engineering, the ME606 and 909. These designs appeared in 1991 and 1992 as the Maersk P class.

The UT722 et Al

The 745 was closely followed by another Ulstein breakthrough, the UT722. The Norwegian offshore brokers 'Seabrokers' had always liked to think of themselves as innovators as well as negotiators and they polled a number of operators to find out what might be required from the ultimate anchor-handler. The result was not far away from what is provided on the UT722. Ulsteins had, by this time also experimented with the triangular wheelhouse, and with the siting of the wheelhouse as far from the bow as possible at the aft end of the accommodation block. These two design features may have been developed from proposals made by the crews of the UT734s, who had suffered from the disadvantages of the rectangular wheelhouse.

The first UT722s were the Far Fosna and Far Grip, both of them constructed at the Ulstein yard at Ulsteinvik on the island of Hareid to the south of Aalesund. These ships were the first of a new style of vessel, larger and a little more powerful than what had previously been available. The ships could store 1500 metres of 72mm wire on each work drum, which gave them considerable, but not astounding, capability.

Possibly the full realisation of the Seabrokers study came with the development of the UT740, also built at Ulsteinvik, which was a recognisably larger and more powerful ship, and appeared in 1996 in the form of the Normand Neptune, the twelfth UT700 to be supplied to Solstad and the sixth to be built at the Ulstein yard. The Normand Neptune was powered by four Wichmanns giving a total power of 20,000 bhp and a bollard pull of 220 tonnes. Commensurate with this power, the ship was provided with a 500-tonne winch which had a storage capacity for 4000 metres of 83 metre wire on two work drums. It was intended that the ships should be able to work water depths of at least 1000 metres.

While the Normand Neptune was to be followed by only one further UT740, the Far Grip and the Far Fosna set the style in anchor-handlers for the rest of the decade and on into the 21st century, although the designers took a leaf from the UT740 book, and added a deck to the accommodation to give a more elegant look, provide accommodation for large numbers of passengers and doubtless offer a greater level of luxury for the crew. The design reached fulfilment with the arrival of the Farstad anchor-handler Far Senior in 1998

The UT740 Normand Atlantic. Later UT722s were to take on some of the features of the 740, making them possibly the best all round anchor handler ever built.
Picture Victor Gibson.

The Admiral Tide, a platform supply vessel built at Moss Point. By 1997 the Americans were making an effort to catch up as the industry ventured into deeper water. Picture: Sandy Stewart.

The Far Senior

By 1998 Far Senior was one of several UT722s being offered for charter from both Scotland and Norway, with 180 tonnes bollard pull and a winch capable of pulling 400 tonnes. Its capacity might have been somewhat in advance of what was then required, since North Sea and Atlantic margin deep-water work had as yet been somewhat limited, but its designers had thought of many ways in which the vessel could be operated efficiently in addition to the massive tow and work drums and the enormous chain lockers with which it was fitted.

Probably its most remarkable, and remarked-on, feature was a small but powerful crane which, at the touch of a button, could be made to rise from the deck next to the towing pins and be used for manoeuvring the heavy shackles required to connect the sort of moorings used in deep water. Its robust construction meant that in addition to lifting it could be used for tugging, turning or pushing. In addition to this crane there was a further lightweight crane, sometimes known as a cherry picker, which could be pulled down the side of the deck. The crane at the aft end was long overdue as a means of assisting the deck crews of anchor-handlers with the problems of connecting and disconnecting the components of mooring systems, and it subsequently became a standard fitting, although the large crane fitted to the Far Senior probably remains unique.

For anchor-handling and towing the winch was provided with a work drum and a tow drum which had a combined capacity of nearly 6000 metres of 96mm wire. The 1300 metres of 83 mm tow wire took up little space on its drum, and each of the drums was divided into a large section and a small section so that connections could be positioned so they would not damage the main part of the wire. The wires could be guided into position with spooling gear controlled from the bridge, which had its own CCTV pointing towards the drum so that the possibility of loose turns could be minimised. In addition to being able to view the drums from the CCTV it was also possible to physically see them from the aft control position - this as opposed to viewing them entirely on CCTV screens. Despite the wonders of technology there is no substitute for a proper view of the equipment.

The Far Senior also featured the latest developments in aft controls. Once more one cannot help making the comparison with the early supply vessels which, despite the fact that the bridge personnel might spend days driving, were either not fitted with any form of seating or else were provided with adapted typists chairs. Over the years seating had gradually improved until, on the Far Senior the ultimate may have been achieved. The seats at the control positions featured a full set of winch controls built into arms of the Chief Engineer's seat and a full set of ship controls built into the arms of the Captain's seat. Both positions were equipped with a joystick. Whether the positioning of the controls in this way was actually an advantage is probably a matter of personal taste, but it looked great.

Liner Services

On 27 August 1992 the Aberdeen Service Company, Asco, issued a press release stating that it had set up a "Marine Services Department to provide marine management as a development of their contract Logistics Service. The Department will be responsible for the operational control, fleet planning and chartering of anchor-handling, platform supply and standby vessels." It should be mentioned here for those unfamiliar with the local topography, that with typical oil industry logic, at that time the Aberdeen Service Company operated principally out of a large purpose-built base on the south side of Peterhead harbour.

This was an announcement which was to influence the operation of platform supply vessels, initially in the Northern North Sea, then in the Southern North Sea and Holland, and then in the Gulf of Mexico.

To understand what the new service would do it is first of all necessary to understand what an oil company marine department does. Firstly and most simply it must provide a standby vessel for each installation which requires one, conforming with all legislative and company safety requirements. It must ensure that the standby vessels are well run, suitably manned and that the ship-owners or managers are capable of supporting them.

Secondly it must provide transport for all materials from the oil company shore base to all the company's offshore installations and mobile drilling units in a way which balances the instant service usually needed by drilling departments with the budgetary constraints of an increasingly efficient industry. This usually involves the long-term charter of a core fleet of supply vessels, which may be as few as one, and the hiring of suitable craft from the spot market to deal with urgent cargoes.

Thirdly it must move the company's chartered mobile drilling units from location to location, using anchor-handlers from the core fleet or hiring them from the spot market. It is a

The Bender Shipyard started to contribute to the technological advance with vessels such as the Agnes Candies, built in 1998 as a PSV, but here obviously carrying out ROV work. Picture Ron Jansen

natural requirement that the vessels hired should be suitable for the task, conforming with any insurance requirements as far as Bhp and bollard pull are concerned, and be taken on for as little money as possible.

What Asco was offering was effectively a means of managing all the marine requirements of the operator. The service was taken on at its inception by Conoco and BP, and Asco, who already operated the South Base in Peterhead Harbour went to work, apparently with a seamless efficiency which confounded the critics, who could see many reasons why the service should not be successful. Predominant amongst these was the theory that as soon as a ship was unreasonably delayed at a platform then such swingeing penalties would be imposed that the oil companies would soon take back the management of their own ships. And to a point this may be so, although the financial arrangements between the service providers and the oil companies have remained shrouded in mystery.

New PSV Designs

As the turn of the century approached the confidence gradually returned in the oil industry and a number of ship-owners ordered VS483s, Vik Sandvik platform ship designs. These ships could possibly be described as the workhorses of the North Sea. They were big lumbering craft but they were provided with a protected working area and were of a robust design. The Clyde shipyards turned out several for Sealion, Farstad and Stirling between 1996 and 1998.

Sealion had also made some major design changes to existing hulls and had carried out five conversions for the standby market,

The VS483 Toisa Intrepid, one of a number built in UK for British and Norwegian ship-owners at River Clyde ship-yards. An unsophisticated but effective design.
Picture: Victor Gibson

and now they were ready to bring out their own design. This initiation resulted in the construction of the Toisa Coral and Toisa Crest, both of which were built at Appledore Shipbuilders in North Devon They entered service in 1999. These two ships were completely up to date and aligned to today's thinking on what support vessels are about, though their concept originated in the Canadian built Balder ships, offering an alterative ROV support or platform supply role. They looked superficially like UT755s but were in fact almost as large as VS483s. They went to work both as supply vessels and in support of ROVs initially for cable laying operations in the Far East.

Meanwhile Ulsteins, apparently prompted by Gulf Offshore, the UK arm of GulfMark, developed the first iterations of the UT755. They appeared as the Highland Piper and Highland Drummer in 1996. It was apparent to no one at the time that the UT755 was to become the second most successful design in the history of Ulstein. Gulf went on to commission the Highland Rover, a 755 with the ability to carry out survey work, with the addition of a moonpool, extra accommodation and DP capability, and that vessel was delivered in 1998.

Tidewater Buy Ships

In 1996 Tidewater, who seemed to have recovered from the hard times from which they had suffered towards the end of the previous decade, purchased Hornbeck Offshore, described by Tidewater as a rival, but actually something of a minnow in the pond, although they did operate a considerable standby vessel fleet in the North Sea.

Earlier, Tidewater had successfully taken over Zapata Gulf Marine, making them a truly gigantic organisation. This purchase included a number of North Sea ships, including the medium sized anchor-handlers the Norwich Service, the Durham Service and the Cambridge Service, which had been built at Wallsend and Goole respectively in 1983, and the Royal Service and Regal Service which were extremely large platform ships.

The fleet also included the original 1970s Offshore Marine vessels which were still trading and very large numbers of Gulf of Mexico ships which had previously been the Jackson Marine fleet and the Gulf Fleet. The Gulf Fleet featured vessels with such inspired names as Gulf Fleet 38, and Gulf Fleet 45, while the Jackson Marine fleet were nominally much more exciting, including the True Grit and the Godfather.

This purchase could hardly be said to be a move forward, except in the acquisition of a large number of ships. The most powerful vessel in the whole fleet, which consisted of upwards of 400 vessels, was the Dee Service, a 1976-built UT704. And this fairly illustrates the problem. What was this enormous number of outdated vessels to do?

In 1997, possibly as a reaction to the previous acquisition, which must have given them an incentive to purchase some more useful vessels, Tidewater purchased OIL, who it will be remembered were now a fleet of considerable size due to their acquisition of OSA in 1988. OIL had become a feature of the worldwide supply vessel industry, being particularly strong in the Far East, where they kept a strong presence, and even in Mexico where a number of old OIL ships had worked for years. At the time of the take-over they were operating a fleet of 30 supply vessels and anchor-handlers plus large numbers of crew boats, standby vessels and tugs. The purchase by Tidewater meant that the latter could become a more positive presence in the heavy duty market and was a sign that the largest supply ship-owner in the world had realised that they had lost their way.

This is not to say that OIL were the most modern ship-owners. Although they had built ships in the early days, when everyone was building, with the passing of time, and the variable fortunes of the industry, they had traded on their stability and had purchased second-hand tonnage from less well-endowed owners during the downturns. The combination of the car boot sale approach and the complete OSA fleet, which had also been of variable age and origins, made the OIL ships a polyglot collection, which could be expected to challenge the resourcefulness of any ship manager. But there is no doubt that Tidewater felt themselves equal to the task.

Later Tidewater were to purchase the ships owned by the tanker operator Sanko, managed from the UK by Gulf Offshore. This fleet consisted of a number of KMAR404s and a couple of late model UT745s, the Ace Nature and the Ace Navigator (which was to become the Russell Tide).

The Russell Tide was almost the ultimate development of the 745. Two Ulstein Bergen

The Sam S Allgood built in 1998 as the Monarch Bay and purchased by Tidewater as part of their modernisation programme. Seen here working off the coast of Australia. Picture Mark Warren.

diesels, housed in an engine room virtually beneath the accommodation, developing an amazing 9600 BHP As well as providing propulsion these engines also powered two shaft generators situated at the aft end of what used to be called the Cement Room. This was a long space containing eight dry-bulk tanks, or at least the bottoms of eight dry bulk-tanks, the tops of these tanks being one deck up, and so close together that even a slim human could not squeeze between them. The available deck area of these ships was 973 square metres, enough space to carry cargo for several platforms at one time.

Like other platform ships constructed since the late 1990s, the Russell Tide was built with one eye on the cable, or ROV market, and this vessel's sister became an ROV mother ship. Hence a Kongsberg DP console capable of interfacing with a number of positioning sources was provided, together with accommodation for 46 persons.

Swire Pacific Expand

Meanwhile – in the Far East, Swire Pacific, who were last mentioned in this narrative as having started up in the late 1970s –decided to branch out. In the early 1980s they purchased a number of UT704s and operated them in the Far East, and ten years later they acquired the UT734 Dong Fang Yong Shi, which had originally been Northern Frontier, the last of the half-dozen or so UT734s which had been built between 1985 and 1987.

The first two 734s were the Star Sirius and Star Spica, built in Stekoder Mekverstad in Kristiansund and Ulsteins at Ulsteinvik respectively, and a few others followed, until all supply-ship construction ceased in the latter years of the 1980s. By the time it started up again in the North Sea things had changed and the 734s, generally considered to be too small, and of limited power in comparison with what was now available, were more or less pensioned off. However the Pacific Frontier was doing such sterling work in the Far East, that Swires decided to go back to Ulsteins for a newbuilding. It was their original intention to upgrade the design in conjunction with the builders, but the final product was so different from the 734 that it was given a new designation, UT720. However, Ulsteins and Swire Pacific still saw it as the vessel to inherit the mantle of the UT704, as the workhorse of the industry. Of course ten years later it became obvious that the inheritor of the 704's title was actually the 722.

The first of the class, the Pacific Buccaneer, looked nothing like its forebears. It had a visual similarity to the first of the UT722s with its high bow, triangular wheelhouse and enclosed winch space. It had no visible funnels, the exhausts going through the wheelhouse on the port

The UT720 Pacific Brigand. This ship is one of a class of six identical vessels, built in Norway for world wide service and proving capable of taking on many tasks despite their moderate power. Picture S C Brand.

The HLX2225 Seacor Vision built in 1997 at Moss Point. At last a firm indication that times were changing in the Gulf of Mexico.
Picture Ron Jansen

side and terminating at the after side of what looked like nothing more than the fire monitor platform. The result was very high visibility from the wheelhouse, both forward when the ship was under way, and aft when operating at offshore installations.

In the engine room two Wartsila Vasa 12V32D engines, each developing 6120 BHP were crammed into a space under the accommodation. The shafts led directly aft to the gearboxes and shaft generators, situated in the mid part of the vessel aft of the mud tanks and forward of the cement tanks. This made the centre part of the vessel available for bulk tanks, ensuring a very large carrying capacity.

This surprising configuration was in part a reflection of the engine builder's art, and their ability to extract incredible power from prime movers of surprisingly small dimensions, and in the case of Wartsila from a surprisingly small number of cylinders. Looking back twenty years the most powerful anchor-handlers of the day had the complete midsection occupied by V-16 engines, the only units developing enough power and still capable of fitting into the space between the engine room bottom plates and the deck above being those originally developed to power railway engines.

The Pacific Buccaneer entered service in 1997. The company had intended to dispatch it to one of their favoured work areas, but it was immediately pressed into service on a variety of anchor-handling jobs, its 12,000 bhp proving to be adequate for many tasks. By this time the operators in the North Sea had decided that medium sized anchor-handlers of 12,000 bhp or so were ideal for moving jack-ups, but one should remember that the rates were pretty low, and later tugs of 5,000 bhp were considered to be appropriate for the task when the cost of hiring ships had risen considerably. However, back in 1998 the Buccaneer was followed by a further five ships of the class, most of which initially worked in the North Sea before gradually dispersing to other parts of the oil patch.

Indeed, the experience of Swires with the Pacific B class was very similar to that experienced by many ship-owners. The industry had moved off the shallows and into deeper waters all over the world, and so ships with the capacity to deal with these conditions were required. The improved sea-keeping capabilities and the improvements in the general levels of marine competence on many vessels made it a straightforward matter for vessels to be relocated from one part of the world to another.

Seacor and Edison Chouest

In the last chapter we mentioned Arcadia Marine and Seacor, and by the latter part of the 1990s they came together, as Seacor abandoned its anonymous role as lessors of vessels and became ship operators in their own right. They purchased Nicor Marine Inc, who by this time were the owners of the former Arcadia Marine fleet, and so took on and operated the larger of these vessels, renaming them as the Seacor "something". Lesser craft one assumes were dispatched into the bareboat fleet, where others could struggle to keep them going.

Additionally over the early part of the decade Seacor purchased the fleet owned by Feronia International Shipping more commonly known as "Fish" and later it acquired a number of ships from Compagnie Nationale de Navigation. Seacor Holdings comprised of 40 subsidiaries by the year 2000. More importantly, the company commissioned a number of well-found anchor-handlers, starting with the 225 ft Seacor Vision in 1997, then three 220 ft 8000 bhp ships and two 255 ft anchor handlers in 1998.

There were surprising differences in design between the 8000 bhp ships and the largest, the 14,000 bhp 255-footers. The smaller craft were built very much in the traditional Halter Marine mould. Most noticeably the engine room was situated as far aft as could be managed. This of course reduced the length of the prop shafts but occupied good cargo carrying space in the hull.

The larger vessels, designated HLX 2255, had a Smatco electric winch which claimed 500 tonnes pull. The most effective winches were, and still are powered by low-pressure hydraulics, but the patents are held by Rolls Royce as part of their Ulstein buy-out, hence other designers looked for other methodologies. When lowering heavy weights to the seabed low-pressure hydraulic winches really come into their own; it is just like heaving in but in reverse. Electric winches are a different case entirely. There is a tendency for the weight to take charge, turning the motors into generators with resulting dire effects on the ship's electrical systems. As a result such winches have to be fitted with some alternative means of braking - sometimes disc brakes, sometimes, as in the case of the HLX 2255, water brakes.

One of the components of the Smatco model 140E is a tension winch. This may well have been the first tension winch fitted to a supply vessel, although a number had been fitted to semi-submersibles for deep water mooring. Their purpose is to always have the first wrap available, and therefore the greatest pulling power. The laws of mechanical advantage result in less pulling power being available at the winch as the drum fills up with wire, as more chain is suspended above the seabed, and therefore as more weight is put on the system. The tension winch is made up of two drums, the first doing the pulling and the second doing the storing. This innovation has not been seen elsewhere possibly because the diameter or workdrums has increased as the requirement for the deployment of very large diameter wires has been identified, hence most modern workdrums are large diameter and of great

The C Acclaim, built in 1998 at Ingalls Shipyard for Edison Chouest, who with a fleet of vessels similar to this one and a base at Fourchon revolutionised the supply business in the Gulf. Picture Ron Jansen.

width; this has resulted in a smaller increase in the diameter of the drum as wire is spooled on.

The HLX 2255 was powered by 4 EMDs producing a total of 14,000 bhp. The engines remained traditionally positioned in the after part of the vessel, in direct contrast to the UT720 and the UT745. Additionally the exhausts still emerged through the deck just aft of amidships, in just the position of the funnels of the early American supply vessels, and were trunked along the deck, over the top of the stores and then vertically into what the Americans call "North Sea Stacks".

In a startling move forward for American designers, the HLX2255 was provided with two CP propellers and three tunnel thrusters, the latter giving 2400BHP of thruster power, all of which could be controlled by a Simrad joystick.

Another major operator in the Gulf was Edison Chouest, who had started from small beginnings in the 1960s and by the middle of the 1980s was operating about 10 small supply vessels. However, by the end of the 1990s the company had expanded and were showing signs of becoming the force they are today. The earlier small ships were disposed of and a building programme started mainly at North American Shipbuilding Inc at Larose, who turned out large numbers of platform ships and anchor-handlers. It is difficult to provide very detailed information about what Edison Chouest have been up to because they are famously shrouded in mystery, it being a policy not to release any details about the ships except to potential clients.

However most of their platform ships bear a striking resemblance to the ME202, particularly the wheel house and the upperworks. To the Europeans this seemed to be a particularly regressive move. One of the things the traditional Halter Marine designs had going for them were the windows in the corners of the wheelhouse which were set at forty-five degrees to the bridge-front, and gave watch-keepers a great view to port and starboard. The ME202 like most North Sea designs of the time had heavy structure in the forward corners of the bridge, preventing those on watch from seeing anything approaching on the port or starboard bow.

So, the only information in the public domain about these ships is their general configuration, and one would think that lack of publicity would be something of a drawback, but this turned out not to be so, and as the turn of the century approached they were a force to be reckoned with.

The Balder Viking engaged in its primary task of icebreaking. One of three KMAR808s built at the beginning of the new century to handle anchors and tow in the summer and break ice in the Baltic in the winter. Picture: Bjart Tronsden

Chapter 9
THE NEW MILLENIUM

Introduction

And so we arrive at the new century. One might think that the most recent decade would be easy to deal with because everything has just happened, but in truth there have been a bewildering sequence of events during the first five years, not least of which the September 11th attack on the New York World Trade Centre in 2001 and the second Iraq war in 2003.

The driving force for the oil industry, and therefore the offshore oil industry, and therefore the marine support industry, is always the oil price. Every time prices fall everyone involved thinks they are never ever going to rise again and so everything stops. The oil companies have a price per barrel at which they deem it worth carrying out exploration and a price per barrel at which they deem it to be profitable to initiate the process of production, so if the oil price falls below this figure then they stop doing as much as possible. Stopping doing things results in a reduction in all subcontracting, which effectively destroys the business. In the corporate climate of the new century, where all directors are more concerned with the share price at the end of a quarter than the long-term success of their business, the result of this process is an alarming stop-start activity, which affects the supply ship business as much as anything else.

After a fairly buoyant period in the late 1990s, when OPEC cut production and there was an increase world demand, prices fell back and it was only at the time of September 11th that prices began to rise again. In general, civil or military unrest is good for the oil price, and through the first five years of the new millennium the price generally fluctuated, as the war with Iraq was threatened, took place and was completed without the complete subjugation of the terrorist elements.

The war effectively caused a reduction in the oil price, as those who gamble in futures assumed that Iraqi production would come on line and satisfy world demand. However, unexpectedly for some, Iraqi insurgents kept blowing up pipelines with such enthusiasm that even in 2005 the situation was not stable.

The other potential major source of hydrocarbons, Russia, was suffering from its own internal problems as the Chief Executive of Yukos was jailed on a charge of fraud, although the reality of the situation remained obscure, particularly for those in the West. It was also rumoured that in at least one place in the country BP lost large sums of money, but this did not deter them from extensive developments in the Caspian Sea, which, at the time of writing have hardly begun to make an impact.

In 2005, the failures of the traditional sources of hydrocarbons and the continuing unrest in Iraq, coupled with the general instability in the middle east, and the unrelenting requirements in China for all sorts of resources, from scrap plastic to fuel, have resulted in an oil price which has not been equalled in real terms since the black days of the mid-1970s when OPEC began to make an impression.

The resulting oil price, of over $50 a barrel, offers almost instant vast profits for every operator with a producing oilfield. In turn this has caused a resurgence in exploration and has made numerous potential developments into big profit centres. As we have come to recognize, as soon as the operators start to expand their activities there is an instant shortage of all contractor's hardware and personnel. Every mobile unit on the planet is dusted off and brought back to life, and to move them about all the anchor-handlers go to work, and to supply them all the platform ships find themselves active. Orders are placed for new ships and old ones are re-activated from lay-up.

This was the situation in the fiftieth year of the supply vessel. During 2005 the John P Laborde arrived in Aberdeen, marking in an effective way the fiftieth anniversary of the supply vessel in the same way as the Ebb Tide marked its birth. The John P Laborde also marked some other global changes. It is the largest anchor-handler in the Tidewater fleet and the most powerful ever, and it was built in China, and it made its first professional appearance in Aberdeen.

This is the decade of the worldwide movement of supply ships, as owners with internationally qualified mariners in charge, move their units from one place on the planet to another, accepting charters sometimes finalised on the internet. The contracts are negotiated by brokers who issue daily lists of available ships to their customers by email, and who negotiate with owners and operators by means of the "Blackberry". There is now no rest for the ship manager, who is expected to keep in touch at all times, and possibly not too much for the shipmaster, who may be required by his owners to phone the company offices by satellite phone to get permission to go ashore.

The winchhouse of the Asso Ventidue an Italian UT722 built at the beginning of the decade. Other UT722s were built with a single enormous workdrum. Picture Victor Gibson

Companies

According the to the Oilfield Publications directory "Anchor-Handling Tugs and Supply Vessels of the World", in 2000 there were 690 companies operating 3190 anchor-handlers and platform ships all over the world. The large number of companies is due in part to the tendency of ship-owners to limit their liability; for instance, it is possible to identify over 30 Tidewater companies on the list, operating collectively over 500 vessels, but in addition to what might be called the traditional European and American ship-owners, there are operators in the Arabian Gulf India, Singapore and China.

It is particularly difficult to get to grips with Chinese companies, which appear to be departments of the government. The Bureau of Oceanic Geological Survey, for instance, operates a number of ships including the Kan 401, which was originally the Weco Supplier 1, and others with the same prefix. The China Offshore Oil Northern Drilling Company operates more than thirty ships with the name prefixed Bin Hai, one of which was the Weco Supplier IV, and another a European 704. And the China Offshore Southern Shipping Company operates 14 ships all prefixed with the words Nan Hai, and all from a variety of sources.

An emerging company during the period was Seabulk Offshore who by 2005 were operating over 100 vessels. The Seabulk fleet was made up of large numbers of ships of considerable age, and there was some controversy about the manner in which they made their

*The MT6000 Olympic Princess. Marinteknikk set a new tend when they developed the MT6000, and stunned the shipwatchers on both sides of the North Sea with the elegance of the design.
Picture Victor Gibson.*

acquisitions towards the end of the 1990s. However in 2005 it all came good for them as they merged with Seacor, one of the other main players in the Gulf of Mexico.

During the latter years of the 1990s Tidewater were seen to be taking account of the design trends in Europe. This whole process began to gather momentum after the turn of the year 2000, and the company actively began to search for new tonnage in Europe. Towards the end of 2000 this search culminated in the purchase of three UT755s off the stocks in Norway and a number of ships in service. Their principle negotiation was with the Japanese company Sanko, from whom they purchased a number of PSVs and four anchor-handlers. All of these vessels were managed on behalf of the owners by Gulf Offshore from their UK headquarters in Aberdeen.

Meanwhile back in Italy Augustea Offshore took deliver of their second UT722, Asso Ventitre. This vessel followed hot on the heels of their first UT722 Asso Ventidue, both being built at the Danish Orskov yard. Italian speakers among us will see that they must be the twenty-

The Bourbon Surf, one of two UT722 LXs the ultimate iteration of the UT722 with a bollard pull of 230 tonnes and a storage capacity of 5500 metres of 83 mm wire.
Picture: Victor Gibson

second and twenty-third vessels in the fleet. To illustrate what a major step forward this was for the company it may be worth mentioning that the Asso Venti (20) is a 1980-built anchor handler of 9000 bhp, which was originally the Maersk Dispatcher, and the company also own the former Skaustream, now Asso Undici (12) which was the first ever UT704.

The twenty-first century has become the time of Brazilian joint ventures, and it is there that much of the Norwegian development has been taking place, particularly for the more established owners, In addition to the inception of Olympic Shipping the name of Havila has become established. Havila first appeared in 1998, as a metamorphosis of Remoy Management and in addition to the Remoy managed vessels almost immediately bought the complete Boa fleet, which had been collected by that company over the previous few years. The result was a diverse assortment of old anchor-handlers and UT705s plus a small number of standby ship conversions, and even painting them all green could not disguise the distinctive lines of the Smit-Lloyd and Wimpey anchor-handlers.

They are included here, because they almost immediately identified the difficulties of operating a large fleet of out-of-date vessels and commissioned new tonnage, and by the end of the first year of the new century they had added two anchor-handlers, the KMAR404 Havila Charisma and the UT722 Havila Crown and two platform supply vessels, the UT745s Havila Hidra and Havila Lista to the fleet.

In the way of the supply vessel industry, the Havila fleet was in turn predated by the French company Groupe Bourbon, to become Bourbon Offshore. At the time they had two new anchor-handlers in the yard, the UT722LXs Havila Surf and Havila Borgstein, which of course became the Bourbon Surf and the Bourbon Borgstein. The UT722LX first entering service in 2003 may be the ultimate development of the UT722, which started with the Far Grip ten years earlier. Bourbon Offshore disposed of a number of the older vessels but retained the Bourbon Castle, built in 1982 by Appledore shipbuilders as the Wimpey Seahunter, so this ship has been in turn the Wimpey Seahunter, Highland Light, Far Sword, Boa Sword and Havila Castle. Most of the Bourbon Offshore fleet still work in the North Sea, but Groupe Bourbon also operate large numbers of vessels in other parts of the world and at the latest count claimed to operate a fleet of 150 vessels.

Developments in the Gulf of Mexico

Readers may remember that in the early 1990s Asco had initiated the concept of the Liner Service, where the operators would contract a service provider who would ship everything they needed. All they had to do was get the stuff to the port. Asco exported the concept to the Gulf of Mexico and the Caribbean, and others started up similar services in Holland. In the Gulf of Mexico Edison Chouest set up "C-Logistics", operating from the "C-port" at Port Fourchon, Louisiana. Edison Chouest took the concept one step further and not only provided the cargo–handling and ship contracting service, they also provided the quay facility itself and the actual ships. The port of Fourchon apparently supports 75% of the offshore activity in the Gulf of Mexico. The C-Port is a covered facility. The ships back under cover and are loaded over the stern by gantries. The whole thing appears more like a submarine pen than the latest state-of-the-art cargo handling operation.

In support of this operation the company ordered a number of new vessels, the names mainly prefixed with the letter "C". Unfortunately for ship-watchers Edison Chouest maintain a policy of keeping the specifications of all their ships secret; however, some details are available. The majority of the new tonnage are platform ships, built to be part of the C-Port service. Typical are the C-Legend and C-Liberty, built at North American SB Inc, Larose. These ships are 85 metres long and are powered by two caterpillars developing a little over 4000 bhp between them. They have two tunnel thrusters and an azimuthing thruster and have DP capability. In contrast the company have also built the Laney Chouest which in 2003 was briefly the most powerful supply vessel in the world, capable, apparently, of laying moorings in 12,000 feet of water.

Elsewhere in 2001 in the Gulf of Mexico, Tidewater named their latest UT755 the Rigdon Tide after one of their senior VPs Larry Rigdon, and it might be surprising to some that later this ship was renamed the Lui Tide. What had happened to Larry Rigdon? He had branched out on

The Laney Chouest sticking out of the shed at Fourchon. It was briefly the most powerful anchor handler in the world at 29,000 bhp. It is however very conventional in style.
Picture Paul Slingsby

The Viking Dynamic, a VS490 built at Aukra in 2002 for Eidesvik. A brief effort by Vik Sandvik to compete with the elegance of the MT vessels.
Picture: Victor Gibson

The Islay, formerly the Stirling Islay, built at Govan on the Clyde in 2002 and subsequently floated through the Russian waterways to the Caspian Sea. A 15,000 bhp utility anchor-handler. Picture Wullie Bemner.

his own to become president and chief executive of Rigdon Marine, and his company commissioned ten PSVs to be designed by Guido Perla and Associates of Seattle and built by the Bender Shipbuilding Corporation. These ships began to enter service in 2004 and epitomised the modern style of Gulf supply vessel, claiming much, while delivering only what would be acceptable in the benign Gulf environment. These craft are 64 metres long, are powered by two Cummins diesels developing 5000 bhp and provided with Z-drives and twin tunnel thrusters forward. All these systems can be collectively controlled by a DP2 control system, offering clients the capability of supply operations in deeper waters.

The old Gulf supply ship company Otto Candies was also building ships and the more recently formed Hornbeck Offshore were also getting in on the act. The new millennium has seen the development of small companies in the Gulf who have had ships in the traditional American mould built for them. The Bollinger Ship yard delivered a number of 145-foot supply vessels to owners on the Gulf coast. Typical was the Wes Bordelon, 145 feet long and powered by two Cummings diesels developing 1500 bhp between them. Observers from outside the country have to assume that there is a cheap source of labour available to man these craft, otherwise it is hard to see how they could operate at all.

The John P Laborde, the VS486 built for Tidewater at Yantai Raffles in China. Its four EMDs produce 24,000 bhp making it the most powerful vessel in the Tidewater fleet. Picture: Victor Gibson

Designs and Designers

As the 21st Century began to get into its stride, with what would now appear to be commendable foresight, a number of companies were ordering new ships, in some cases using radical designs. The designers appear to have determined that there were two trends in the requirements for anchor-handlers, the first the need for deep-water mooring of all sorts, particularly the mooring of offshore installations such as FPSOs, and the second the moving and mooring of semi-submersibles.

At the beginning of this new millennium a number of new designs were jostling for attention in each of these categories. Possibly the most striking was the arrival on the scene of the Tor Viking II, the first of three ships originally designed by Kvearner and known as the KMAR808s, but after purchase of the design house by Moss Maritime re-designated the MOSS 808. These vessels were owned by B&N Viking, B&N being a Swedish shipping company and Viking Supply the vastly experienced and well-resourced Norwegian ship-owners who had sold their fleet during 1995, much to the distress of ship-watchers, who had enjoyed the somewhat irreverent colour scheme of black and yellow stripes. This colour scheme was most evident, by the way, in the 1978 film "North Sea Hijack" which had stared Roger Moore and the Viking anchor-handler Ben Viking.

The designers of the MOSS808s had learnt from the mistakes made by the designers of the Finnish ships Fennica, Botnica and Nordica. One of the major activities of the ice-breaker in thick ice is to haul the rescued ships up into a notch in their stern and then drag them bodily through the frozen sea until they reach the destination. The Finnish ships were built with the notch in the stern which made it more or less impossible for them to engage in any sort of serious anchor-handling, although they were provided with structures which allowed them to launch anchors over the side. The Viking ships, on the other hand, were provided with a conventional roller, together with a substantial anchor-winch and wire and chain storage, and when they were converted to break ice the notched stern was bolted on and a helideck added in the middle of the afterdeck. The 18,000 bhp provided by four MAKs provide 200 tonnes of bollard pull, making these large ships both decorative and efficient.

Absolutely at the other end of the spectrum, one of the few remaining British companies, Stirling Shipping, commissioned a VS473, designed by Vik-Sandvik and built at Fergusons on the Clyde. This ship, the Stirling Iona, was the first anchor-handler to be built in the UK for 20 years, and had a sort of utility air about it. The concept seems to have been to get as close as possible to the general purpose ships which existed in the 1970s, so that it could be operated economically and relatively cheaply. It would therefore be capable of towing and mooring semi-submersibles in up to 300 or 400 hundred metres of water, and be cheap enough to be hired to move jack-ups. If required it could also carry a good deck load. The accommodation is moderately dimensioned for 16 people, instead of the small regiment for which berths seem to be provided on most modern ships and the modestly sized winch can be viewed from the bridge instead of being hidden in a cavernous hangar, as has become the fashion.

This ship was followed by two others of the same class, Stirling Islay and Stirling Jura, but both these vessels were bought by BUE and exported to the Caspian Sea, and of course, the movement of Western technology to the Caspian Sea has become another saga of the twenty-first century. At the same time as the Stirling Islay and Stirling Jura were being completed BUE awarded a contract to Ulstein Verft for the construction of an unusual shallow draft ice-breaking anchor-handler for the Caspian Sea. The order illustrates the unusually varied conditions which the ship operators have to address, and the fact that BUE seem to have the franchise more or less wrapped up there.

In addition to the VS473s, Vik-Sandvik also designed the VS486, of which the John P Laborde was the first. The order was placed in 2001, so the gestation period was fairly extensive. The naval architects had also developed the VS468, of which two examples were built for Boa, the Boa King and the Boa Queen, and the VS480 which entered service as the Boa Giant and Boa Hercules, subsequently to become part of a Boa District Offshore co-operative and renamed the Skandi PMS 1 and the Skandi PMS II. These four ships were built at the Dalian shipyard in China. All had a bollard pull of more than 200 tonnes.

One of the big stories of the era was the sale of the UT brand of supply vessels by Ulstein to Rolls Royce. Everything was sold but the yard itself and of course it was not long before they produced their own design for an anchor-handler and a platform ship. The anchor-handler designated the Ulstein A101 was intended to be a ship which could do everything and the first was ordered by Olympic Shipping of Fonsavaag, Norway. Olympic had recently entered the offshore market with the by now aging ME303 the Olympic Supplier, originally the Barra Supplier.

In addition to the ongoing development of the UT722 Rolls-Royce continued to develop their ship types with the UT710 and the UT719, 738 and 721. These were smaller anchor-handlers and were ordered in large numbers particularly by Swire Pacific.

More Platform Ships

Both the UT755 and the VS483 had featured raised bulwarks, to protect those working on deck from adverse weather. Gone were the days when the crew, readying themselves for cargo work, would don oilskins and seaboots and use gaffer tape to seal the join between the leggings and the tops of the footwear. All the Norwegian designers could be seen to follow this style with Marin Teknikk being the most noticeable because of the elegance of their work. Their first offering was the Skandi Marstein, which had stunned ship watchers when it first appeared in Torry in 1997. By 2006 they had developed the MT6016, essentially an even larger version of the MT6000, maintaining the same qualities of manoeuvrability, economy and carrying capacity. Their most enthusiastic supporters, District Offshore (DOF), continued to equip their fleet with more almost identical vessels, several of them occupying pivotal roles in the Shell logistics operations in the North Sea. The Skandi Marstein was joined by the Skandi Rona and Skandi Foula, and occasionally by the Skandi Barra and Skandi Chieftain. But DOF were not alone, and Olympic Shipping also purchased a number of MT designs culminating, as far as this story is concerned, in the Olympic Commander, delivered at the beginning of 2007.

Unstein Verft produced the A104, which was a robust design, showing the same DNA as the A101, uniquely up to that time provided with a dismountable section of bulwark to allow it more easily to engage in subsea operations over the side. All of these vessels were capable of delivering large quantities of cargo in less than ideal conditions, to the point that the personnel interacting with them on board the oil rigs and platforms they lay close to had no idea about the skill and nerve it took to put the ship in position, and the tenacity it took to maintain station for long periods of time close to fixed objects.

Rolls-Royce continued to field various versions of the UT745 which were now so different from the original Maersk Fighter that they might as well have had a different designation,

The MT6000 Skandi Buchan working at a semi-submersible. As well as elegance of design these ships set new standards for available deck space and crew protection. Picture: Victor Gibson

and it was around this time that the designers began to realize that they could have as many designs as there were letters in the alphabet. However, various versions of the 745 continued to be seen in the northern ports of Europe, including Solstad's Normand Flipper, officially a UT745E, where the E stands for Environmental, and the Northern Canyon, supposedly a standard UT745 but looking entirely different from all the early 745s and for that matter from the Normand Flipper, even though they were built only twelve months apart.

Almost unnoticed amongst these attractive superships the Vik-Sandvik VS470 appeared on the scene in the form of the Eidesvik-owned Viking Surf. This ship was followed almost immediately by the VS470 Mark II, four of which were ordered by the upstart SBS (Shetland Base Services), which had developed as an offshoot of the company of that name, and which had been set up to operate the remains of the port services in Lerwick. The first Mark II to be delivered was the SBS Nimbus, resplendent in its black livery with red and white striped funnel, eerily reminiscent of the OIL colour scheme. This ship was followed by numbers of others for a variety of owners, its popularity based more on its carrying capacity than its looks.

Another Vik-Sandvik design, the VS 493 Avant made its appearance in 2004. It was the second supply vessel after the Oil Challenger to go against convention and have its accommodation sited at the aft end rather than the forward end of the vessel. It was operated by Eidesvik and called, inspirationally, the Viking Avant. The rational for this innovation was apparently a reduction in the number of control positions – from two to one – and greater comfort for the crew. It was also designed to act as a standby vessel with a daughter craft housed in the stern and launched down a slipway. One assumes that this would not have been possible if the accommodation had been conventionally placed at the bow. The vessel went into service supporting exploration in the Barents Sea and was voted ship of the year by the Norwegian shipping magazine "Skipsrevyen". It was provided with a cover for the cargo area to protect the stuff on the deck. This was not quite a hatch cover, but little more than a tarpaulin, and seemed to some to indicate a weakness in the design, the protection of the cargo. Of course, since it was provided with a dynamic positioning system, it would only be necessary, in theory, for the Captain to drive up close to the installation being services and flick the switch and allow the ship's systems to take over.

SBS Nimbus one of the many VS470 Mk IIs designed by Vik Sandvik as an alternative to the UT755. This one was built at Karmsund in 2003.
Picture: Victor Gibson

Millennium Anchor-Handlers

Although delivered in 1999 it is probable that the UT742s Normand Pioneer and Normand Progress set the scene for what the industry was to expect in the future. At 95 metres long they were larger than any anchor-handler previously commissioned and were provided with helidecks. Their four engines provided 27,800 bhp giving them a bollard pull of 286 tonnes. The winch could pull 500 tonnes at the first wrap and could store 2000 metres of 83mm wire.

In August 2000 the Normand Pioneer became briefly famous when it was commissioned to carry the British rescue submarine LR5 to the Barents sea to be part of the attempt to rescue the trapped sailors on the Kursk. In the event the submarine was never deployed, and the Normand Pioneer went back to its day job, which was towing trenching ploughs across the seabed ready for submarine pipeline installations. Together with the enormous power, large working decks and extraordinary winch capability, these vessels were provided with high-quality accommodation for large numbers of contractors and extensive office and conference facilities. Their charterers could therefore put large numbers of personnel on board, and keep in touch with them on a minute to minute basis by means of satellite phones and email. The Captain might still be the master of the ship, but he was no longer the master of his destiny.

Also in 1999 Maersk Supply Service introduced the Maersk S class. The S Class were also ships for the new millennium, and in their own way suitable for whatever task they were given, including as we will see, anchoring a semi-submersible in over 4000 ft of water at the edge of the UK continental shelf.

The six "S" class vessels were delivered in the latter part of 1999 and early in 2000.

They were built at Keppel Singmarine in Singapore and once their trials were completed all in turn made their way to Aberdeen via the Suez Canal.

Although the S class were later additions to the Maersk fleet than the impressive B class, from which their design was obviously derived, their 4 MAK engines developed slightly less power, providing 18,250 BHP and offering a bollard pull of 210 tonnes. It may have been the first time that the Maersk Company had brought out a class of anchor-handlers of lesser power than the previous newbuildings, and it was felt at the time that 200 tonnes of bollard pull was enough for what-ever needed to be done.

In addition to the main propulsion the vessels were provided with a 1200 bhp tunnel thruster at the bow and the stern and a 1200 bhp azimuthing thruster at the bow. The azimuthing thruster was thought to be particularly useful in adverse weather because it was deeper in the water and so less likely to draw air as the ship pitched. One of the downsides of operating such large vessels is the windage created by the accommodation, and sometimes all the thrust available would be required to maintain station. An innovation on the joystick was "anchor-handling mode". This reduced thruster activity, apart from the azimuthing thruster, which was set to thrust astern with small changes to port and starboard to maintain the heading.

Yet another UT722 being launched in South America for Brazilian deep water service in 2005. Its workdrum has a capacity of 5000 metres of 76mm wire. Picture Christian Borges

The heart of any anchor-handler is the winch and, due initially to the known lead time required for low-pressure hydraulic winches, the company opted for electric winches. The winches proved to be extremely effective and seemed to have overcome the traditional difficulties of electric winches. When lowering anchors to the seabed the old electric winches had to be operated on the brake because otherwise the motors would turn into generators and blow up parts of the ship's electrical systems. These winches were designed to turn the motors into generators, excess power being dissipated through resistor banks which turn it into heat.

The S class were provided with work drums large enough to take the 2000 metres of work wire required for deep-water jobs, and it was possible to use one of the two tow drums as a work drum for lesser activities, so that the main work-wire would remain undamaged from contact with shackles, links and other connections.

Like all the very large ships which were being provided to service the needs of the oil industry, the specification of the Maersk S class seemed to include anything that anyone could possibly require for any job. They had split rollers to ease the task of connecting two parts of a mooring system, and two enormous chain lockers with provision to handle chain sizes from 3" to 6". They had three cranes, two at the forward end of the deck for heavy work and one small Palfinger two-tonne crane at the port side aft, to assist with making and breaking connections at the Triplex sharks jaws.

For the carriage of cargo the ships offered over 600 square metres of deck space (which for some reason seems to be the magic figure when it comes to hiring platform ships) and could carry large quantities of bulk cargo, the most significant of which might be the ability to carry over 4000 barrels of liquid mud in four cylindrical tanks. This is the sort of quantity required for drilling a deep-water well, due to the extra length of riser.

Up on the bridge the master and chief engineer were provided with a bewildering number of VDUs to look at everything from the ship's position on the surface of the earth to the gearing of the winch. The chief had four screens for the winch alone,.

The Maersk A Class followed the S Class. Anyone who thought that they had already

The Aker Yards 9000bhp AH03 Donnelly Tide which entered service for Tidewater in 2005. It briefly visited Aberdeen before disappearing to Angola. Picture Victor Gibson

seen everything, only had to look at the Maersk Assister, which arrived in Aberdeen during 2000, to realise that things were changing for ever. There were nine decks from the lowest to the bridge, which apart from anything else must have ensured that the ships were crewed by very fit personnel. Some of the specifications of these vessels may be worth stating. The 24,000 bhp apparently offered a bollard pull of 278 tonnes and the work-drum could store 12,000 metres of 84 mm wire, enough one would think, to carry out any marine operation connected with the oil industry on the planet.

Initially these very large vessels seemed to be underemployed, but as the oil price rose so they became more popular, and in times of shortage of anchor-handlers to move mobile units, they were pressed into service along with other large and extremely sophisticated vessels. There seemed to be something almost incongruous in one of the Maersk A class, possibly the most sophisticated, modern and powerful vessels in the industry, backing up to a semi-submersible thirty years old to take the anchor pennant and run an anchor. Indeed it was becoming something of a problem for the operators of the now ageing fleet of mobile units, to limit the power used both the run and recover anchors and to lift them from the seabed. All moored semis were by now using fabricated high-holding power anchors, and the 400-tonne pulling power of the Maersk A class winches was sufficient, if used incautiously, to pull an anchor out of the mud with a force which would result in its destruction.

The Loss of the Stevns Power

One would think that by the turn of the new century the offshore industry might have identified most of the threats to the safe operation of the ships servicing it, but this proved not to be the case. On 19th October 2003 the anchor-handling tug Stevns Power was lost with all hands in calm conditions while supporting the pipe-laying vessel Castoro Otto offshore Nigeria. The circumstances surrounding this event were investigated by the Danish Authorities, whose report was published in June 2004. The only response by the marine press seems to have been 200 words on page 6 of the NUMAST Telegraph, the first paragraph of which states "A report on accident in which an anchor-handling vessel sank in just one minute off Nigeria has raised concerns about commercial pressures."

The Castoro Otto was a ship-shape vessel built in 1976. It was almost 200 metres long and had a heavy lift crane on the aft end. It was owned by the Italian company Saibos Construceos Maritimas. Its task off Nigeria was to lay pipe in 75 metres of water.

There are a number of ways in which pipe can be laid and that employed on the Castoro Otto was the most traditional. The pipes are transported to the vessel in lengths and craned aboard from the attendant supply vessel, then the lengths are welded together and deployed over the stern on a fabricated ramp known as a stinger. In order to keep the production line on the move the vessel is eased slowly forward by means of its moorings.

The Castoro Otto had twelve anchors, so the contracted anchor-handling tugs had to move the anchors forward one at a time. Two vessels were usually employed, one on each side, constantly lifting anchors, being heaved in towards the ship, then re-running them on a new heading.

On 19th October the Stevns Power was running anchors on the port side of the ship, and the Maersk Terrier was working on the starboard side. On the Castoro Otto the winches were actually operated from the bridge and a crew member was positioned on deck adjacent to the

The Stevns Power was formerly the Maersk Beater, one of the first Maersk B class. The new paint job cannot disguise its origins.
Picture: Oddgeir Refvik.

winch being operated to inform the winch driver if things go wrong. The Stevns Power had picked up No 10 anchor, and it was being recovered towards the pipe-layer. The actions of the tug are slightly different depending on which anchor is being deployed. The two forward anchors lead virtually ahead, and the two aft anchors virtually astern. In these cases the tug picks up the anchor and moves in the direction of travel of the pipe-layer. In the case of the beam anchors, the tug lifts the anchor from the seabed and the Castoro Otto then heaves the anchor in until the wire is virtually off the seabed. Up to now the tug had been stern on to the pipe-layer, but when sufficient wire has been heaved in it turned in the direction of the new anchor position and began to move in the direction of travel of the pipe. Soon the winch driver began to pay out the wire (this action saves a minute or two in the operation).

Also present at the location was the pipe carrier the Oil Traveller, which was tied up to the Castoro Otto on the starboard side, and the survey vessel the Inspector, which was trailing astern of the pipe layer checking the pipe on the seabed with an ROV.

The report on the loss of the Stevns Power states that at 1705 the tug had lifted No 10 anchor off the seabed and that the mooring was being recovered at 1710. At 1715 the Stevns Power began to move towards the new anchor position by canting the ship to port with the intent finally of moving astern in the direction of travel of the pipe.

At this time the report states that "the Third Officer (at the winch) saw that the Stevns Power began to heel over to port side and a bit to the stern. Thereby the Stevns Power got a more aft trim."

The Third Officer spoke to the bridge, telling them to stop heaving because it was apparent to him that the tug was in trouble, and the winch operator immediately stopped the winch. However, the report goes on to say that the Chief Officer "saw that the Stevns Power heeled over to port and was taking in water on the aft deck in the port side. Immediately after Stevns Power heeled over to one side and sank very fast with the stern first." There were no survivors.

The Stevns Power, and its sister ships, are well known to everybody who has worked in the marine sector of the offshore industry. It was originally the Maersk Beater and together with five sister ships supported pipe-layers and exploration rigs from 1976 onwards. They were a ship type which was briefly in favour because due to their small size and relatively high power, they were able to carry out anchor-handling operations faster than the conventional anchor-handlers of the period, which always had trouble with windage, and deck length.

The crew of the tug consisted of three Danes, six Philippinos and two Congalese. The master had considerable experience in the business, the mate was on his first trip on an offshore vessel and the navigating officer (second mate) was on his second trip on the Stevns Power.

Both the engineers and the motorman were from the Philipines and all had served on anchor-handlers before, two of them having undertaken several trips on the Stevns Power. One of the ABs had also done a previous trip on the ship and the cook and the Second AB had just signed on.

The two Congalese were required to be there by the Republic of Congo, part of the usual agreement in Africa to employ persons native to the country where the units are operating.

Lacking anyone to talk to from the ship, the Danish investigators interviewed personnel from the other anchor-handler, the Maersk Terrier, the Inspector and a number of former masters of the ship and some other Danish anchor-handler masters.

The results of these discussions and the interviews with the crew of the Castoro Otto, indicate that the Stevns Power was probably trimmed too far by the stern and that the engine room escape hatch at the port aft corner of the ship was probably open. The mooring was being recovered at high speed and on a number of occasions, including the day of the accident, the Stevns Power had indicated to the Castoro Otto that the recovery speed of the moorings gave them problems.

From the various calculations and observations which took place, the Danish investigators determined that the speed of recovery of the mooring resulted in the Stevns Power travelling astern at a speed of between 6 and 8 knots.

In all accidents there are many factors which must be concurrently in place for them to occur. We usually suggest during our major accident risk assessments that overtaking a bus on a blind right hand bend is not in itself dangerous. There has to be a vehicle coming the other way. The factors to be considered and in the case of the Stevns Power included the following – in no particular order:

The tug was trimmed too far by the stern, giving little freeboard at the roller.
The speed of recovery of the mooring was extremely fast.
The Safety Management System of the Company did not mention anchor-handling.
It is possible that the rudders went hard over due to the influence of sternway.
It is possible that the Master of the Stevns Power failed to react by operating engines or the winch when problems started.
The Chief Officer lacked necessary training in anchor handling.
But regardless of all of the above there was a single factor which could have prevented this terrible tragedy. This is stated in the report as follows:

"an open hatch and maybe open watertight doors resulted in water flooding the engine room. Therefore the vessel sank very fast."

Into the Unknown

Having almost reached what at the time of writing is the present day, it is possible to see a couple of years into the future, and visualise, up to a point, what may be happening by 2009 and 2010. This chapter is therefore followed by one which identifies a few of the pointers. It is not unlike having to comment on a reality TV show on a Tuesday for a paper which will print the copy on a Sunday, so generalisations are inevitable, but if we wait to see what will happen, then we'll never publish.

The view from the bridge – a very large fabricated anchor on the deck, and the crew waiting for something exciting to happen. Picture: Tony Poll

Chapter 10
DEEP WATER MOORING

Introduction

Back in the days of the Sea Quest the ships found it extremely difficult to deck anchors in 300 ft of water, and fifteen years ago they found it difficult to deck anchors in 2000 ft of water; today the craft are so powerful that they can deck anchors in virtually any depth of water. Manufacturers of mooring systems have been energised to find means by which very large floating objects can be attached firmly to the seabed, which can be managed by the ships available. This chapter follows one where many of the ships capable of carrying out this work have been described. They have lots of power and very large winches, and some have the means of storing the miles of wire or fibre mooring that will be required to carry out the task.

The systems available fall broadly into two categories; the suction mooring and the fabricated anchor, with the possible addition of the torpedo anchor (which does not quite fit into either).

The advocates of suction anchors and the pre-laid moorings presented many papers at mooring conferences in the late 1990s to describe the manner in which a single anchor-handler could be used to deploy suction moorings. One such paper conference was concerned with the pre-laying of suction pile moorings for the Transocean Marianas in the Gulf of Mexico using the Edison Chouest AHTS Gary Chouest. The piles were 60 ft long, 12 ft in diameter and connected to 12000 ft of 96 mm wire. Details of the ship were not made available (as we have come to expect from the ship-owner); however, the paper said that the ship was able to carry and deploy three moorings before going back to port to load a further set.

This meant that the vessel had a drum capacity of 5500 meters of 96 mm wire. Since an ROV was used extensively during the mooring operation it must also have been provided with some means of deploying it. Additionally there was a good chance that it was, and probably still is, fitted with some form of basic DP system to maintain station while engaged in landing the suction pile and sucking it into the seabed. Of course little bollard pull was required because all that is required once the rig is on station is to connect up the rig mooring to the pile mooring, although almost certainly twin sharks jaws, or Karmforks would also be fitted to make this particular part of the job easy.

Suction anchors may be less suitable for use in the North Sea, where the seabed is a little harder, and hence the conventional high-holding power anchors marketed by Bruce and Vryhof are likely to come into their own. It has become almost commonplace to moor semi-submersibles in 5000 ft of water using conventional mooring techniques and in the Gulf of Mexico the Deepwater Nautilus has been moored with suction anchors and polyester mooring lines in 8009 feet. This is the record for a moored rig.

A suction anchor starting on its way to the seabed courtesy of a Solstad anchor-handler in the Gulf of Mexico. Picture: Graham Medhurst

The Ships

Some of the ships capable of carrying out the work have been described in the previous chapter, and for the charterer it is just a matter of getting the correct power, the right winch configuration and the right positioning system. Of the European designs there are a number of ships with 280 tonnes bollard pull anchor-handlers, and a large number of slightly lesser vessels, all of them capable of deploying moorings in 5000 ft of water.

In the Gulf of Mexico things are a bit more of a mystery, but the largest vessels appear to be the Trinity Marine 255-footers, of which the Gerard Jordan and the Seacor Vanguard are two. They are HLX255s and have 14,000 BHP available. These vessels can store 41,200 ft (12500 metres) of 3.5" (76 mm) wire have two triplex sharks jaws and are provided with a Kongsberg-Simrad DP system. By European standards the ships would seem to be a little underpowered, but they would certainly be adequate for the suction anchor task.

In addition to the Laney Chouest, which was mentioned in the last chapter, Boa have commissioned a second vessel to join the Boa Deep C, which was constructed in Spain. These vessels are VS4201s from Vik-Sandvik. They are 120 metres long over all, with a beam of 27 metre.(393.7 ft x 88.58 ft). They are slightly less powerful than the Laney Chouest at 27,000 bhp, but are will be equipped with an anchor-handling and towing winch of 500 tonnes.

Some of the Problems

Some problems of running conventional anchors became evident once the depth became a significant component in relation to the total length of the mooring. It would for instance be perfectly acceptable today for the anchors to be placed 1500 metres (5000 ft) from the rig in most water depths. In water depths of 100 metres (300 ft) the depth can be shown as 6% of the distance; but in water depths of 800 metres (2600 ft) the depth is 53% of the distance, and so on.

There has been a tendency for those in charge of mooring activities to require the anchor-handling vessels to continue to steam out to the required 1500 metres, or whatever, with the anchor at the stern roller, but what was possible when the water depth represented 6% of the distance may not be possible if the depth represents 50% of the distance.

In this case the combined forces act on the anchor-handling drum while it is completely full of wire and as a result there is a tendency for the brakes to slip in the middle of the operation, causing general distress. Often out in the Atlantic this has resulted in a second ship with a J-hook being placed in the middle of the mooring to reduce the load, and the use of two ships extends the total mooring time. This can be crucial if an Atlantic low is rushing towards the location. In deeper water, initially in the Gulf of Mexico, but now in many parts of the world, the technique of "load sharing" has become more common. Using this technique the anchor is gradually lowered towards the seabed as the ship gets further away. However, in order to load share and

The Boa Deep C one of the new generation of super anchor-handlers capable of working in any water depth. Picture Robert Nilsen.

still get the anchor out to the notional 1500 metre distance, the ship needs to be able to store great lengths of large diameter wire.

Another problem which has become evident only as semi-submersibles have moved into deeper water, is the vulnerability of the rig bolsters. Bolsters are the means of stowing the anchors when the rigs are under way.

Of necessity the bolsters stick out from the columns of the rigs well beyond the sides of the pontoons, and as a result it is almost inevitable that the mooring will damage the bolster if insufficient pull is used. Experience has shown that the chain may wear through the horizontals of the bolsters and become trapped or possibly cause damage to the actual structure of the rig.

High-Holding Power Anchors

Once rigs start to work in deep water, it ceases to be viable to lay back-up anchors behind the main anchors or to have to go through the process of lifting and rerunning them. It all takes too long. Hence it has become essential to use high-holding power fabricated anchors and the ships laying them follow the manufacturer's procedures to ensure that they are laid correctly.

Both the Bruce and Vryhof high-holding power anchors are complex fabrications, such that the chasers lodge at the end of the shank rather than travelling down the shank towards the crown. Hence in order to place them correctly on the seabed the ship must lower away gently and apply just the right amount of pull. Bruce Anchors claim that theirs will turn over, regardless of how they are laid, which is probably why the ends of the flukes look more like some sort of origami. However Vryhof's anchors rely on the skill of the shipmaster doing the laying.

Additionally, in order to use these drag embedment anchors in deep water it is an absolute requirement to use considerable lengths of chain to prevent uplift. Usually either 1000 or 1500 metres are used before changing over to wire, since wire is always included in the system in one way or another once we get much deeper than 700 metres.

Further problems have become evident as the bollard pull and lifting capacity of the new tonnage has been applied to the recovery of high-holding power anchors. The anchors are extremely efficient and given the right fluke angle they will bury themselves deeply into the seabed during the insurance tensioning process. When the moorings are chased out the chaser will not travel up the shank of the anchor as has already been mentioned. Instead it will lodge on the end of the shank. Hence it is possible for the force from the AHTS to be inappropriately applied. The anchors need to be gently eased out of the mud, and probably in deep water not decked until the rig has recovered the mooring. Any other plan may well result in considerable damage to the anchor - or even their complete destruction.

Suction Anchors

One identified answer to these and many other problems is to pre-lay the moorings, and so far suction anchors have been favoured, particularly in the Gulf of Mexico where the seabed is particularly soft. There are proposals for systems which use suction anchors to embed plate anchors at specific depths and precise positions and proposals for what might be called self-drilling piles, although the latter would seem to require a rig which seems to defeat the purpose.

Torpedo anchors are a dramatic alternative to other mooring methods. They are launched over the stern and bury themselves deep into the seabed. Picture: Tony Poll

A Bruce VLA – Vertical Lift Anchor on the deck of the ship. This and other designs rely on the power of the ship to break a weak link and change the attitude of the flukes.
Picture: Tony Poll.

The basis of the whole suction anchor process is to lower a steel pile to the seabed connected by a suitable hose to a pump on the deck of the ship. The end of the pile is allowed to sink into the mud, and then the pump is started to evacuate the seawater inside it. As the water is removed, the pressure forces the tube into the seabed. Eventually, when only the top is exposed, a ROV disconnects the pump hose. If it is not already connected it can also connect up the mooring.

Suction anchors used to be deployed by barges or large construction or crane vessels, but the technique has been refined so that now a sufficiently large anchor-handler to house a number of piles on deck and enough wire on its storage reels can do the job. In addition it requires a means of launching and recovering and operating an ROV.

The motivation for this approach is of course that the moorings can be laid independent of the rig, so that if day rates for semi-submersibles are particularly high some money can be saved. Whether such an approach would be valid in the Atlantic margin is debatable since a couple of top of the range anchor-handlers might equal the day rate of a semi-submersible, and the weather window is all.

Vertical Lift Anchors

In addition to pre-laying suction anchors it is possible to pre-lay conventional anchors and high holding power anchors and to pretension them using one of the patented tensioners produced either by Vryhof or Bruce. This operation has been limited to shallower waters in the past and, all in all, the technique is not really practical, since the lengths of chain required are unacceptable.

However, as if by magic these two difficulties are overcome by the Vertical Lift anchor, which ceases to be dependent on the horizontal component of the mooring to hold it in position. Vertical Lift anchors may be placed on the seabed hanging from the mooring wire; the ship can then apply the required forces by bollard pull to break a tension link. The anchor then takes up a new attitude. This allows a single but powerful vessel to lay and tension anchors, which in themselves are dimensionally easy to deal with. An alternative might be for the ship to embed the anchor in the seabed but leave the rig to carry out the tensioning operation.

Use of Fibre Moorings

The sales pitch for fibre moorings is that eventually the weight of the length of wire between the surface and the seabed will be such that it will be sufficient to exceed the breaking strain. But, they say, fibre moorings have neutral buoyancy in water, and therefore they are a much better bet.

The downside is that they are dimensionally much larger than wire for the same strength and have a greater bending radius. As a result very large winches are required to store them, and very large reels required to move them. But there are already ships which can store great lengths of fibre rope, and easily deploy them from the storage reels, since there is little stress involved. In Europe fibre ropes are frequently used to allow moorings to safely span pipelines or subsea architecture. This technique replaces that which uses wires and subsea buoyancy.

The ships involved will usually remove the anchor from the mooring and then pay a measured amount of chain in to a chain locker. The deck crew will then capture the chain in the shark's jaw and separate it, either at a joining link, or by cutting it with oxy-acetylene equipment, known universally in the offshore industry as the "gas axe". If they are at the correct distance from the rig, they will then connect the end of the fibre mooring and pay it out carefully as they move slowly away from the rig, passing over the subsea pipeline. Once the other end of the fibre rope is at the stern they connect up the chain and pay it out from the chain locker until they are at the anchor position. Often the speed at which the ship can pay out the chain exceeds that possible by the rig.

Fibre ropes are beginning to be used as an alternative to chain or wire, but reeling it on can be a tedious business. Picture: Victor Gibson

Some Operations

Workdrums for deep water need to be capable of storing may thousands of feet of large diameter wire. Picture: Victor Gibson.

Although Europeans look out in amazement at the extraordinary feats being carried out in Brazil and in the Gulf of Mexico, both these areas of operation have one thing in their favour: proximity to the shore. Water of considerable depth may be only a few hours from a suitable base port, or at least shallow water, where moorings and anchors may be conveniently stowed on the seabed for later collection.

No such serious testing of existing vessels has taken place in the Atlantic, where there still appears to be considerable difficulty in 2000 ft (750 metres). In the northern North Sea and out in the Atlantic all activities are controlled by the weather and so one would expect that enough ships would be hired to carry all the equipment at once, whatever sort it was.

Some work has been done mooring FPSOs and shifting some mobiles, and operators have often been caught out by the weather. Since they are under the impression that they need very large vessels indeed, these have turned out to be extremely costly operations in all cases. It should also be emphasised that the activities took place in the shallows - compared with the Gulf of Mexico.

However a number of Atlantic operations have taken place, and one is described here to illustrate some of the difficulties faced by the ships, and indeed the semi-submersibles.

The complex winches require even more complex controls. This is the winch operator's console on the Maersk Assister. Picture: Victor Gibson.

An Atlantic Rig Move

At the beginning of April 2000 the Sovereign Explorer featured prominently in the British national press when it was boarded by members of Greenpeace, who scaled the legs and bivouacked an external ledge at main deck level, in the style of mountaineers over-nighting on the North face of the Eiger. At the time it was 'stacked', the oil industry term for being laid up, in the Cromarty Firth and was being prepared for a Marathon Oil deep-water charter.

Marathon Oil UK, the charterers and Transocean Sedco Forex, the owners, obtained an injunction to have the protestors removed and as silently as they had arrived they disappeared and are probably still being sought by the police. The visit followed a similar attack on the R&B Falcon semi-submersible Jack Bates, where the protestors chained themselves to parts of the moorings.

Greenpeace were targeting rigs bound for the Atlantic, claiming that their presence would have an adverse effect on marine life of all sorts. Such claims appear to be entirely subjective, but it is possible to say that an oil rig takes up very little space on the surface of the planet, and marine life appears to thrive in the immediate vicinity of oil rigs, platforms and pipelines.

Both the Jack Bates and the Sovereign Explorer were heading for water depths of about 1320 meters (4500 ft) 60 miles west of Harris, one of the better known of the Scottish Western Isles. On the UK continental shelf this is deep water in a hostile environment.

Marathon and Enterprise decided to co-operate on the venture, since the schedules for the two rigs were compatible. The Jack Bates was to be taken out and moored first, and the Sovereign Explorer second, the same ships being used for both operations.

The ships chosen were the venerable Maersk Master and the newer S Class Maersk vessels, Maersk Seeker and Maersk Searcher. The latter two vessels were built to Maersk designs derived from their B class vessels, in Singapore. For the Sovereign Explorer operation Marathon

*The driver's controls on the Olympic Pegasus. Most of the controls are sited in the arms of his seat.
Picture: Neil Holland.*

also hired the Swire Pacific UT720, Pacific Blade. The capacities of these craft appear elsewhere in this volume.

The Sovereign Explorer was originally designed to work in a maximum depth of 3500 feet, and so had to have an additional 200 metres of chain fitted. This gave the rig 1400 metres of 76mm chain and 1800 metres of 90 mm wire. The bitter end of the chain is permanently connected to the outer end of the wire, which is stored on reels in the pontoons and paid out, tensioned and recovered by means of tension winches mounted above the windlasses on the corner columns. The anchors are 12 tonne Stevpris. Despite the extreme environment in which the rig is intended to work it is not dimensionally large, extending to 90 meters in each direction.

Having ensured the removal of the pressure group members and having had the extra 200 meters of chain added to the mooring system, the rig departed the Cromarty Firth, towed by the Maersk Master, at 1600 on 4th April. Apart from 24 hours hove to in adverse weather the tow northward through the Fair Isle passage was uneventful, and the rig with its attendant vessels arrived at the location at 0130 on 16th April.

Shortly after 0200 the job of locating the rig was started in earnest with the chasing pennants for Numbers 1 and 5 anchors, the forward starboard and port aft moorings being passed down to the Maersk Seeker and Maersk Searcher. The two ships, at opposite corners of the rig, started out, the operation following the designed procedures which are undertaken for every rig move.

Deep-water rigs with combined wire and chain systems must be provided with a means of changing over from the windlass to the winch, which is always difficult in one way or another because the chain is piled up in a locker and the wire is stored on a drum. Some systems are automatic, complex and expensive and some are conducted entirely by the rig crew, who split the chain and connect up the end of the wire, often working on a small platform below the windlass and sometimes with no mechanical aids.

The Sovereign Explorer falls somewhere between the two. The end of the wire is

*The Sovereign Explorer and the Maersk Seeker starting their anchor job in the deep water of the Atlantic.
Picture: Victor Gibson*

permanently attached to the end of the chain, but the transfer of load from the windlass to the tension winch is undertaken with the assistance of a guiding system which is hydraulically driven and manually controlled. The system was designed to accept the vertical loading from the anchor chain of 90 tonnes, which had now been exceeded by the addition of 200 meters of chain. Hence the presence of the Pacific Blade.

When the moorings reached what is known as the transition point, the Pacific Blade was required to J-hook the chain close to the rig and reduce the weight on the guiding system. This initially proved to be difficult because the rig was not fixed in any way, apart from the two anchor-handlers pulling in opposite directions. It is easy to J-hook a horizontal mooring and impossible to J-hook a vertical mooring and so achieving any horizontal component required some co-ordination. However the initial difficulties were overcome and by 1500 on the first day both the initial anchors had been laid.

To illustrate the process the running of No 8 anchor by the Maersk Seeker is described in greater detail.

The chasing pennant for No 8 anchor was passed to the Maersk Seeker at 1522 on 16th

*The Maersk Shipper – sister ship to the Seeker and Searcher together three of a class of six vessels built for deep water work.
Picture: Andrew Woodrow.*

The Pacific Blade which acted as the support vessel on the Sovereign Explorer move – J-hooking the chain to reduce the stress on the winches. Picture: Victor Gibson.

April, about 13 hours after the start of the mooring operation. The ship's crew connected the end of the pennant to the link at the end of the 2000 metre work wire with a 120-ton shackle and the anchor was lowered off the bolster. The ship heaved up on the work drum until the anchor could be sighted at the roller.

100 meters of chain was then paid out to allow the ship to run out and re-spool its work wire and this task was completed by 1938 when the rig crew started to pay out No 8 chain and the Maersk Seeker started to run the anchor. At around 2030 the 1400 metres of anchor chain had been paid out and the Pacific Blade was J-hooking for the bight so that the transition from chain to wire could be accomplished. Once the chain was hooked the transition took place and was completed at 2106; the Pacific Blade then released itself from the chain.

The rig and the ship then resumed alternately paying out wire. When the rig stopped paying out wire at 2122 the Maersk Seeker paid out 650 meters of wire, maintaining the bollard pull required by the programme. When this was completed the ship was 1775 metres from the rig. The rig then paid out a total length of 900 metres of wire and the ship paid out a further 650 metres wire while still maintaining the required bollard pull and thereafter increased power to achieve a distance from the rig of 2900 meters. The rig then paid out a further 950 metres of wire, which was completed at 2346. At this stage of the operation the ship was 3500 meters from the rig and was being required to apply 105 tonnes of pull, the highest level necessary during the whole operation. The Maersk Seeker then paid out a further 480 meters of wire and moved away to a maximum distance of 4000 meters. This is two and a half miles away in old money! At twelve minutes past midnight number eight anchor was on the bottom and for that mooring it was all over bar the shouting, except for the return of the chasing pennant to the rig. The chasing back and the return took a further one hour and forty minutes.

On the morning of 17th, with only two anchors to run the weather blew up. In the western Atlantic and the northern North Sea depressions can change direction unpredictably and since each anchor was taking something approaching 12 hours to run it was possible for a ship to be caught part way through a run by a change in the weather. So it was for the Maersk Searcher which was forced to abandon the operation for weather six hours into running Number 2 anchor. However, modern navigation and positioning systems are sophisticated and the ship was able to lie to the rig anchor, bow to the weather until the morning of 19th when it completed the laying of Number 2 and then go on to lay the last anchor, which was Number 6.

So, the job was done. The insurance tensioning of the moorings was completed at 1900 on 19th April and the Maersk Searcher, now the only anchor-handler left on the location, was allowed to depart for Aberdeen. Both vessels were required to de-tension their work wires before returning to port. De-tensioning is now routinely carried out after deep-water operations because otherwise the motorised reels used to recover the wires from the work drums are just not up to pulling out the turns. The usual technique is to drop a five-tonne anchor over the stern on the end of the wire and then pay it out, in shallow water - or deep water, depending on how the mood takes you. Whatever technique is used, the operator is particularly keen to get the wires back in good condition. They are, after all, longer and stronger than the average tow wire, and while shipmasters treat tow wires as if they were delicate parts of their anatomy, they have not yet learnt to adopt the same approach with very long work wires.

The whole operation was carried out with very few problems apart from two winch failures, due to the electronics refusing to believe that the chain length had been increased from 1200 to 1400 meters. When it came to recovering the moorings the whole job was carried out equally successfully and the rig moved on to do other work.

Manning the Ships

One of the changes caused by the mooring of semi-submersibles in deep water is the duration of individual anchor jobs. In the early days it was common for the man on the bridge to spend days at the controls, as the operation of laying anchors staggered onwards, the ships stumbling from one difficulty to another. On the deck the same crew might work continuously, cat-napping when the opportunity arose. In order to ease these difficulties the Department of Transport in UK issued an instruction, known as an "M" notice, recommending an increase in the manning for anchor work. The increase was to be an extra deck officer, and extra engineer and an extra seaman. These additional personnel allowed watches to change down in the engine room, although the Chief Engineer would still be more or less continuously working the winch, and also allowed there to be two sets of deck crew, each controlled by a mate. This in turn might give the master the opportunity for some rest if the job was stopped for a time.

The Norwegians had adopted a set of rules which resulted in anchor-handlers being manned by less personnel than platform ships because they were smaller. In addition to all this shipmasters were very reluctant to hand over control of their vessel in close proximity to fixed objects to others, despite formal encouragement from the marine authorities.

Now that very large vessels are working in deep water for extended periods of time, it is necessary for there to be sufficient competent personnel on board for there to be complete changes of watch, and "driving mates" are the norm. Of course it remains questionable whether the driving mates are receiving the appropriate levels of training, and the increase in the numbers of these large vessels and an increase in the numbers of deep water mooring operations means that an increased number of mariners will be required.

In response to this requirement there are now limited simulator facilities for the training of mariners in the operation of supply vessels. Maersk have their own facility, and there are also simulators in Norway, and in Lowestoft and South Shields in UK. There is no formally approved syllabus for the training of mariners in the ship-handling requirements for offshore support vessels so, for the time being, the skills gained depend on the perception of the trainers as to what will be required to make deep water anchor-handling more effective and safer.

The Ulstein A102 Bourbon Dolphin, the loss of which, while anchor-handling in April 2007, may be the greatest motivation for change ever seen in the offshore support industry. Picture Victor Gibson

Chapter 11
TO BOLDLY GO

Introduction

In the last few years shipyards all over the world have been producing new supply vessels at a rate which has not been seen since the 1970s. The Norwegian shipyards, together with the less sophisticated metal bashers of the former Eastern bloc shipyards, have been producing Rolls Royce UT designs of all sorts, but particularly variants of the UT755. The Aker yards have designed their own small anchor-handler and Ulstein Verft, having sold the UT designs and all their subsidiaries to Rolls-Royce, have produced their own very large anchor-handlers and platform vessels.

The well-known Norwegian designer Maritime Engineering became part of the Aker empire, which during the 1990s produced the KMAR404 and KMAR808, and was then passed on to Moss Maritime to disappear altogether from the scene, but was replaced in Norway by Marin Teknikk with their "MT" designs, which have a particularly head turning streamlined superstructure and are well known for their economy.

In South America, yards are building UT722s one after the other, and in the Far East Jaya Holdings are developing and building their own designs and selling them to others or operating themselves. In America things have continued to change as exploration and production has moved into deeper and deeper water, and now it is expected that vessels servicing rigs in the Gulf of Mexico will be provided with some form of DP system and the anchor-handlers will be capable of deploying suction piles in 10,000 feet of water. In India a number of yards are building what might be termed "conventional" supply vessels and anchor-handlers locally designed in the 4000 to 6000 bhp range.

Now, as the world supply of oil is for the first time seen to be finite and the requirements of the developing nations infinite, the offshore oil industry may be entering its most focused period. Onshore, even the Saudis seem to be struggling to meet demand and in other areas the supply is, to say the least, less than reliable. Hence offshore Europe, America and Africa business is booming. All the exploration rigs in the world are becoming active and as the day rates move upwards the more adventurous companies are commissioning new units. New and ingenious ways of recovering the hydrocarbons which are discovered are being employed and all of this requires the use of more and more ships.

The large deepwater anchor-handlers are achieving such high rates that rig owners are co-operating with the oil companies to install the large A-frames and other equipment which are required to install subsea completions on board semi-submersibles, thereby bypassing this requirement. But nevertheless the steady progress into deeper and deeper water requires a constant review of the capabilities of the modern fleet and what can be done with a ship.

The Far Sound UT712L built in 2007. This is a medium sized anchor-handler with all possible accessories, and its 16,000 bhp shows that the way forward may not always be to build bigger. Picture: Victor Gibson

Newbuildings

By the end of 2006 there were over 500 supply vessels of one sort or another being built all over the world. Previously unheard-of companies were paying large sums of money for nothing more than an interest in a newbuilding. Siem Offshore, which had been formed out of the small diving ship company DSND, ordered six enormous anchor-handlers from Kleven Verft in Norway with options for a further 6. These vessels were in addition to orders for eight platform ships, a combination of Marin Teknikk and Vik Sandvik designs.

The increased activity around the shores of India stimulated an increased interest by Indian ship-owners in the offshore sector. Great Eastern had seven offshore support vessels of various sorts on order in the autumn of 2006, and like other companies was looking round for strategic purchases. In October of 2006 they purchased the venerable UT712 Skandi Bergen off District Offshore, renaming it the Malaviya 36.

In the midst of all this activity Groupe Bourbon announced such a large building programme for vessels all over the world that there must be some doubt as to whether it can ever be completed

Despite the apparent success of the Laney Chouest, no other American company or yard has ordered further very large anchor-handlers. Edison Chouest on the other hand have commissioned a further two of the type, with the Dino Chouest due for delivery in 2008. Courtesy of the video resources of "YouTube" the traditional secrecy of Edison Chouest has been overcome and a clip of the Carol Chouest, a 280 foot PSV, has been shown being launched sideways at North American Fabricators. This ship is the first of a number of very large PSVs due to enter service with the company over the next few years. Other American companies are purchasing European-designed ships which continue to be built in the Far East, and are having platform ships built by local yards, which promise much but cannot actually achieve the best of both worlds, economy and effectiveness.

Design Activity

Back in Europe, Rolls-Royce began to lose their grip on the whole market as the UT designs continued to be assailed by rivals, not least by the former owners of the design house, Ulstein Verft. The Aker Group, having become the owners of a number of Norwegian yards, have produced their own designs for a small anchor-handler, a number of which have been built, and a platform ship, the streamlined forepart of which is reminiscent of the extremely successful MT designs. The great advantage of this process is a freedom to search the market for cost-effective components rather than having to use hardware manufactured by Rolls-Royce subsidiaries.

Ulstein Verft have broken new ground with the XBow, which is an entirely different front end, firstly on an Ulstein A101 anchor-handler and then on a platform ship. Bourbon have commissioned two anchor-handlers and two platform ships, and the old rivalry between BP and Shell in Aberdeen surfaces as the former have chartered the XBow platform ships for a prolonged period. Shell on the other hand have almost single-handedly provided employment for all the elegant MT6000s owned by District Offshore.

The XBow is a throwback to designs where the bow profile curves back from the waterline rather than forward. It was probably last used on World War One battleships, and presumably it has never really found favour on commercial ships because it would tend to make the decks very wet. On a conventional ship, as it pitches into a sea, the flare on the bow pushes the water away. This tends to keep the deck dry as long as the vessel is not moving too fast, but it uses energy and every time the ship pitches into the sea it slows down. By changing the bow profile so that there is no flare, the vessel will drive through the water, without loss of speed. Ulsteins have videos of their tank tests showing this process and it seems to work, and at the end of 2006 the first XBow ship, the Bourbon Orca entered service . There is this nagging feeling that if this idea was so great then why are all ships not like this, and it might be because the design can't work in very heavy weather. Time will tell and readers of this volume may be able to look out on numerous XBows and know it all worked wonderfully.

At the other end of the XBow anchor-handler there is the manifestation of the Norwegian obsession with automation. Strange-looking articulated arms, not unlike those which stick out of the space shuttle, can be seen on either side of the afterdeck, and the primary function of these is to drop the lasso over the anchor-buoy. Once the anchor has been recovered to the roller, the after end of the ship articulates to bring the anchor aboard. It is difficult to precisely explain the process. First the anchor slides up the forty-five degree slope which apparently forms the stern of the ship, and once it is in position the after part hinges upwards so almost magically

The XBow ship Bourbon Orca approaching Aberdeen for the first time. Tank tests have proved that the design allows the ship to travel faster through heavy seas. But they are a bit more difficult to tie up. Picture: Victor Gibson

the sloping bit becomes part of the deck, and the crew can walk about on it. Once more, only time will tell whether this is a good idea.

Other manufacturers and designers have developed other sorts of automation which they have punted for a variety of tasks. In 2006 the UT712L Olympic Octopus arrived with the latest anchor-handling gear from Rolls-Royce, which despite the fanfare seemed to consist of two cranes, each running on rails down the sides of the deck and being fitted with all sorts of manipulators for different tasks. The designers suggested that the cranes could be used to drop the lasso over a buoy, or collect the pennant being offered by a rig crane. The move towards capturing the pennants in the shark's jaw, before releasing the crane, instead of capturing the pennant with a tugger, releasing the crane, and then closing the jaw on the wire is still considered by some to be a process which has just moved the risk from one place to another. Things might be safer for the guys on the deck, but the risk of collision, or damage to the crane have possibly increased. Similarly there will be a point when the crane on the rig is connected to the ship by another crane. It would seem to be less than appropriate if the ship is not fitted with DP2.

It is difficult to work out what is currently driving the designers forward, but it appears that the quest for greater and greater power has, at least for a time, been subordinated by a desire for economic construction. Maersk, usually taking the lead in trends, and having constructed the A class which are amongst the largest anchor-handlers in the world, have ordered eight VS472s to be constructed in Denmark. At 16,000 bhp they are an easy fit into the mid range of anchor-handlers and are doubtless aimed at the old task of moving semi-submersibles form one place to another, a task which has been rather neglected due to the downturn in drilling, which may have been the reason for the proliferation of very large multi-role vessels. However, building on the success of the wonderful Ulstein A101s, Olympic Pegasus and Olympic Hercules, Ulstein Verft and Olympic have got together again and announced the construction of the Ulstein A122, billed as the largest anchor-handler ever built by the yard and to be delivered in 2009. The idea, say Olympic, is to build a ship which is not limited to anchor-handling and therefore will be less vulnerable to the cyclic nature of the oil industry. This craft has the usual mind-boggling specifications, not least of which is an overall length of 93.8 metres and a bollard pull of 260 tonnes.

Like other recently designed anchor-handlers there are cranes running on rails down the

The stern of the Bourbon Orca. The whole centre section changes attitude to become a ramp onto which the anchor can slide, it is then levelled up and the anchor is then magically on deck. Picture: Victor Gibson

sides of the after deck, the purpose of which is to assist with anchor and chain-handling activities. It may be worth noting that if one looks back to the earliest British anchor-handler designs, they were provided with portable 'strongbacks' which could be assembled and fitted across the afterdeck, to allow the unobstructed transit of the tow wire when turning. These were seldom used, but conventional towing techniques still required the facility for the tow wire to pass round quarters and up the sides as far as the stag horns during turns.

The availability of towing pins at the edges of the main deck of anchor-handlers has allowed masters to discard this traditional technique, but apparently despite the power now available they can still be caught out during acute turns when they are unable to overcome the restraint of the tow wire.

The Loss of the Bourbon Dolphin

On 12th April 2007 the Bourbon Dolphin capsized apparently without warning while running an anchor from the Transocean Rather, in water depths of 1100 metres to the west of the Shetland Islands. Eight of the fifteen crew members were lost.

A few words are included about this terrible accident because it is certain that when the Norwegian Royal Commission reports in 2008, the result will be many changes to the way in which anchor-handlers are designed and operated.

The Bourbon Dolphin was a unique vessel, the first Ulstein A102, a sort of compact version of the A101. It had 16000 bhp available which apparently gave it a bollard pull of 190 odd tonnes. It had a very large winch and so was thought generally suitable for deep water work. As well as two propellers in kort nozzles with high lift rudders, the ship was equipped with one tunnel thruster and one azimuthing thruster forward and two tunnel thrusters aft.

A public enquiry was conducted in Norway and some witness testimony has been translated into English. The most important witness was one of the two second mates, because he was driving the winch at the time of the accident. The master was at the ship's controls. He had just relieved the mate who had been on the sticks since the 1200 shift change. The second mate described a situation where the Bourbon Dolphin was being unable to get back to the correct line, having pulled out 900 metres of rig chain, and deployed most of the 900 metres of additional chain it had been carrying. The complete length of chain was therefore partly supported by the Bourbon Dolphin and partly by the winch of the rig, the Transocean Rather. In these circumstances the tension which shows on the ship's gauges is a combination of bollard pull, and chain weight, and according to the second mate the tensions on the ship's readouts exceeded 300 tonnes at one point.

The UT722 Highland Valour had been given the task of grappling the chain astern of the Bourbon Dolphin. If successful the Highland Valour would have taken some of the weight of the chain and this would have allowed the Bourbon Dolphin to take up a heading which would have got it back on line. Unfortunately, according to the witness there was a near collision between the two ships and during this the grapple fell off, so no progress was made. Also about this time the Chief Engineer called up to say that the starboard engines were overheating.

Towards the time of the capsize there seem to have been a number of significant events .The starboard inner towing pin was lowered, and the chain allowed to slide across the stern, coming to rest against the port outer pin with some force, according to another witness. Also one of the ABs thought there had been a blackout , and lastly the second mate testified that after the master had relieved the mate, the latter started transferring ballast.

According to the second mate, he had the job of writing the departure draft, and the departure GM in the log book. The draft was 6.5 metres and the GM was 0.26 metres. If you ask any experienced master in this business he will say that he would like there to be a GM of more than 1 metre.

The position of the chain may have been particularly relevant, and hence the recollections of the witnesses are particularly important in this respect. Unfortunately the two who noticed the position of the chain disagree. The second mate recollected that as the ship went over to 90 degrees he saw the chain leading over the crash barrier, however the AB felt that the chain was trapped by the port outer pin.

Most of the relevant evidence was provided by a young man who was on the bridge, although he had only qualified for the position he held at the end of 2006. He is also recorded as having said that the starboard rudder was in the midships position and the port rudder was to starboard, however others have thought from the pictures of the ship upside down that the rudders were positioned so as to turn the ship to port, and and yet others have thought that both rudders were midships.

Construction

The new millennium has heralded a new means of building supply vessels. Out in the Far East the Chinese shipyards are booming, and owners seem to accept the delays involved, which are sometimes numbered in years. The suppliers of marine equipment find themselves quoting for vessels to be constructed in yards which themselves do not yet exist. In Europe the Norwegian yards are taking advantage of the cheaper labour costs in the eastern bloc countries. Typically the hull of the Dina Merkur, a UT755L built for the new Norwegian ship-owner Myklebusthaug, was welded together in four pieces in the Polish shipyard of Maritim Ltd of Gdansk. It was then transported on a barge to the Simek yard in Flekkefjord. At the same time Simek were constructing another UT755L with a specially low superstructure so that it would be able to get under the bridges over the canal system connecting the Caspian Sea with the outside world.

The Ulstein A122 two of which are to be delivered to Olympic in 2009. They are 94 metres long, develop 25,000 bhp and offer 260 tonnes bollard pull. They will be good for any task the designers claim. Picture: Ulstein Verft

The People

With the massive increase in the offshore fleet, and the impending retirement of many of the seafarers who entered the industry as it developed in the 1970s and 1980s, it began to dawn on the owners of the ships that when they were finished there might be no-one to take them to sea.

In Europe the availability and use of DP systems continued to exercise the intellect of the marine specialists in the oil companies. The question was, why, in this modern world with the increasingly sophisticated systems and greater power and larger ships, were collisions still taking place between ships and the floating and fixed objects they were trying to supply. The use of DP systems of any sort was more limited in the Gulf of Mexico and hence many of those operating the ships retained the traditional skills of "driving" the ships, by operating propulsion rudders and thrusters using the individual controls on the aft console. On the other hand those who commanded the smaller craft would be unlikely to be sufficiently qualified to take large ships out into the ocean.

A standard dynamic positioning control desk, showing the duplication of the keyboards, joysticks and screens. Dynamic positioning will feature more and more in offshore operations as time passes. Picture: Victor Gibson

The 12,000 bhp Magnus. This ship – new in 2007 – shows that there are still tasks for small ships to carry out. On delivery it was immediately hired by Shell for jack-up moving. Picture Victor Gibson.

It can be seen therefore at the beginning of 2007 that a large number of well trained and courageous seafarers are required to take all these new ships to sea, all of them qualified to sail worldwide on vessels of considerable tonnage. In addition to the formal seafaring skills of watch-keeping, engineering and marine management, they will also be required to be competent in all aspects of the operation of offshore support craft, an activity which is perhaps becoming more complex rather than more simple.

In all of this, the most traditional skill of driving the ship, facing the stern close to fixed objects out in the sea is being lost, and this may be why ships are colliding with offshore installations; because the guys out there do not know what to do when the DP systems fail.

Equipment

In addition to the work carried out by Ulstein in the development of automated anchor-handling equipment, Triplex, best known for their sharks jaws, developed what is billed as a completely automated system of anchor work and cargo operations. This system is based on a travelling bridge crane which spans the after-deck and is capable of moving forward and aft. On the bridge crane are two manipulator arms which can reach down to work on the deck. The equipment can apparently be controlled from the bridge of the ship, or by the use of remote

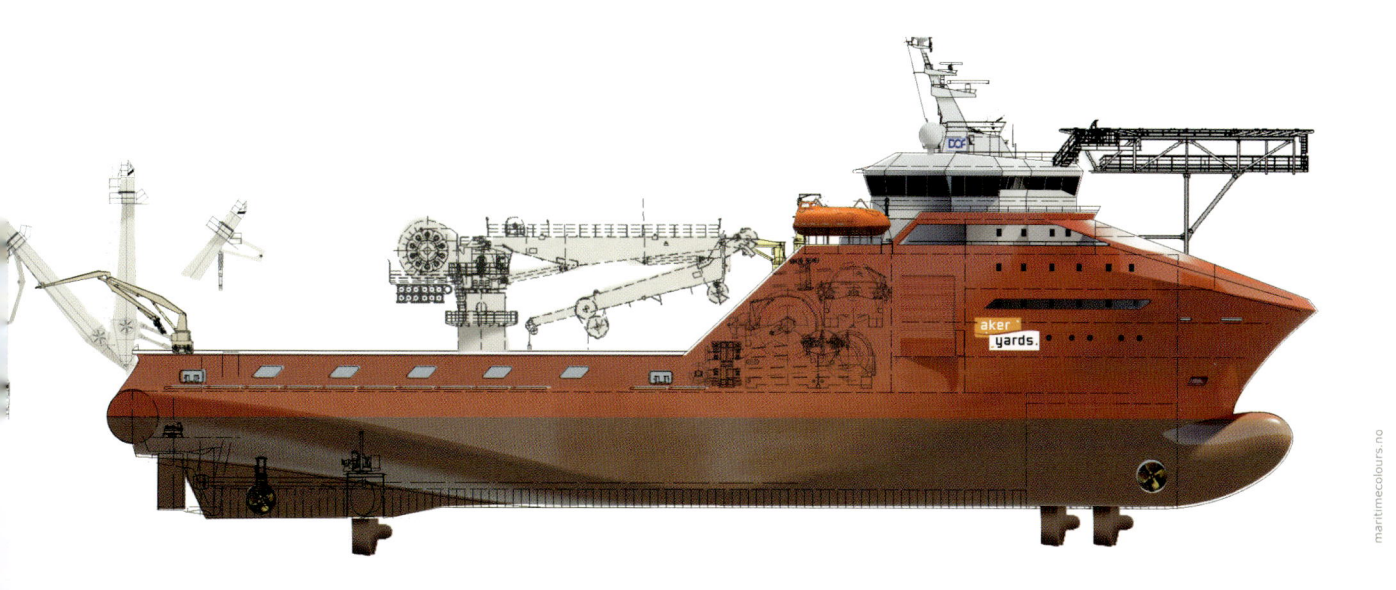

Aker have also been slaving over their drawing boards and have produced a number of futuristic designs including this AH04which is to be delivered to District Offshore in 2009. Picture: Aker Yards.

operating panels held by the seaman on deck. Triplex also claim to be developing remote hose-handling equipment. This crane is not unlike that installed on the Mammoth Tide and the Giant Tide back in the 1970s.

As well as the equipment on the deck of the ship receiving attention the industry, especially in Norway, continues to look at means by which the crane can be automatically connected and disconnected from the lifts, and if it is going to do this, the manner in which the lifts can be oriented. In order to land tubulars, say, the crane driver will have an extra control in addition to the lift, luff and slew options already available. This control will alter the orientation of the lifts, so that the driver will be able to line up, drill pipe, or long open top containers, with the ship's rail, or other lifts, and once landed he will be able to press a button and the hook will disengage. One assumes that in combination with the Triplex gear the lifts will be able to be hooked on without anyone going near them.

Other areas of supply are also receiving attention, and once more the Norwegians are in the lead. Dry-bulk cargoes have always presented problems in both their carriage and transfer, and oil-based mud continues to irritate operators, because it has become more or less essential for many sections of the hole, but is difficult to carry, is subject to high losses and is very expensive. In addition it is the mud which contaminates the drill cuttings and makes it essential that they either be re-injected into the substrata or transported to the shore.

Over the years the carriage of dry bulk has more or less standardized, and tends to be carried in large vertical hoppers and discharged to the offshore installations by being pressured into the pipe-work through the cone in the bottom and blown onwards by compressed air, jetted into the tubing at the bends. The trick is to maintain the pressure in the hopper while injecting just the right amount of air. Too little and the powder will stop moving and create a blockage which can take hours to shift, too much and all the rig will get is the air, and the hopper will lose pressure because the amount of air being produced by the compressed air system is finite. Other systems have been tried, notably one which moved a quantity of powder from a large low-pressure hopper into a small high-pressure hopper. Once the small hopper was full, it was pressurized and the cargo ejected upwards as a slug.

Meanwhile the carriage of drilling fluid, mud, has moved from being a haphazard hit or miss operation, utilizing poorly converted fuel tanks, to a pretty sophisticated process utilizing tall

The crewboat Milton R McCall taking off for the beach. Crewboats can now carry large quantities of deck cargo as well as numerous passengers at high speed, making them an attractive alternative to the PSV. Picture: Robert Smith

Sister ships to the unusual Viking Avant have been ordered, but it seems unlikely that the all aft supply vessel will replace the conventional PSV, if for no other reason, it is too unlike the Ebb Tide. Picture Robert Nilsen

cylindrical tanks ranged down the sides of most platform ships. However, all these cylindrical tanks make for poor utilization of space and so in 2007 alternative systems are being offered. These are rectangular tanks which can be converted for different types of cargo, hence they can be utilised for dry powders, mud or even drill cuttings. The innovators of these systems remain understandably coy about the precise manner in which they work, but one assumes that they operate in some way similarly to the big low-pressure container/small high-pressure container system, with additional connections to pumps and augers for different bulk cargoes.

In addition to the idea of special tankage on board platform ships for the carriage of drill cuttings, the concept of the offshore island has re-emerged as a means of reducing voyage time. This, it is thought would look something like an aircraft carrier and would contain all the plant necessary to remove the oil from the cuttings, which could then be legally returned to the sea. If such an object was strategically positioned, voyage times for the supply vessels could be halved and all the peripheral port costs would be reduced. There are downsides to such a scheme, even without considering the cost. The interface between the ship and the point of loading or discharge would be dependent on good weather at both ends of the voyage, and in order to comply with the legislation (in the UK), the cuttings from every location would have to be segregated from all other cuttings so that they could be totalled up and reconciled with the quantity removed from the hole.

The Edge of the World

Finally it behoves the author to look forward into uncharted regions, where no-one has yet boldly gone, to try to predict the possible direction of the industry. Here there are many opportunities for ridicule, and it seems to be the fate of inventors to invent things which are supposed to make things better at sea in some way, to find, if they ever get off the drawing

The Acergy Energy loading a suction anchor, showing that apparently an anchor-handler is not the only sort of ship which will be used for mooring offshore installations of all sorts. Picture: Stephen Green

board, that the sea has more tricks up its sleeve than the innovator anticipated, and so another good idea is consigned to the bin. Fifty years ago it seemed, even to the more cynical mariners, that the hovercraft was going to revolutionize the carriage of passengers and freight by sea, but how many are there about today? The hovercraft has been followed by the hydrofoil, the catamaran, the swath vessel and other great ideas, but in general their use has been limited. Offshore, some completely lunatic proposals have been made, and sometimes design work has been done, but in the end we have seen operators revert to the use of conventional hull forms, full of conventional equipment. They know it works.

Looking towards the future, is it likely that the ships currently in use, and being constructed will be sufficient to keep the business running until things begin to slow down? In other words, is this the last major input of new vessels likely to take place? Possibly the answer is, that as long as hydrocarbons are being discovered in deeper and deeper water, larger and more sophisticated ships will be required to support the means being used to recover these reserves. It is also reasonable to assume that as hydrocarbons become more difficult to recover, it will be cost-effective to collect smaller quantities.

It is therefore likely that for a while the holes will be drilled further offshore by dynamically positioned drill ships, other vessels will install the subsea structures necessary to allow the oil to be recovered and thereafter it will be piped to FPSOs, platforms or even the shore. It is even likely that the mobile recovery vessel will be re-introduced, the only one built now operating in the Campos Basin as an FPSO.

Paradoxically, very deep water activities which are likely to result in the increase in the price of hydrocarbons, should also discourage the use of drill ships and other DP drilling vessels, because of the cost of keeping them fuelled. Moored semi-submersibles have already been put to work in the Gulf of Mexico in water depths of about 10,000 feet. The mooring systems have generally consisted of suction piles and fibre ropes, so it is possible that instead of the industry

The Supply Express and the Rig Express two ships, brand new in 2007, built in Rumania for Vroon, showing that traditional shapes will be with us for many years to come.
Picture: Victor Gibson

being reduced to a bunch of fuel carriers, more very large anchor-handlers will be required with the ability to single-handedly launch suction piles and connect and disconnect moorings using their own remotely operated vehicles (ROVs). It might be that these vessels would also need to be able to launch the latest in mooring equipment, the torpedo anchor. In both cases, this would seem ideally to involve some sort of ramp, onto which the anchor could be placed. It would then be elevated, and the anchor would be launched over the stern.

Will the oil industry ever learn to plan more than five minutes ahead? Will the current business models allow the purchasing departments to buy things ahead of time, which will then be stored on large ships for extended periods? Will they ever build sufficient redundancy into the equipment they are using to ensure its reliability, and therefore avoid the constant need for spares to be rushed to the location? If the answer to these questions is a resounding no, perhaps we are going to see an extension in the use of the crew boat. These craft are becoming larger and more powerful, so that the latest models are capable of travelling at more than 30knots and carrying several hundred tons of cargo in addition to fifty or sixty passengers.

Since there are already two more VS493 Avants on order it seems likely that there will be an increase in the number of all aft supply vessels, but it is unlikely that they will take over the business. If there is one common trait which oil men have it is conservatism.

On the periphery of our vision of the future, is the possibility of drilling taking place remotely on the seabed. There is already a prototype production unit being tested in the Gulf of Mexico. The process would almost certainly be a development of coiled tubing operations. One could visualize the complete unit being lowered to the seabed by a large crane and then it carrying out its task without human intervention. After all, drilling a hole in the planet sounds more straightforward than being required to wander about on the surface of the red planet as the next generation of Mars rovers is going to be required to do.

Finally it seems possible that the ships which are currently being used in the oil industry may move sideways into the production of environmentally friendly power. Currently there seems to be limited interest in power produced by the sea, possibly due to the enthusiasm for power produced by the wind, but one assumes that eventually half the planet will be covered with windmills, each one providing enough power to boil a kettle, and then someone will call a halt. Meanwhile models of tidal and current driven devices generally languish in the store-rooms of the e-energy companies whose funding has been removed by an impatient government. One of the problems is that the designers are enthusiastic, but their knowledge of the marine environment is limited, and they are unable to visualize the power of the sea. Some years ago a prototype marine power generating device was built and towed out to a point in the Pentland Firth, where it promptly sank. It weighed 7000 tonnes. But that's not the end of it. Once the problems are better understood, marine expertise will be needed. Taking all the unanswered questions into consideration, the designers will continue to try to anticipate the needs of the industry while producing shapes pleasing to the eye. In general there is, in 2007, a move to more or less enclose the bow. This is taken to the extremes in the XBow, but has been used to a lesser extent by other designers who effectively cover over the forecastle, probably making the means of tying up difficult for the deck crew. The signs of things to come are already present in vessels such as the UT787 Island Vanguard, which is provided with its own ROV hanger as well as a permanently installed A-Frame, which when not in use folds up behind the bridge. This vessel and other late model UT designs are fitted with a curved bridge front, which one assumes is seen to be an improvement on the triangular shape used for the last twenty years by the Norwegians. Of course the curved bridge front was last used in the 1950s in the Gulf of Mexico, and it may at this point be worthwhile looking back at the picture of the Ebb Tide, which used the pilot house from an old tug. Yes, its just the same only bigger. Perhaps there really is nothing new under the sun.

The UT787CD Island Vanguard is, in 2007, the latest offering from the Rolls-Royce UT design team. Picture: Jan Plug.

AFTERWORD

During the final phases of the writing of this book the Bourbon Dolphin sank West of the Shetland Islands during anchor-handling operations, with the loss of the lives of eight of the crew, and as the date of publication approaches the Norwegian Royal Commission investigation in to the causes of the accident continues, and witness statements appear occasionally in the public domain. Meanwhile the Norwegian maritime authorities and the International Maritime Organisation have issued guidance for the use of those engaged in anchor handling, and in UK the Marine Safety Forum has set up a number of committees to look at aspects of anchor handling activities. The final effect of all this input is unknown and it is likely that the way ahead will not be clear until the Royal Commission publishes its findings early in 2008. It is probable that ship-owners are hoping that the changes will be limited to the way in which anchor-handlers are operated, rather than the way in which they are designed.

Throughout this book there are details of other disasters with which the industry is associated, sometimes with an equally distressing loss of life. Investigations have been carried out and findings published, but it seems that the recommendations which have been made have had little influence on the industry as a whole. Common themes have been the urgency with which the tasks have been undertaken, failure to consider weather conditions and inexperience of some part of the team involved, whether it be those on the ships or those on the units being serviced.

It could be argued that servicing oil rigs is less dangerous than tramping over the oceans in deep sea ships, and this may well be right, since a perusal of the pages of Lloyds List will reveal that ships sink almost daily. Oil rig support vessels have always been substantially constructed and if the doors are kept closed it is difficult to sink them. However, some of their activities are frightening for those on board the ship, and it is only familiarity which makes the job easier.

It is a sobering thought that as the end of 2007 approaches, there are, according to one enthusiast who keeps records of these things, more than 1000 offshore support vessels being built or on order. There are those who believe that this enormous newbuilding programme, coupled with a shrinking workforce will result in pressure internationally to offer qualifications to those who might be less than suitable to take up the task. The last time this happened was during the Second World War, when the western nations were desperate for seafarers to take merchant ships across the Atlantic. People were given certificates of competency, when possibly they might have been too inexperienced, or lacked the mindset to carry out the task safely. In the end we must rely on the international legislation which promotes the maintenance of levels of expertise, and requires training for the tasks which are to be carried out, as well as the integrity of the oil companies hiring the ships.

It should also be born in mind that the search for oil takes place in parts of the world which are far from the centres of civilisation, and often these far flung areas allow operators to use older tonnage, owned and managed by inexperienced or unprincipled organisations and manned by vulnerable personnel, in some cases unfamiliar with the environment. A trawl through the comments made by seafarers on the internet reveals that there are places where the Plimsoll line is frequently disregarded. Its use has been internationally required since 1930. If it is still possible to disregard a simple regulation, like not submerging a line on the side of the ship, what hope for more complex rules.

But on the bright side, there are the new ships. Every one of them is a jewel, and they will engender loyalty amongst the people working on them and a fan base amongst the enthusiasts ashore. The Chinese yards will get better at making them, just as the Brits and the Koreans did before them. Once, even the Norwegians were uncertain about how to put a supply boat together.

The new ships are wonderful examples of modern technology, and in their own way have developed a following amongst seafarers and non-seafarers alike. No one has so far adopted one for posterity but the day is coming. It is to be hoped that this book has filled in some of the gaps, and made some of the information there is available, more accessible, and that in the future it will provide a record where for whatever reason other records have been lost.

TIMELINES

1947	Wimpey said to have built offshore platform for Shell Brunei
1947	Kerr McGee drilled a well 10.5 miles of Louisiana in 18 ft water.
1949	First offshore submersible barge (Breton Sound 20 – Hayward)
1954	First jack-up built the Barge No 1 – Delong design
1954	First mat supported jack-up mobile unit (Mr Gus)
1954	First purpose built submersible (Mr Charlie – Odeco design)
1955	George Bush Senior becomes president of Zapata
1955	Platform installation depth reaches 100 ft
1955	5 mobile drilling units in operation
1955	First three legged jack-up (Scorpion – Le Tourneau design)
1955	The Ebb Tide designed Laborde – Tidewater
1956	First deepwater bottle submersible (Rig 46 – Kerr-McGee)
1956	First drill ship launched (CUSS 1 – California)
1958	First purpose built pipe layer (BAR 207 – Brown & Root)
1958	First commercial helicopter flights
1960	First multi-platform complex
1960	OPEC founded
1961	the First Semi-Submersible
1963	The Ocean Driller
1963	Wimpey first to drill offshore UK in Lulworth cove for BP
1964	May Mr Louise drilling in German sector
1964	Dec. Mr Cap starts drilling in North Sea
1965	Offshore drilling fleet reaches 75 units
1965	Dec 28th Sea Gem sinks
1965	Sedco 135 (Earl & Wright)
1965	The Offshore Company owns 16 units
1966	2 x jack-ups sunk the Gulf of Mexico
1966	Tidewater operating 200 vessels (of all sorts)
1966	Second generation pipe-laying barge – North Sea
1966	Ocean Traveler Holed in Norwegian sector
1967	Oil strike in Prudhoe Bay Alaska
1967	BP's West Sole ready for production (first Sea gem find)
1968	200 platforms offshore Gulf of Mexico
1968	Tidewater buys Twenty Grand Marine now 350 vessels
1968	Ocean Prince – submersible lost when drilling on Dogger Bank
1968	Nov 15th Hewitt A blow-out and loss of Hector Gannet
1969	Pentagone 81 (Neptune)
1969	First semi-submersible pipe-laying vessel Choctaw 1 – Santa Fe
1969	Oil found in Norway by Ocean Viking drilling for Phillips Ekofisk.

1969	Zakum subsea production for BP – till 1972
1970	Oct Forties Field discovered
1971	Ocean Prospector – 12 columns first of the Victory class
1972	Seaforth Maritime incorporated
1972	OIL incorporated
1973	Western Pacesetter 6 columns Friede and Goldman
1973	End of Vietnam War
1973	Middle east crude oil embargo
1974	Deep Sea Driller. First Aker H-3
1974	Glomar Explorer recovers bits of soviet sub from 11,000 ft
1974	Pipe-laying takes place in over 1000 ft (Castoro V – Saipem)
1974	Drilling water depth 2150 ft in Gabon – Shell
1974	Drill ship Sedco 445 drilling record depth of 1969 ft
1974	Forties A Greythorpe 1 and C Highland 1 jackets installed
1974	Statfjord discovered
1975	Floating production system Transworld 58 on Argyll Field
1976	Viking Piper- ETPM 1601 pipe-layers with 1000 ft capability
1976	Exxon Hondo platform installed in 850 ft of water off California
1977	Drill ship Sedco 472 drills in record water depth of 7467 ft
1977	First tanker production system Castellon for Shell
1978	Shell Cognac platform in 1025 ft of water in the Gulf of Mexico
1979	Apache enters service
1979	Iranian Revolution
1980	Iran Iraq war starts
1980	The Alexander Keilland Disaster
1981	Union's Cerveza platform installed in 935 ft of water
1982	Union's Liger platform installed in 925 ft of water
1982	BP Magnus platform installed in 600 ft of water in the North Sea
1982	The Loss of the Ocean Ranger
1982	The Falklands War
1983	Shell's Lena platform in 1000 ft of water, the first guyed tower.
1983	Sealion enter the Offshore Industry
1986	Star Offshore Strike
1987	Tidewater suffers extremely high losses
1988	The Piper Alpha disaster
1988	Drill ship Discoverer Seven Seas drills in water depth of 7467 ft
1988	End of Iran Iraq war
1988	OIL buys OSA
1989	Seabulk formed by Hvide

1990	The first Iraq War
1991	Oil process slide
1993	Oil 15$ a barrel
1993	UK tax changes reduce drilling activity.
1992	Condeep concrete platform Sleipner A sinks in Norwegian fjord
1992	Tidewater purchase Zapata Gulf Marine
1992	Development of the UT745
1993	The development of the UT722
1994	Auger TLP installed in 2860 ft water (Shell)
1994	John P Laborde retires from Tidewater
1995	The Brent Spar Incident
1996	Drill ship Discover 534 drills in water depth of 7612 ft
1996	Oil prices exceed $20 per barrel
1996	Ulsteins develop the UT740
1996	Tidewater acquires Hornbeck Offshore (now 600 vessels)
1997	Tidewater acquire OIL (now 700 vessels)
1997	Shortage of deep water semi-submersibles
1997	10 newbuilding and 24 rig upgrades taking place
1997	First production in more than 5000 ft of water.
1999	Drill ship Deepwater Expedition drills in water depth of 9111 ft.
2000	The Maersk Assister enters service
2001	Discoverer Spirit sets deep water drilling record at 9727 ft
2003	Discoverer Deep Seas deepwater drilling record at 10011 ft
2005	Oil Price exceeds $50 per barrel
2006	July 13th Oil price reaches $78.40 per barrel
2006	Exxon sets the record for the greatest profit ever at $39.5 billion.

REFERENCES

Books

1. North Sea Oil – The Great Gamble. Bryan Cooper and Dr T.F.Gaskell. 1966
2. The Oil Rig Moorings Handbook. Captain J.Vendrell. Brown Son & Ferguson
3. Jane's Ocean Technology 1974-75
4. Taken at the Flood. The Story of Tidewater. Charles L Dufour. 1980.
5. Offshore Supply and Support Vessels Worldwide. Offerpace. 1985
6. The Story of P&O. David and Stephen Howarth. 1986.
7. Blow-out. Robert Orrell. 2000.
8. The Great Alliance. A History of O.I.L. Rodger MacDonald 1996.
9. 50 Years Offshore. Hans Veldman, George Lagers. 1997.
10. Anchor- Handling and Supply Vessels of the World.
11. Anchor-Handling Tugs and Supply Vessels of the World.

Reports

1. Ocean Express Capsize and Sinking. US Coastguard Marine Board. 1976
2. The Public Enquiry into the Pier Alpha Disaster. Oct 1990.
3. Danish Maritime Authority Casualty Report. Loss of Stevns Power. June 2004

Magazines and Papers

Ocean Energy. June 1975.
Lloyds List. Various dates between 1980 and 1990.
Reed's Tug World Annual Review Various in late 1980s.
The Offshore Support Journal. Various Issues

Some Websites Visited

www.tugspotters.com
www.coltoncompany.com
www.eureka-firefighting.com
www.kingdomdrilling.co.uk
www.marcon.com
home.hccnet.nl/w.verwoerd
oljepioneerene.no/index_eng.php
people.zeeland.net/jduivend

GLOSSARY OF TERMS

A-FRAME
A frame angled over the stern of an anchor-handler allowing things to be lifted above the sea surface and then pulled aboard, or alternatively launched from the deck.

ANCHOR-HANDLER
Offshore vessel designed to undertake the deployment of mobile unit anchors and other mooring systems, as well as towing and normal supply work.

ARTEMIS
A position fixing system which measures changes in position by linking an aerial on the ship with one on a fixed station. The aerials tracked each other the therefore identified changes in direction and distance.

BARYTE
A mineral which can be added to drilling fluid to weigh it up.

BASE OIL
The oil which is used as a basis for mud – to which the baryte and other chemicals are added.

BITTER END
The inner end of an anchor chain, either on a ship or a rig.

BLOWOUT PREVENTER
The collection of rams and valves which can be closed at the seabed to ensure that control is maintained over the well being drilled.

BOW-THRUSTER
A propeller in a tube in the forward end of the vessel, capable of moving the bow to port or starboard.

CASING
The tubing of decreasing sizes which are used to "case" the well, to stop the sides falling in.

CHAIN CHASER
A cast ring fitted round an anchor chain connected to a wire, which the anchor handler will run along the chain to the anchor as part of the recovery process, or vice –versa during deployment. Also known as a chasing collar.

CHASE VESSEL
A craft used by seismic operators to keep passing merchant ships and fishing vessels away from the streamers.

CHERRY PICKING
The practice of picking out individual items of cargo from a stow, often requiring the crew to climb onto the tops of adjacent containers.

CLUMP WEIGHT
A weight on the end of a wire deployed from vessels engaged in DP operations. The system measures the change in the angle of the wire and signals the ship's propulsion system to return it to the original position.

COILED TUBING
Systems based on the use of small diameter steel pipe on reels which can be used to re-enter wells and carry out work-over activities.

CP PROPELLER
A controllable pitch propeller which allows the shaft to be rotated in one direction at a constant speed. The thrust is controlled by altering the pitch of the propeller blades.

CROSS TENSIONING
Tensioning up opposing moorings of a semi-submersible to test whether the anchors are holding.

DACON SCOOP
A large net extended from the side of the standby vessel by crane, intended to scoop people in the sea to safety.

DAUGHTER CRAFT
Fast rescue craft with covered wheelhouses, capable of remaining on station close to offshore installations for several hours for safety purposes.

DELONG DOCK/BARGE
A floating barge from which legs could be extended raising the hull from the seabed.

DP
See dynamic positioning.

DRILL BIT
The cutting tool on the end of the drill string.

DRILL CUTTINGS
The chips of rock which are scraped off the interface between the drill bit and the rock and recovered to the surface in the drilling fluid.

DRILL SHIP
A drilling unit consisting of a derrick and support systems on a monohull, sometimes positioned with anchors, sometimes dynamically positioned.

DRILL STRING
The pipe which is screwed together to make the tubing which is used to drill the well.

DRILL WATER
Fresh water used in the drilling process, which may not be suitable for human consumption.

DRILLING FLUID
See oil based mud.

DRILLING PACKAGE
The derrick and associated equipment on the drill floor of a jack-up.

DRY BULK
Cement and other bulk powers carried in silos below deck on supply vessels and discharged with the assistance of compressed air.

DRY HOLE
A well which does not contain recoverable quantities of crude oil.

DUSTER
An oilfield name for a well which on completion does not yield any oil.

DYNAMIC POSITIONING
The means by which a marine craft maintains station on the surface of the earth, sometimes in proximity to other objects, by means of electronics and propulsion, most simply using GPS.

ELASOMAR FOAM
A special material from which anchor buoys were and are sometimes constructed.

ERRV
Emergency Response and Rescue Vessel. Small vessels capable of rescuing personnel from the sea.

EXPLORATION RIG
See oil rig.

FANBEAM
A system consisting of an aerial on board the vessel and a reflector fitted to the installation, with which the aerial reacts to provide bearing and distance to the DP system.

FIBRE ROPE
Lengths of high quality bundled monofilament line which can be used in semi-submersible mooring systems, to replace chain or wire.

FPSO
Floating Production Storage and Offtake vessel, a vessel, often a former tanker which acts in the same way as a platform and additionally can pump oil to visiting vessels.

FRAC VESSEL
A ship capable of pumping acids and other specialised fluids down oil wells under pressure.

FRC
Fast rescue craft. Small craft launched from standby vessels to rescue people from the water.

GEOPHONE
The receiver of acoustic signals broadcast by the seismic vessels.

GPS
Global positioning system – a satellite system which can be used to locate mobile units of all sorts.

GROSS TONNAGE
The volumetric measurement of all the totally enclosed spaces of a vessel.

HELIDECK
The fabricated deck, usually conforming to airport legislation on which crew transfer helicopters are able to land.

JACKET
The steel structure, or base, of a platform which is floated out and upended on the seabed, and on which the production and accommodation units are situated.

J-HOOK
A fabricated hook weighing several tons used to recover moorings when the buoys have been lost, or the chaser, or chasing pennant has failed. Also sometimes known as a "shepherd's crook".

JOYSTICK
A single control which can be used to operate the engines thrusters and rudders of a supply ship, principally in order to maintain station during offshore operations.

LASSO
A wire connected at both ends to the end of the workwire and thrown over the anchor buoy by two crew members.

LOAD SHARING
A technique used in deep water, requiring the anchor handling vessel to gradually lower the anchor as it gets further away from the rig.

LOCATION
The position where the well is to be drilled.

LST
Landing Ship (Tank). A US military craft developed for landing tanks on the beaches of German and Japanese beaches in the Second World War.

MANIFOLD
The point on the seabed where the well emerges and from which the well fluids are directed by valving.

MEDITERRANEAN MOOR
A mooring technique where the vessel drops and anchor forward and backs up to a landing stage. Hence any activity must take place over the stern.

MUD PIT
The tank for holding the mud on board the rig. They are usually open topped.

OIL BASED MUD
Drilling fluid, which is pumped down the drill string and provides a hydrostatic head, lines the hole and returns drill cuttings to the surface.

OIL RIG ALSO MOBILE DRILLING UNIT
A mobile offshore drilling unit, used to drills wells for exploration and development of offshore oil fields.

PELICAN HOOK
Early means of securing wires and chain on the deck, proior to connection or disconnection from the vessel work wire.

PENNANT
A wire used to connect an anchor to something, usually a buoy or in the case of a chain chaser, the ship. Also sometimes known as a "pendant".

PIGGY BACK
Additional anchors laid ahead of the main anchor if the tensioning up process had caused the main anchor to drag. Also known as "back-up anchors".

PIPE CARRIER
A type of supply ship designed to carry pipe to the construction vessels laying pipe from the oil fields to the shore.

PIPE-LAYER
Monohull or semi-submersible vessel used to lay pipe connecting wellheads to platforms, fields to platforms and fields to the shore.

PLATFORM
A structure on which crude oil is processed. And which also sometimes is provided with a drilling derrick.

POTABLE WATER
Fresh water which is suitable for human consumption.

PRE-LAID MOORINGS
Moorings which are laid in advance of the arrival of the vessel which is intended to use them.

RESERVOIR
The area under the surface of the earth containing the oil.

RISER
The large diameter pipe which connects the drilling rig with the well within which the drill string is deployed, and which provides a means of returning the mud to the surface.

SAFETY CASE
A formal safety document required for all offshore installations, mobile and fixed, by the Health and Safety Executive in the UK sector of the North Sea.

SCRAMBLING NET
A large net constructed of rope which will allow personnel to climb down from the deck of a rig to the water in an emergency.

SEISMIC DATA
The information collected by survey vessels in order to establish the presence of oil bearing strata under the seabed.

SEMI- SUBMERSIBLE
A mobile unit which is partially submerged so that only its vertical columns are exposed to wave action at the sea surface.

SHALE SHAKERS
Powered screens over which the mud passes, which collect the drill cuttings and shake them off into chutes for disposal.

SHALE SHAKERS
Vibrating screens over which returned drilling mud is passed, to remove the debris brought back to surface.

SHARK'S JAW
Generic name for the deck equipment fitted to secure wire or chain at the aft end of the working deck, to allow the crew to make or unmake connections.

SHIP AND SKIP
Name for the process of transporting drill cuttings to the shore.

SLIP JOINT
The uppermost section of the riser, which allows for the vertical movement of the rig.

SNATCHING
The technique of maintain station under offshore cranes while loading or unloading takes place without tying up.

SPLIT ROLLER
A two part stern roller, allowing for the recovery and deployment of moorings at different rates on each side of the deck. Commonly used for connecting prelaid moorings to MODUs and FPSOs.

SPUDDING IN
The time when the drill bit rotates and excavates the first few feet of the hole.

STAG HORNS
Tubular structures fitted half way along the crash barriers of anchor handlers to stop the tow wires moving forward of midships.

STANDBY VESSEL
ERRVs in all other parts of the world than the North Sea.

STINGER
A long chute deployed from the stern of a pipe-layer down which the newly welded pipeline would slide into the sea.

STREAMER
The cable towed behind the seismic ship containing the geophones and means of depth control.

SUCTION PILE/ANCHOR
A type of anchor consisting of a tube which is sucked into the seabed as a result of the vacuum caused by the pumping out of the water it contains.

SUPPLY SHIP
A generic terms for vessels which directly support fixed and mobile offshore installations.

SURVEY SHIP
Vessel used to collect information about the seabed or the substrata.

SYLEDIS
A long range positioning system, using aerials and a form of cross referencing. Seldom used today.

TENSION LEG PLATFORMS
Floating semi-submersible units where the moorings extend vertically down to the seabed, holding the unit in position by the vertical tension.

TENSION WINCH
A winch on which only one layer of wire is present, hence it operates in conjunction with a storage drum. The advantage of the design is that maximum pull is always available.

TOPSIDES
The structure which is placed on top of the jacket, usually in a single lift by a heavy lift vessel.

TOWING PINS
Hydraulic pins which rise out of the deck at the aft end of an anchor-handler limiting the movement of any wire. Also known as "pop-ups".

TOWING SPRING
A large diameter rope, usually nylon inserted between the towing bridle and the tow wire of the tug, for the purpose of absorbing shock loading.

TRANSITION POINT
The point at which there is a change from chain to wire in the mooring systems of deep water semi-submersibles.

TRENCHING PLOUGH
A device towed behind very powerful anchor-handlers to make a trench in the seabed along which pipe can be run.

VARIABLE DECK LOAD
The chemicals tubular, food and movable items which are stored on the deck of a mobile unit.

WELL TESTING
The process of recovering well fluids – crude oil – from the well, checking its volume and form and burning off the results to avoid the need to store them.

WELLHEAD CONNECTOR

The connection on the top of the 30" casing to which the hardware which connects the well with the drill floor is affixed.

WHITTAKER CAPSULE

A type of lifeboat which is almost circular and lowered to the sea on a single wire. The propeller and rudder still allows it to be directed when under way.

YARD-FIGHTER BARGE

A US military barge purchased by the oil industry for transporting supplies.

YOKOHAMA

A very large fender often used to protect pipe carriers and pipe-layers from each other, while the pipe is being discharged.

INDEX

4D seismic 9
"50 Years Offshore" 27
A&P Appledore 126
Aarhus Flydok 57, 78
Aberdeen 49
Aberdeen Service Company (Asco) 129, 141
Abidjan 54
Ace Nature 131
Ace Navigator 131
Acergy Energy 177
Admiral Tide 128
Agnes Candies 129
Aker Group 169
Aker H-3 74
Aker Yards 148
Alden J (Doc) Laborde 26, 30, 32
Alexander Shipyard 32
Alexander Towing 105
American Marine Corporation 65
Amoco 122, 123
Anchor-handling 84
Anchor-Handling Tugs and Supply Vessels of the World" 138
Apache 20
Appledore Shipbuilders 57, 130, 140
Aramco 33
Arcadia Marine 73, 104, 134
Argyll Field 72
Artemis 16, 43
Arthur Levy 56
Asso Venti 140
Asso Ventidue 138, 139
Asso Ventitre 139
Atlantic Conveyor 108
Atlantic Marine Corporation 55
Augustea Offshore 139
B & L Boat Rentals 73
B&N Viking 143
BA and VA Islander 60, 61
Baku 122
Balblair 119
Balder 18

Balder Baffin 109
Balder Viking 136
Barge No 1 30
Barnsdall 29
Barra Supplier 144
Baton Rouge 27
Bayou Chico 49
Beaudril 109
Beaufort Sea 109
Ben Line 74
Ben Viking 143
Bender Shipbuilding Corporation 129, 142
Berlinertor 54
Bill LeBlanc 31
"Blowout" 58
Blue Star 71
Bluewater One 36
Boa 140, 154
Boa Deep C 154, 155
Boa Giant 144
Boa Hercules 144
Boa King 144
Boa Queen 144
Boa Sword 140
Bob Orrell 58
Bolson's shipyard 52
Borneo Straits Offshore 65
Boston Hornet 58
Boston Putford 58
Botnica 143
Bo-Truc Rentals 65
Bourbon Castle 140
Bourbon Dolphin 166, 171, 172
Bourbon Offshore 140
Bourbon Orca 169, 170, 171
Bourbon Surf 140
BP 33, 49, 51, 117, 137
BP Shipping 119, 126
Brent Field 21
Breton 20 29, 30
British Auk 106

British Forties 106
British Offshore Supply Vessel Association (BOSVA) 113
Brodrene Olsen A/S 113
Brown and Root 29, 33
Brownfield activities 21
Bruce anchors 155
Bruce Vertical Lift Anchor 157
Bryan Cooper 52
BUE 106, 122, 123, 124, 143
Bugge Supply Ships 65
Bureau of Oceanic Geological Survey 138
Burton Shipbuilding Company 34
C Acclaim 134
Caldwell Well Services 33, 35
Cambridge Service 131
Cameron 28
Camlocks 46
Campos Basin 115
Canberra 108
Carl Rolaston 123
Carol Chouest 169
Carriage of bulk 45
Caspian Sea 122, 123, 137
Castoro Otto 148, 149, 150
Centurion Service 48
Charles Hill 52
Chasing 93
Chasing collar 90
Cheramie Bros 73
Cherry picking 44
Chevron 75
China Offshore Northern Drilling Company 138
China Offshore Southern Shipping Company 138
Claymore platform 116
Clearwater 49
C-Legend 141
C-Liberty 141
Cliff Roberts 115
C-Logistics 141
Cochrane's shipyard 52
Coffee club 114
Colton Company 36
Compagnie National de Navigation 134
CP propellers 43, 71
C-Port 141
Cunard 56

Dacon scoop 23
Dalian 144
Damon B Bankston 68
Daughter craft 23
Dave Bland 61
Decca Hifix 89
De-commissioning 22
Dee Service 131
Dee Service 70
Deep Sea Driller 74
Deep water mooring 153
Deepwater Nautilus 153
Delong dock 30
Den Helder 54
Dina Merkur 172
Dino Chouest 169
District Offshore (DOF) 144, 169
Diver intervention 16
Dogger Bank 51
Don Durant 32
Dong Fang Yong Shi 132
Donnelly Tide 148
DP systems 16
Drag embedment anchors 15
Drill cuttings 46
Drilling fluid 13
Drypool Engineering 66
DSND 168
Dubai 54
DUC 57
Dundee 54
Durham Service 131
Eakring 49
Earl and Wright 53, 74
East Tide 50, 51
Ebb Tide 26, 32, 33, 34, 56, 68. 110
Edda Sun 108
Edison Chouest 56, 134, 135, 141, 153, 169
Ekofisk 59
El Leon Grande 77
Elvis Presley 32
Emergency Response and Rescue Vessels (ERRVs) 23
Enterprise Oil 160
Essex Shore 52
ETPM 1601 75
Exploration Drilling 29

Exxon 36
Faldentor 85, 118
Falklands War 108
Fanbeam 16
Far Fosna 124, 127
Far Grimshader 8, 43
Far Grip 123, 127, 140
Far Scout 92
Far Senior 95, 127, 128, 129
Far Sound 168
Far Sword 140
Farstad 130
Farstad UK 126
Fast Rescue Craft (FRCs) 23
Fennica 143
Fergusons shipyard 126
Feronia International Shipping (Fish) 105, 134
Fibre moorings 158
Flekkefjord 121
Flood Tide 32, 34
Forex Neptune 74
Forties Alpha 72
Forties Charlie 72
Forties Field 53, 71
Fourchon 54
FPSOs 19, 159
Frac vessel 21
Fred Olsen 74
Friede and Goldman 74
Gary Chouest 153
George Bush 32
George Craigen 49
George Wimpey 33, 57
Gerard Jordan 154
German and Milne 109
Giant Tide 175
Gill Jet 52, 66
Global positioning system (GPS) 15
Godfather 77, 131
Goliath Atlantic 105
Goliath Tide 68
Great Eastern 168
Great Yarmouth 48
Greenpeace 160
Gregory Callimanopolous 109
Groningen 49

Groupe Bourbon 140, 168
Guido Perla 142
Gulf Backer 1 73
Gulf Explorer 80, 81, 82
Gulf Fleet 1 65
Gulf Fleet 38, 45, 131
Gulf Knight 80, 81, 82, 83
Gulf Mississippi Marine Corp 80
Gulf Offshore 118, 130, 131
Gulf Rambler 76
Gulf Viking 80, 81, 82, 83
GulfMark 118
Hall Russell 56, 106
Halter Lockport 104
Halter Marine 34, 50, 62, 99
Halter Moss Point 65, 104
Hamilton Brothers 72
Harland and Wolff 53
Harrisons Clyde 61
Hatch Tide 104
Havila 140
Havila Borgstein 140
Havila Castle 140
Havila Charisma 140
Havila Crown 140
Havila Hidra 140
Havila Lista 140
Havila Surf 140
HBCarlton 33, 34, 35
Heavy lift barge 18
Hector Gannet 50, 57, 58
Hercules 32
Herdentor 118
Hewett A 57, 58
High holding power anchors 155
High Tide 31, 36
Highland 1 72
Highland Champion 77, 119
Highland Endurance 94
Highland Fortress 119
Highland Legend 43, 118
Highland Light 140
Highland Piper 130
Highland Pride 118
Highland Rover 130
Highland Sprite 118

Highland Star 118, 119
Highland Valour 172
Hirenturm 78
HLX2225 133
HLX2255 134, 135
Hogarth Shipping 66
Hornbeck Offshore 131, 142
Humble CT 36
Humble Oil Company 29, 36
Huntetor 118
Hutton TLP 22
Ian Noble 66
Ikaluk 109
Inchcape Group 65
Ingalls Shipyard 34, 36
International Offshore Services (IOS) 56
International Support Vessel Owner's Association (ISOA) 121
Invincible Tide 102
Iolair 117
International Offshore Services (IOS) 65
Iran 84
Iraq War 121
Irwin Jacobs 114
Island Vanguard 179
Islay 142
J Ray McDermott 29, 33
J Samuel White 51
Jack Bates 98, 160
Jackson Marine 65, 77, 114, 131
"Jane's Ocean Technology" 73
Jaya Holdings 167
J-hook 93
Johannes Ostensjo 106
Johannes Solstad 113
John P LaBorde (AHTS) 138, 142, 144
John P Laborde 34
John Ross 110
Jones Act 33
Joystick 43
Kalvik 109
Kan 401 138
Karmforks 97, 153
KasperNeftflot 122
Kaubturm 118
Kent Shore 52
Keppel Singmarine 147

Kerr-McGee 29
Kingsnorth UK 116
KMAR404 86, 131, 140, 167
KMAR808 136, 143, 167
Kongsberg-Simrad 154
Kongsgaard 112
Kongstein 112
Kort nozzles 89
Kreuzturm 118
KS schemes 112
Kulluk 109
Kursk 146
Kvaerner 143
Lady Margaret 59
Lake Caddo 27
Lake Eirie 27
Lake Maracaibo 27, 28, 33
Landing Ship Tank (LST) 29
Laney Chouest 141, 154, 169
Larry Rigdon 141
Lauritz Eidesvik 113
LeTourneau 30, 35
Lehman Brothers 118
Leith 54
Liberty ships 33
Lister Blackstone 52
Lloyds List 113, 114
Lloydsman 72
Loch Carron 116
Loch Kishorn 18
Loch Shuna 116
Lord Cullen 117, 125
Louis Giliasso 28
Low Tide 35
Lowland Cavalier 116
Lui Tide 141
LWT anchor 92
Lyle Shipping 66
M L Levy 81
Maersk A Class 147
Maersk Assister 22, 148, 160
Maersk B Class 77
Maersk Beater 149, 150
Maersk Chieftain 112
Maersk Company 57, 60, 75, 107, 111, 126
Maersk Cutter 107, 116

Maersk Dispatcher 140
Maersk Feeder 44
Maersk Fighter 120, 126, 144
Maersk Launcher 114
Maersk Leader 117
Maersk Logger 117
Maersk Mariner 111, 113, 115
Maersk Master 111, 113, 115, 161
Maersk Ranger 107
Maersk Retriever 80, 107
Maersk Rider 107
Maersk Rover 107
Maersk S Class 146, 147
Maersk Searcher 160, 161, 164
Maersk Seeker 160, 161, 162, 163
Maersk Shipper 162
Maersk Supplier 48, 57
Maersk Supply Service 146
Maersk Tender 68
Maersk Terrier 149
Maersk Topper 68
Maersk Trimmer 66
Magnitor 78
Magnolia Petroleum Company 29, 30
Magnus 174
Magnus Sea 118
Majestic Tide 106
Malaviya 36 168
Mammoth Tide 68, 175
Mangone Shipbuilding Co 65
Manta 122
Marathon Oil 81, 160
Marcon International 104
Marin Teknikk 139, 144
Maritim Ltd 172
Maritime Engineering 75, 80, 106, 107, 127
Maureen platform 18, 22
Maureen Sea 118
MCP-01 116
ME202 75, 135
ME303 104, 107, 112, 124, 144
ME303 Mk II 121
ME606 127
ME909 127
Milton R McCall 175
Miscaroo 109

Mobil Oil 33
Molikpaq 109
Monarch Bay 131
Montrose 54
Moray Firth 49
Morgan City 54
Moss Maritime 143, 167
MOSS808 143
Mr Cap 50
Mr Charlie 26, 32
Mr Gus 30, 81
Mr Louis 50
MT6000 139, 145, 169
MT6016 144
Myklebusthaug 172
Navajo 77
Neftegaz-62 122
Nicole Martin 80, 83
Nicor Marine 134
Ninian Central 19
Noble Lynda Bossler 38
Nordica 143
Normand Atlantic 127
Normand Drott 91
Normand Flipper 145
Normand Neptun 127
Normand Pioneer 146
Normand Progress 146
North American SB Inc 141
North Prince 85
North Sea Assets 66
North Sea Hijack 143
"North Sea Oil – The Great Gamble" 52
North Star 51
Northern Canyon 145
Northern Fortress 119
Northern Frontier 132
Northern Seeker 45
Norwegian Ship-owners Association 113
Norwich Service 131
NUMAST 111
"NUMAST Telegraph" 149
Occidental 117
Ocean Driller 50, 74, 86
"Ocean Energy" 78
Ocean Express 80, 81, 83

Ocean Fleets 65
Ocean Inchcape Ltd (OIL) 65, 75, 118, 131
Ocean Prince 57
Ocean Ranger 125
Ocean Traveler 59
Ocean Victory 74
Ocean Viking 59
Odeco 26, 30, 50, 81
"Offerpace" 103
Offshore Company 30, 55
Offshore Jefferson 36
Offshore Logistics 118
Offshore Marine 52, 65
Offshore Orleans 36
Offshore Supply Association (OSA) 54, 56, 60, 64, 75, 118
Offshore Transporation Corp 36
Offshore Trawlers 65, 104
Oil & Gas Rentals 121
Oil based mud 47
Oil Challenger 75, 145
Oil Champion 112
Oil Discoverer 66
Oil Driller 66
Oil Explorer 65
Oil Mariner 66, 71
Oil Producer 65
Oil Prospector 65
Oil Supplier 65
Oil Traveller 150
Oil Venturer 66
Olympic Commander 144
Olympic Octopus 170
Olympic Pegasus 161, 170
Olympic Princess 139
Olympic Shipping 144
Olympic Supplier 107, 144
Orskov shipyard 112, 139
Otto Candies 56, 73, 142
Oy Laivarteolisuus 69
P&O 56, 65
Pacific Blade 161, 162, 163
Pacific Brigand 132
Pacific Buccaneer 132, 133
Pacific Frontier 132
Pacesetter 74
Parli Augusonn 105

Pelican hook 96
Pentagon 41, 42, 84
Peter Gibson 113
Petromar 104
Phillips Petroleum 29, 58
Piggy-back 92
Pike 99
Pipelaying 20
Piper Alpha 116, 117, 125
Point Baker 82
Port Fourchon 141
PRB Offshore 104
Pure Oil 28
Queen Elizabeth 56
Queen Mary 56
R&B Falcon 160
Ray J Hope 86
Raymond Concrete Pile Company 27
Raz Tanura 54
Red River 27
Regent Quay 54, 107
Regal Service 131
Remote Operating Vehicles (ROVs) 20, 22
Remoy Management 140
Richard Dunstan 108
Rig 40 30
Rig 51 30
Rig Express 178
Rig shifting 86
Rigdon Marine 142
Rigdon Tide 141
Rioni 124
Rip Tide 29, 32, 34
River Tay 118
Robert Allen 109, 110
Rock dumpers 19
Rolandwerft 48, 57
Rolls-Royce 144, 167, 170
Royal and Regal Service 67
Royal Service 131
Russell Tide 131, 132
Safety Case 116
Saibos Construceos Maritimas 149
Salvesens 74
Sam S Allgood 131
San Pedro Gulf 65

Sandhaven 116
Sanko 131
Sanyo Shipping Company 78
SBS Nimbus 145, 146
Scheepswerf De Hoop 56
Schepelsturm 118
Schoorturm 118
Scorpion 33
Scotoil 1 to 6 74
Scott platform 18
Sea Explorer 65
Sea Gem 51, 117, 125
Sea Quest 53, 67, 153
Seabrokers 127
Seabulk Offshore 138
Seacor 65, 104, 105, 134
Seacor Vanguard 154
Seacor Vision 133, 134
Seaforth Centurion 107
Seaforth Chieftain 66
Seaforth Crusader 107
Seaforth Hero 66, 67
Seaforth Maritime 66, 107, 113
Seaforth Prince 66
Seaforth Victor 68
Seagair 109
Seahorse Inc 65
Sealion Shipping 108, 130
Seaway Falcon 43
Sedco 700 type 74, 116
Sedco F 53
Sensor 33
Shark's Jaw 88, 96
Shell 30, 32, 50, 65, 117, 169, 174
Shetland Base Services (SBS) 145
Shetland Service 67
Ship and skip 47
Ship Shoal 29
Sidlaw Industries 66
Siem Offshore 168
Sigjorn Iverson 121
Silver Pit 116, 117
Simek 172
Skandi Barra 144
Skandi Bergen 168
Skandi Buchan 145

Skandi Chieftain 144
Skandi Falcon 47
Skandi Foula 144
Skandi Marstein 144
Skandi PMS 1 144
Skandi PMS II 144
Skandi Rona 144
Skaustream 69
"Skipsrevyen" 146
Smit brackets 96
Smit-Lloyd 1 56
Smit-Lloyd 43, 56, 60, 70, 106, 121
Snatching 13, 24, 43
Socony Vacuum 33
South Shore 52, 56
Southeaster Drilling Company (Sedco) 53
Sovereign Explorer 160, 161, 162, 163
Stadive 117
Standard Oil Company 33
Standby Vessel Code 125
Standby vessels 23
Stanolind Oil and Gas 29
Star Aquarius 72
Star Offshore 71, 75, 108, 111
Star Polaris 88, 114
Star Sirius 106, 132
Star Spica 106, 132
Star Taurus 71, 72
Star Vega 41
State Boat Company 56, 65
Statesman 72
Stavanger Tank 126
Steamboat 54
Stena 74
Stena Don 12
Stena Seaspread 108
Sterkoder MV 106, 132
Stevns Power 148, 149, 150, 151
Stirling Dee 38
Stirling Islay 142, 143
Stirling Jura 143
Stirling Shipping 130, 143
Storfonn 112
Straits Steamship Company 65
Suction anchors 15
Suction mooring 153

Summerland 27
Sun Wrestler 13
Superior Oil 28, 29
Supply Express 178
Sverr Farstad 121
Swire Pacific 80, 132, 144, 161
Syledis 16
T.F.Gaskell 52
Takapu 114
Tangen Verft 105
Tartan platform 116
Tempest 78
Tension leg platforms 18
Terry Fox 109, 110
Texaco 28
Texas Oil Company 33
Tharos 116, 117
The Abyss 17
The submersible 28
Theriot 73, 74
Theriot One 118
Thor Flademark 121
Tidewater 32, 34, 35, 36, 50, 60, 65, 68, 73, 77, 104, 114, 115, 131, 138, 139, 141, 142, 148
Tilman J 36
Tilman Offshore 36
TNT Cougar 109
TNT Gryphon 109
TNT Leopard 108
TNT Lion 108
TNT Mariner 109
TNT Panther 108
TNT Sentinal 109
TNT Tiger 108
Toisa Coral 130
Toisa Crest 130
Toisa Intrepid 130
Tor Viking II 143
Torpedo anchor 153, 156
Totovo 106
Towing pins 96
Trafalgar Service 104
Transocean Marianas 153
Transocean Rather 171
Transocean Sedco Forex 160
Transworld 58 72

Trenching machines 20
Trinity Marine 34, 121, 154
Triplex gear 93, 97, 174
True Grit 77, 131
Typhoon 78
Ulstein 75, 107
Ulstein A101 144, 169, 170, 171
Ulstein A102 166, 171
Ulstein A104 144
Ulstein A122 173
Ulstein Hatlo 68
Ulstein Verft 143, 167, 169
Ulsteinvik 127
Unit 222 79
United Towing 71
USS Lexington 83
UT704 68, 69, 80, 132
UT705 47, 75, 80, 118, 121, 126
UT706 43
UT708 80, 107
UT710 144
UT712 80, 168
UT712L 168, 170
UT719 144
UT720 132, 135, 161
UT721 144
UT722 123, 127, 128, 132, 138, 140, 147, 167
UT722LX 140
UT734 106, 127, 132
UT738 144
UT740 127
UT742 146
UT745 44, 118, 120, 126, 127, 135, 140, 144
UT745E 145
UT755 130, 141, 144, 167
UT755L 172
UT787CD 179
Verolme 56
Vertical lift anchors 157
Vesty Group 71
Victory ships 33
Viking Avant 145, 176
Viking Dynamic 141
Viking Piper 19, 75
Viking Supply Ships 121
Viking Surf 145

Vik-Sandvik 80, 106, 130, 143, 144, 145

Vroon 178

VS468 144

VS470 145

VS470 MkII 145

VS472 170

VS473 112, 124, 143, 144

VS480 144

VS483 130, 144

VS486 142, 144

VS490 141

VS493 Avant 145, 178

Vulcan Service 125

Warri 54

Weco Supplier 1 78, 138

Weco Supplier IV 138

Well testing 14

Werdertor 118

Wes Bordelon 142

Western Pacesetter 6 74

Western Regent 10

Whittaker capsule 80, 82, 83

Wilhelmsen Offshore 65

William E Bright 68

Wimbrown 1 57

Wimpey Marine Ltd 57, 78, 113

Wimpey Seafox 75, 78

Wimpey Seahorse 108

Wimpey Seahunter 140

Wimpey Seatiger 78

Wolraad Woltemade 110

XBow 169, 170

Yantai Raffles 142

Yard Fighter (YF) Barge 29

Yukos 137

Zakum Field 33

Zapata Corporation 32, 56

Zapata Gulf Marine 48, 73, 114, 121, 131

Zapata Heritage 105